The ABCs of Political Eco

The ABCs of Political Economy

A Modern Approach

Robin Hahnel

Pluto Press

LONDON • STERLING, VIRGINIA

First published 2002 by Pluto Press
345 Archway Road, London N6 5AA
and 22883 Quicksilver Drive,
Sterling, VA 20166–2012, USA

www.plutobooks.com

British Library Cataloguing in Publication Data
A catalogue record for this book is available from the British Library

ISBN 0 7453 1858 4 hardback
ISBN 0 7453 1857 6 paperback

Library of Congress Cataloging in Publication Data
Hahnel, Robin
    The ABCs of political economy : a modern approach / Robin Hahnel.
        p. cm.
    ISBN 0–7453–1858–4 (hardback) — ISBN 0–7453–1857–6 (pbk.)
    1. Economics. I. Title.
    HB171 .H22 2002
    330—dc21

                                                                    2002006491

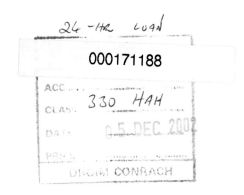
10   9   8   7   6   5   4   3   2   1

Designed and produced for Pluto Press by
Chase Publishing Services, Fortescue, Sidmouth EX10 9QG
Typeset from disk by Stanford DTP Services, Towcester
Printed in the European Union by Antony Rowe, Chippenham, England

Contents

List of Illustrations

Preface

The ABCs of Political Economy: A Modern Approach is an accessible introduction to modern, radical, political economy. It draws on the work of Karl Marx, Thorstein Veblen, John Maynard Keynes, Michael Kalecki, Piero Sraffa, Joan Robinson, and other great political economists, but requires no prior familiarity with political economy, and concentrates on modern concepts and models best suited to understanding economic issues today. *The ABCs* provides readers who are dissatisfied with the economics of competition and greed and mistrustful of conventional economic theory with the essential tools they need for a critical evaluation of the major economic institutions and policies of our day. *The ABCs* also teaches readers who want to make our economies more democratic, equitable, sustainable and efficient what they need to know to evaluate how effective different policies and institutional reforms are likely to be at accomplishing their goals. In other words, *The ABCs of Political Economy* empowers people who are dissatisfied with today's economies and mainstream theories to think through how we can move from the destructive economics of competition and greed toward an economics of equitable cooperation.

No previous economics background is assumed, and everything is explained verbally in eight core chapters. Simple theoretical models that illustrate the logic of key relationships are confined to three chapters which are not necessary to follow the rest of the text. Even the models in these three chapters require no mathematical skills beyond arithmetic and high school algebra. But while technique has been reduced to a minimum, and confined to chapters that can be skipped or postponed, there is much to be learned about important aspects of modern economies and policy debates from the simple political economy models in chapters 3, 5, and 9. I urge readers who want to empower themselves as economic thinkers, that is, readers who want to be able to analyze economic issues and debates for themselves rather than always look to others to provide them with a "politically correct" conclusion, to invest the time to explore the simple models in these three chapters. These chapters help you to become a "player" rather than a "spectator" in the game of modern political economy.

Chapter 1 develops a social theory designed to understand the relationship between economic, political, kinship, and cultural activities, and the forces behind social stability and social change in a way that neither over nor underestimates the importance of economic dynamics, and neither over nor underestimates the importance of human agency compared to social forces.

Chapter 2 carefully examines what is meant by economic justice, economic efficiency, economic democracy, and environmental sustainability. Since these are the measuring sticks we will use to judge economic performance, it is crucial to be clear about our goals.

Chapter 3 uses a simple corn model to explore the relationship between efficiency and inequality. The corn model allows us to see how labor and credit markets affect efficiency and inequality, and provides a convenient context to see how conservative, liberal, and radical conceptions of economic justice give rise to different conclusions about when unequal outcomes are unfair and when they are not.

After teaching readers the laws of supply and demand necessary for understanding how markets work, chapter 4 explores what lies behind the debate between enthusiasts, who see markets working as if they were guided by a beneficent invisible hand, and critics, who see markets often working as if they were guided by a malevolent invisible foot.

Chapter 5 presents three micro economic models. The concept of a dominant strategy equilibrium in a simple, static "public good game" illustrates how the free rider problem leads markets to produce too little public goods. Backward induction in a simple, dynamic "Price of Power Game" illustrates how the logic of preserving an unequal power advantage can lead to a loss of economic efficiency in both patriarchal households and capitalist firms. Finally, a Sraffian model using an input–output framework illustrates why there is a negative relationship between the wage rate and rate of profit, why the relative prices of goods depend on the bargaining power between capitalists and workers, and why profit maximizing capitalists sometimes make socially counterproductive technological choices.

Chapter 6 explains the importance of aggregate demand in explaining why economies sometimes fail to produce all they could, the origins of cyclical unemployment and demand pull inflation, and the logic of fiscal policy. The chapter also explains why wage-led growth is possible in the long run and dispels popular myths about inflation and the national debt.

Chapter 7 unravels the mystery of money and banks and explains the logic of monetary policy. Besides explaining how the financial sector *can* improve productivity in the "real" economy, the chapter also explains how the financial sector *can* lead to efficiency losses in the real economy – something mainstream finance theory seldom bothers to point out.

Chapter 8 tackles the question of whether international trade and investment deserve to be described as mutual benefit – the mainstream view – or imperialism – the political economy view. Understanding how international trade and investment can affect global efficiency both positively and negatively, and how international trade and investment affect inequality between and within countries, is crucial for people who want to understand the raging debate about globalization. While the balance of payment accounts and a simple open economy macro model prove critical to understanding controversies surrounding IMF conditionality programs.

Chapter 9 contains a number of simple macro economic models illustrating the logic of bank runs and international financial crises, the problematic relationship between the financial and real economies, both domestically and internationally, and the logic of fiscal and monetary policies in both closed and open economy models. The chapter concludes with a long run political economy macro model incorporating the insights of Keynes and Marx that illustrates the possibility of wage-led growth.

Chapter 10 provides a critical appraisal of the main features of capitalism. Contrary to the claims of Milton Friedman who argues that free enterprise and markets promote economic freedom, efficiency, and fairness while reducing economic discrimination, we discover how and why free enterprise and markets obstruct economic democracy, efficiency, and justice. The chapter ends with a brief evaluation of what went wrong with attempts to replace the economics of competition and greed in the twentieth century.

Chapter 11 begins a discussion of how to move towards an economics of equitable cooperation. A variety of reforms within capitalism are discussed, as well as reforms that would move us beyond capitalism by replacing private enterprise with worker-owned and managed firms, and replacing markets with a system of participatory, democratic planning. The chapter ends with a discussion of reasonable doubts people have about whether it is possible to organize our economic activities democratically, fairly, and efficiently.

Over the past quarter-century radical political economy has changed dramatically. Few who see themselves as radical political economists today use tools like the labor theory of value to explain prices, wages, and profits in capitalist economies. Consequently primers on Marxist economic theory no longer provide an adequate introduction to *modern* political economy. Readers with chapters written by different modern political economists on subjects in their areas of expertise can provide insightful analyses of particular issues. But such Readers provide conclusions rather than tools of analysis. Therefore they also fail to teach people who are not professional political economists how to *think* economic issues through for themselves. Finally, introductory texts that cover the same theories and materials covered in mainstream texts written by a group of political economists can provide a welcome relief from the extreme conservative bias that permeates standard intro texts today. But competent texts that avoid a conservative bias do not provide an introduction to *radical* political economy. I can only hope that *The ABCs of Political Economy: A Modern Approach* fills a void for those who want to sharpen their ability to critically evaluate economic issues so they can help decide how we can best go about replacing the economics of competition and greed with the economics of equitable cooperation in the years ahead.

Robin Hahnel, Professor of Political Economy
American University
Washington DC
July 26, 2002

Acknowledgements

I have taught political economy to students at American University in Washington DC for more than twenty-five years. I would like to thank all of the students in my political economy classes over the years whose reactions and suggestions are largely the basis for this book. What they found more or less insightful, important, compelling, and helpful, has had a great impact on what follows.

I also thank Professors Robert Blecker, Maria Floro, Mieke Meurs, and John Willoughby with whom I have the pleasure of teaching political economy at American University. While other professors of political economy have been victims of isolation and discrimination in economic departments where they serve as token radicals, or have suffered through demoralizing, internecine squabbles with other political economy faculty over curriculum content, I have been blessed with a remarkably stimulating and collegial group of fellow political economists with whom to work.

I thank my fellow activists in the still young anti-globalization movement who encouraged me to write a book that would equip people with progressive values, but with little or no prior formal economics education, to think through economic issues for themselves without falling prey to the myths and biases prevalent in the mainstream of my chosen profession. Honest, civic minded people deserve such a book, whether or not I have succeeded in providing it.

Thanks to the people at Pluto Press – Roger van Zwanenberg, Robert Webb, Julie Stoll, Ray Addicott, Oliver Howard, and Melanie Patrick – who showed faith in this project when others did not, and whose good cheer throughout was always appreciated.

Finally, special thanks to four PhD graduate students who worked with me as research assistants and provided invaluable concrete assistance: Assen Assenov, Aaron Pacitti, Arslan Razmi, and Stanislav Vornovitsky.

As much as I owe to those thanked above, and others, the views expressed here are entirely my own responsibility.

1   Economics and Liberating Theory

Unlike mainstream economists, political economists have always tried to situate the study of economics within the broader project of understanding how society functions. However, during the second half of the twentieth century dissatisfaction with the traditional political economy theory of social change known as *historical materialism* increased to the point where many modern political economists and social activists no longer espouse it, and most who still call themselves historical materialists have modified their theory considerably to accommodate insights about the importance of gender relations, race relations, and the "human factor" in understanding social stability and social change. The *liberating theory* presented briefly in this chapter attempts to transcend historical materialism without throwing out the baby with the bath water. It incorporates insights from feminism, national liberation and anti-racist movements, and anarchism, as well as from mainstream psychology, sociology, and evolutionary biology where useful. Liberating theory attempts to understand the relationships between economic, political, kinship and cultural activities, and the forces behind social stability and social change, in a way that neither over nor underestimates the importance of economic dynamics, and neither over nor underestimates the importance of human agency compared to social forces.[1]

PEOPLE AND SOCIETY

People usually define and fulfill their needs and desires in cooperation with others – which makes us a *social species*. Because each of us assesses our options and chooses from among them based on our

1. For a fuller treatment see *Liberating Theory* (South End Press, 1986) by Michael Albert, Leslie Cagan, Noam Chomsky, Robin Hahnel, Mel King, Lydia Sargent, and Holly Sklar.

1

evaluation of their consequences we are also a *self-conscious species*. Finally, in seeking to meet the needs we identify today, we choose to act in ways that sometimes change our human characteristics, and thereby change our needs and preferences tomorrow. In this sense people are *self-creative*.

Throughout history people have created *social institutions* to help meet their most urgent needs and desires. To satisfy our economic needs we have tried a variety of arrangements – feudalism, capitalism, and centrally planned "socialism" to name a few – that assign duties and rewards among economic participants in different ways. But we have also created different kinds of kinship relations through which people seek to satisfy sexual needs and accomplish child rearing goals, as well as different religious, community, and political organizations and institutions for meeting cultural needs and achieving political goals. Of course the particular social arrangements in different *spheres of social life*, and the relations among them, vary from society to society. But what is common to all human societies is the elaboration of social relationships for the joint identification and pursuit of individual need fulfillment.

To develop a theory that expresses this view of humans – as a self-conscious, self-creative, social species – and this view of society – as a web of interconnected spheres of social life – we first concentrate on concepts helpful for thinking about people, or the *human center*; next on concepts that help us understand social institutions, or the *institutional boundary* within which individuals function; and finally on the relationship between the human center and institutional boundary, and the possible relations between *four spheres of social life*.

THE HUMAN CENTER

Except for creationists most consider the laws of evolution straightforward and non-controversial. Unfortunately popular interpretations that emphasize the advantages of aggression and strength, but neglect equally important factors for passing on one's genes like good parenting skills and successful cooperation, sprinkle more ideology over the scientific basis of Darwin's theory of evolutionary biology than most realize.

The laws of evolution reconsidered

Human nature as it now exists was formed in accord with the laws of evolution under conditions pertaining well before recorded human history. Fossils discovered in Ethiopia and Kenya now date human ancestors back at least 5 or 6 million years. Distinctly human species arose in Africa at least 2 million years ago, while present evidence indicates that modern humans are only about 100,000 years old. Therefore the conditions relevant to which genetic mutations were advantageous and which were not are the conditions prevailing in central Africa between 6 million and 100,000 years ago. It is often noted that the last 10,000 years of human history – so called "historic time," the time period we know much about – has been fraught with war, conquest, genocide, and slavery. And it is often speculated that *under those conditions* people with a genetic disposition to aggression and vengeance, for example, might have been well suited to survival. But historic time is only a tenth of the time modern humans have roamed the earth, and is only an evolutionary instant compared to the 6 million years during which the human species evolved from our common ancestry with apes and chimpanzees. This means it is impossible for the historical conditions we know something about to have selected genetic characteristics significantly different from those humans already had 100,000 years ago. Therefore, it is not possible that the human history we know something about – our history of war, oppression, and exploitation – has made our genetic "nature" hopelessly aggressive, vindictive, or power hungry. Throughout the 10,000 years of recorded history we have been, and remain, genetically what we were at the outset. To believe otherwise is to believe that a baby plucked from the arms of its mother, moments after birth, 10,000 years ago, and time-traveled to the present would be genetically different from babies born today. And this is simply not the case.

But what is the relevance of this to perceptions about "human nature?" The point is that whether conditions during the past 10,000 years favored survival of the more aggressive and vindictive, or survival of those who cooperated more successfully, is irrelevant to what "human nature" is really like. Because the conditions during known history played no role in forging our genetic nature. The relevant conditions for speculations concerning genetic traits promoting survival were the conditions that prevailed in Africa 6 million to 100,000 years ago. And whether or not the conditions human ancestors lived in during that lengthy period favored genetic traits conducive to aggression any more than traits conducive to successful cooperation, is very much an open question.

This does not mean that our 10,000-year history of war, oppression, and exploitation has had no impact on people's attitudes and behavior today. These aspects of our history have had important effects on our consciousness, culture, and social institutions that cannot be ignored or "willed away." But the point is that known history has left ideological and institutional residues, *not* genetic residues. Only conditions in Africa 6 million years ago had any influence on genetic selection. So it is perfectly possible that under institutional conditions that are very different from those we have today, and the different expectations that go with them, that human behavior – the combined product of our genetic inheritance and our institutional environment – could be quite different than it is presently. This simple fact is something apologists for capitalism ignore when they argue that people are doomed to the *economics of competition and greed* by "human nature." Instead it is just as plausible that an *economics of equitable cooperation* is compatible with our genetic make-up, and perfectly possible under different institutional conditions – popular opinion to the contrary, not withstanding.

Natural, species, and derived needs and potentials

All people, simply by virtue of being human, have certain needs, capacities, and powers. Some of these, like the needs for food and sex, or the capacities to eat and copulate, we share with other living creatures. These are our *natural needs and potentials*. Others, however, such as the needs for knowledge, creative activity, and love, and the powers to conceptualize, plan ahead, evaluate alternatives, and experience complex emotions, are more distinctly human. These are our *species needs and potentials*. Finally, most of our needs and powers, like the desire for a particular singer's recordings, or the need to share feelings with a particular loved one, or the ability to play a guitar or repair a roof, we develop over the course of our lives. These are our *derived needs and potentials*.

In short, every person has natural attributes similar to those of other animals, and species characteristics shared only with other humans – both of which can be thought of as genetically "wired-in." Based on these genetic potentials people develop more specific derived needs and capacities as a result of their particular life experiences. While our natural and species needs and powers are the results of past human evolution and are not subject to modification by individual or social activity, our derived needs and powers are subject to modification by individual activity and are very dependent on our social environment – as explained below. Since a few species needs and powers are especially critical to understanding how humans and human societies work, I discuss them before explaining how derived needs and powers develop.

Human consciousness

Human beings have intellectual tools that permit them to understand and situate themselves in their surroundings. This is not to say that everyone accurately understands the world and her position in it. No doubt, most of us deceive ourselves greatly much of the time! But an incessant striving to develop some interpretation of our relationship with our surroundings is a characteristic of normally functioning human beings. We commonly call the need and ability to do this *consciousness*, a trait that makes human systems much more complicated than non-human systems. It is consciousness that allows humans to be self-creative – to select our activities in light of their preconceived effects on our surroundings and ourselves. One effect our activities have is to fulfill our present needs and desires, more or less fully. But another effect of our activities is to reinforce or transform our derived characteristics, and thereby the needs and capacities that depend on them. Our ability to analyze, evaluate, and take the human development effects of our choices into account is why humans are the "subjects" as well as the "objects" of our histories.

The human capacity to act purposefully implies the need to exercise that capacity. Not only can we analyze and evaluate the effects of our actions, we need to exercise choice over alternatives, and we therefore need to be in positions to do so. While some call this the "need for freedom," it bears pointing out that the human "need for freedom" goes beyond that of many animal species. There are animals that cannot be domesticated or will not reproduce in captivity, thereby exhibiting an innate "need for freedom." But the human need to employ our powers of consciousness requires freedom beyond the "physical freedom" some animal species require as well. People require freedom to choose and direct their own activities in accord with their understanding and evaluation of the effects of that activity. In chapter 2 I will define the concept "self-management" to express this peculiarly human species need in a way that subsumes the better known concept "individual freedom" as a special case.

Human sociability

Human beings are a social species in a number of important ways. First, the vast majority of our needs and potentials can only be satisfied and developed in conjunction with others. Needs for sexual and emotional gratification can only be pursued in relations with others. Intellectual and communicative potentials can only be developed in relations with others. Needs for camaraderie, community, and social esteem can only be satisfied in relation with others.

Second, needs and potentials that might, conceivably, be pursued independently, seldom are. For example, people could try to satisfy their economic needs self-sufficiently, but we seldom have done so since establishing social relationships that define and mediate divisions of duties and rewards has always proved so much more efficient. And the same holds true for spiritual, cultural, and most other needs. Even when desires might be pursued individually, people have generally found it more fruitful to pursue them jointly.

Third, human consciousness contributes a special character to our sociability. There are other animal species which are social in the sense that many of their needs can only be satisfied with others. But humans have the ability to understand and plan their activity, and since we recognize this ability in others we logically hold them accountable for their choices, and expect them to do likewise. Peter Marin expressed this aspect of the human condition eloquently in an essay titled "The Human Harvest" published in *Mother Jones* (December, 1976: 38).

> Kant called the realm of connection the kingdom of ends. Erich Gutkind's name for it was the absolute collective. My own term for the same thing is the human harvest – by which I mean the webs of connection in which all human goods are clearly the results of a collective labor that morally binds us irrevocably to distant others. Even the words we use, the gestures we make, and the ideas we have, come to us already worn smooth by the labor of others, and they confer upon us an immense debt we do not fully acknowledge.

Bertell Ollman explains it is the individualistic, not the social interpretation of human beings that is absurd and unscientific when examined closely (*Alienation*, Cambridge University Press, 1973: 108):

> The individual cannot escape his dependence on society even when he acts on his own. A scientist who spends his lifetime in a

laboratory may delude himself that he is a modern version of Robinson Crusoe, but the material of his activity and the apparatus and skills with which he operates are social products. They are inerasable signs of the cooperation which binds men together. The very language in which a scientist thinks has been learned in a particular society. Social context also determines the career and other life goals that an individual adopts. No one becomes a scientist or even wants to become one in a society which does not have any. In short, man's consciousness of himself and of his relations with others and with nature are that of a social being, since the manner in which he conceives of anything is a function of his society.

In sum, there never was a Hobbesian "state of nature" where individuals roamed the wilds in a "natural" state of war with one another. Human beings have always lived in social units such as tribes and clans. The roots of our sociality – our "realm of connection" or "human harvest" – are both physical–emotional and mental–conceptual. The unique aspect of human sociality is that the "webs of connection" that inevitably connect all human beings are woven not just by a "resonance of the flesh" but by a shared consciousness and mutual accountability as well. Individual humans do not exist in isolation from their species community. It is not possible to fulfill our needs and employ our powers independently of others. And we have never lived except in active interrelation with one another. But the fact that human beings are inherently social does not mean that all institutions meet our social needs and develop our social capacities equally well. For example, in later chapters I will criticize markets for failing to adequately account for, express and facilitate human sociality.

Human character structures

People are more than their constantly developing needs and powers. At any moment we have particular personality traits, skills, ideas, and attitudes. These *human characteristics* play a crucial mediating role. On the one hand they largely determine the activities we will select by defining the goals of these activities – our present needs, desires, or preferences. On the other hand, the characteristics themselves are merely the cumulative imprint of our past activities on our innate potentials. What is important regarding human characteristics is to neither underestimate nor overestimate their permanence. Although I have emphasized that people derive needs, powers, and characteristics over their lifetimes as the result of their activities, we are never completely free to do so at any point in time. Not only are people limited by the particular menu of role offerings of the social institutions that surround them, they are constrained at any moment by the personalities, skills, knowledge, and values they have accumulated as of that moment themselves. But even though character structures may persist over long periods of time, they are not totally invariant. Any change in the nature of our activities that persists long enough can lead to changes in our personalities, skills, ideas, and values, as well as changes in our derived needs and desires that depend on them.

A full theory of human development would have to explain how personalities, skills, ideas, and values form, why they usually persist, but occasionally change, and what relationship exists between these semi-permanent structures and people's needs and capacities. No such psychological theory now exists, nor is visible on the horizon. But fortunately, a few "low level" insights are sufficient for our purposes.

The relation of consciousness to activity

The fact that our knowledge and values influence our choice of activities is easy to understand. The manner in which our activities influence our consciousness and the importance of this relation is less apparent. A need that frequently arises from the fact that we see ourselves as choosing among alternatives, is the need to interpret our choices in a positive light. If we saw our behavior as completely beyond our own control, there would be no need to justify it, even to ourselves. But to the extent that we see ourselves as choosing among options, it can be very uncomfortable if we are not able to "rationalize" our decisions. This is not to say that people always succeed in justifying their actions, even to themselves. Nor do all circumstances make it equally easy to do so! Rather, the point is that striving to minimize what some psychologists call "cognitive dissonance" is a corollary of our power of consciousness. The tendency to minimize cognitive dissonance creates a subtle duality to the relationship between thought and action in which each influences the other, rather than a unidirectional causality. When we fulfill needs through particular activities we are induced to mold our thoughts to justify or rationalize both the logic and merit of those activities, thereby generating consciousness-personality structures that can have a permanence beyond that of the activities that formed them.

The possibility of detrimental character structures

An individual's ability to mold her needs and powers at any moment is constrained by her previously developed personality, skills, and consciousness. But these characteristics were not always "givens" that must be worked with; they are the products of previously chosen activities in combination with "given" genetic potentials. So why would anyone choose to engage in activities that result in char- acteristics detrimental to future need fulfillment? One possibility is that someone else, who does not hold our interests foremost, made the decision for us. Another obvious possibility is that we failed to recognize important developmental effects of current activities chosen primarily to fulfill pressing immediate needs. But imposed choices and personal mistakes are not the most interesting possibil- ities. At any moment we have a host of active needs and powers. Depending on our physical and social environment it may not always be possible to fulfill and develop them all simultaneously. In many situations it is only possible to meet current needs at the expense of generating habits of thinking and behaving that prove detrimental to achieving greater fulfillment later. This can explain why someone might make choices that develop detrimental character traits even if they are aware of the long run consequences.

In sum, people are self-creative within the limits defined by human nature, but this must be interpreted carefully. At any moment each individual is constrained by her previously developed human characteristics. Moreover, as individuals we are powerless to change the social roles defined by society's major institutions within which most of our activity must take place. So as individuals we are to some extent powerless to affect the kind of behavior that will mold our future character traits. Hence, these traits, and any desires that may depend on them, may remain beyond our reach, and our power of self-generation is effectively constrained by the social situations in which we find ourselves. But in the sense that these social situations are ultimately human creations, and to the extent that individuals have maneuverability within given social situations, the potential for self-creation is preserved. In other words, we humans are *both* the subjects *and* the objects of our history. The concept of the *Human Center* is defined to incorporate these conclusions.

- The **Human Center** is the collection of people who live within a society with all their needs, powers, personalities, skills, and consciousness. This includes our natural and species needs and powers – the results of an evolutionary process that occurred long before known history began. It includes all the structural human characteristics that are givens as far as the individual is concerned at any moment, but are, in fact, the accumulated imprint of her previous activity choices on innate potentials. And it includes our derived needs and powers, or preferences and capacities, that are determined by the interaction of our natural and species needs and powers with the human characteristics we have accumulated.

THE INSTITUTIONAL BOUNDARY

People "create" themselves, but only in defined settings which place important limitations on their options. Besides the limitations of our genetic potential and the natural environment, the most important settings that structure people's self-creative efforts are social institutions which establish the patterns of expectation within which human activity must occur.

Social institutions are simply conglomerations of interrelated roles. If we consider a factory, the buildings, assembly lines, raw materials, and products are objects, and part of the "built" environment. Ruth, Joe, and Sam, the people who work in, or own the factory, are people, and part of society's human center. The factory as an institution is the roles and the relationships between those roles: assembly line worker, maintenance worker, foreman, supervisor, plant manager, union steward, minority stockholder, majority stockholder, etc. Similarly, the market as an institution consists of the roles of buyers and sellers. It is neither the place where buying and selling occurs, nor the actual people who buy and sell. It is not even the actual behavior of buying and selling. Actual behavior belongs in the sphere of human activity, or history itself, and is not the same as the social institution that produces that history in interaction with the human center. Rather, the market institution is the commonly held *expectation* that the social activity of exchanging goods and services will take place through the activity of consensual buying and selling.

We must be careful to define roles and institutions apart from whether or not the expectations that establish them will continue to be fulfilled, because to think of roles and institutions as *fulfilled* expectations lends them a permanence they may not deserve. Obviously a social institution only lasts if the commonly held expectations about behavior patterns are confirmed by repeated actual behavior patterns. But if institutions are defined as fulfilled expectations about behavior patterns it becomes difficult to understand how institutions might change. We want to be very careful not to prejudge the stability of particular institutions, so we define institutions as commonly held expectations and leave the question of whether or not these expectations will continue to be fulfilled – that is, whether or not any particular institution will persist or be transformed – an open question.

Why must there be social institutions?

If we were mind readers, or if we had infinite time to consult with one another, human societies might not require mediating institutions. But if there is to be a "division of labor," and if we are neither omniscient nor immortal, people must act on the basis of expectations about other people's behavior. If I make a pair of shoes in order to sell them to pay a dentist to fill my daughter's cavities, I am expecting others to play the role of shoe buyer, and dentists to render their services for a fee. I neither read the minds of the shoe-buyers and dentist, nor take the time to arrange and confirm all these coordinated activities before proceeding to make the shoes. Instead I act based on expectations about others' behavior.

So institutions are the necessary consequence of human sociability combined with our lack of omniscience and our mortality – which has important implications for the tendency among some anarchists to conceive of the goal of liberation as the abolition of all institutions. Anarchists correctly note that individuals are not completely "free" as long as institutional constraints exist. *Any* institutional boundary makes some individual choices easier and others harder, and therefore infringes on individual freedom to some extent. But abolishing social institutions is impossible for the human species. The relevant question about institutions, therefore, should not be whether we want them to exist, but whether any particular institution poses unnecessarily oppressive limitations, or promotes human development and fulfillment to the maximum extent possible.

In conclusion, if one insists on asking where, exactly, the *Institutional Boundary* is to be found, the answer is that as commonly held expectations about individual behavior patterns, social institutions

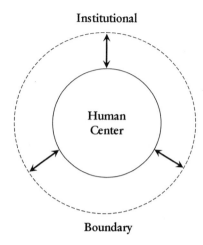

Figure 1.1   Human Center and Institutional Boundary

are a very practical and limited kind of mental phenomenon. As a matter of fact they are a kind of mental phenomenon that other social animals share – baboons, elephants, wolves, and a number of bird species have received much study. But just because our definition of roles and institutions locates them in people's minds, where we have also located consciousness, does not mean there is not an important distinction between the two. It is human consciousness that provides the potential for purposefully changing our institutions. As best we know, animals cannot change their institutions since they did not create them in the first place. Other animals receive their institutions as part of their genetic inheritance that comes already "wired in." We humans inherit only the necessity of creating some social institutions due to our sociability and lack of omniscience. But the specific creations are, within the limits of our potentials, ours to design.[2]

2. Thorstein Veblen, father of institutionalist economics, and Talcott Parsons, a giant of modern sociology, both underestimated the potential for applying the human tool of consciousness to the task of analyzing and evaluating the effects of institutions with a mind to changing them for the better. This led Veblen to overstate his case against what he termed "teleological" theories of history, i.e., ones that held on to the possibility of social progress. The same failure rendered Parsonian sociology powerless to explain the process of social change.

- The **Institutional Boundary** is society's particular set of social institutions that are each a conglomeration of interconnected roles, or commonly held expectations about appropriate behavior patterns. We define these roles independently of whether or not the expectations they represent will continue to be fulfilled, and apart from whatever incentives do or do not exist for individuals to choose to behave in their accord. The Institutional Boundary is necessary in any human society since we are neither immortal nor omniscient, and is distinct from both human consciousness and activity. It is human consciousness that makes possible purposeful transformations of the Institutional Boundary through human activity.

COMPLEMENTARY HOLISM

A social theory useful for pursuing human liberation must highlight the relationship between social institutions and human characteristics. But it is also important to distinguish between different areas, or spheres of social life, and consider the possible relationships between them. In *Liberating Theory* seven progressive authors called our treatment of these issues "complementary holism."

Four spheres of social life

The economy is not the only "sphere" of social activity. In addition to creating economic institutions to organize our efforts to meet material needs and desires, people have organized community institutions for addressing our cultural and spiritual needs, intricate "sex-gender," or "kinship" systems for satisfying our sexual needs and discharging our parental functions, and elaborate political systems for mediating social conflicts and enforcing social decisions. So in addition to the *economic sphere* of social life we have what we call a *community sphere*, a *kinship sphere*, and a *political sphere* as well. In this book we will be primarily concerned with evaluating the performance of the economic sphere, but the possible relationships between the economy and other spheres of social life are worthy of some consideration.

A *monist* paradigm presumes some form of dominance, or hierarchy of influence among the spheres of social life, while a *pluralist* social theory studies the dynamics of each sphere separately and then attempts to sum the results. A *complementary holist* approach assumes any form of dominance (or lack of dominance) among the four spheres of social life is a matter to be determined by empirical study of particular societies. All four spheres are socially necessary. Any society that failed to produce and distribute the material means of life would cease to exist. Some Marxists argue that this implies that the economic sphere, or what they call the economic "base" or "mode of production," is necessarily dominant in any and all human societies. But any society that failed to procreate and rear the next generation would also cease to exist. So the kinship sphere of social life is just as "socially necessary" as the economic sphere. And any society that failed to mediate conflicts among its members would disintegrate. Which means the political sphere of social life is necessary as well. Finally, since all societies have existed in the context of other, historically distinct societies, and many contain more than one historically distinct community, all societies have had to establish some kind of relations with other social communities, and most have had to define relations among internal communities as well. This means that the community sphere of social life is as necessary as the political, kinship, and economic spheres.

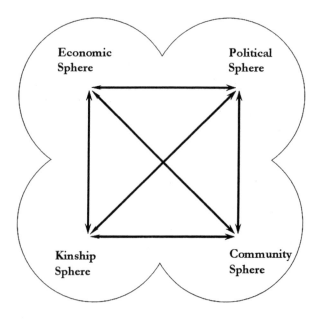

Figure 1.2   Four Spheres of Social Life

Besides being necessary, each of the four spheres is usually governed by elaborate social institutions that can take many different forms and have significant impacts on people's characteristics and behavior. This, more than their "social necessity" is why complementary holism recognizes that all four spheres are important, but that any pattern of dominance that may or may not result cannot be determined by theory alone. Instead of *a priori* presumptions of dominance, complementary holism holds there are a number of possible kinds of relations that can exist among spheres, and which possibility pertains in a particular society can only be determined by empirical investigation.

Relations between center, boundary and spheres

The human center and institutional boundary, and the four spheres of social life, are useful conceptual building blocks for an emancipatory social theory. The concepts human center and institutional boundary include all four kinds of social activity, but distinguish between people and institutions. The spheres of social life encompass both the human and institutional aspects of a particular kind of social activity, but distinguish between different primary functions of different activities. The possible relations between center and boundary, and between different spheres, are obviously critical.

It is evident that if a society is to be stable people must generally fit the roles they are going to fill. Actual behavior must generally conform to the expected patterns of behavior defined by society's major social institutions. People must choose activities in accord with the roles available, and this requires that people's personalities, skills, and consciousness be such that they do so. We must be capable and willing to do what is required of us. In other words, there must be conformity between society's human center and institutional boundary for social stability.

Suppose this were not the case. For example, suppose South African whites had shed their racist consciousness overnight, but all the institutions of apartheid had remained intact. Unless the institutions of apartheid were also changed, rationalization of continued participation in institutions guided by racist norms would have eventually regenerated racist consciousness among South African whites. Or, on a smaller scale, suppose one professor eliminates grades, makes papers optional, and no longer dictates course curriculum nor delivers monologues for lectures, but instead, awaits student initiatives. If students arrive conditioned to respond to grading incentives alone, wanting to be led or entertained by the instructor, then the elimination of authoritarianism in the institutional structures of a single classroom in the context of continued authoritarian expectations in the student body would result in very little learning indeed.

Social stability and social change

Whether the result of any "discrepancy" between the human center and institutional boundary will lead to a remolding of the center to conform with an unchanged boundary, or changes in the boundary that make it more compatible with the human center cannot be known in advance. But in either case *stabilizing forces* within societies act to bring the center and boundary into conformity, and lack of conformity is a sign of social instability.

But this is not to say that the human centers and institutional boundaries of all human societies are equally easy to stabilize. While we are always being socialized by the institutions we confront, this process can run into more or fewer obstacles depending on the extent to which particular institutional structures are compatible or incompatible with innate human potentials. In other words, just as there are always stabilizing forces at work in societies, there are often *destabilizing forces* as well resulting from institutional incompatibilities with fundamental human needs. For example, no matter how well oiled the socialization processes of a slave society, there remains a fundamental incompatibility between the social role of slave and the innate human potential and need for self-management. That incompatibility is a constant source of potential instability in societies that seek to confine people to slave status.

It is also possible for dynamics in one sphere to reinforce or destabilize dynamics in another sphere of social life. For example, it might be that the functioning of the nuclear family produces authoritarian personality structures that reinforce authoritarian dynamics in economic relations. Dynamics in economic hierarchies might also reinforce patriarchal hierarchies in families. In this case authoritarian dynamics in the economic and kinship spheres would be mutually reinforcing. Or, hierarchies in one sphere sometimes accommodate hierarchies in other spheres. For example, the assignment of people to economic roles might accommodate prevailing hierarchies in community and kinship spheres by placing minorities and women into inferior economic positions. It is also possible that role definitions themselves in a sphere are influenced by dynamics from another sphere. For instance, if the economic role of secretary includes tending the coffee machine as well as dictation, typing, and filing, the role of secretary is defined not merely by economic dynamics but by kinship dynamics as well.

On the other hand, it is possible for the activity in one sphere to disrupt the manner in which activity is organized in another sphere. For instance, the educational system as one component of the kinship sphere might graduate more people seeking a particular kind of economic role than the economic sphere can provide under its current organization. This would produce destabilizing expectations and demands in the economic sphere, and\or the educational system in the kinship sphere. Some argued this was the case during the 1960s and 1970s in the US when college education was expanded greatly and produced "too many" with higher level thinking skills for the number of positions permitting the exercise of such potentials in the monopoly capitalist US economy – giving rise to a "student movement." In any case, at the broadest level, there can be either stabilizing or destabilizing relations among spheres.

Agents of history

The stabilizing and destabilizing forces that exist between center and boundary and among different spheres of social life operate constantly whether or not people in the society are aware of them or not. But these ever present forces for social stability or social change are usually complemented by conscious efforts of particular social groups seeking to maintain or transform the status quo. Particular ways of organizing the economy may generate privileged and disadvantaged *classes*. Similarly, the organization of kinship activity may distribute the burdens and benefits unequally between *gender groups* – for example granting men more of the benefits while assigning them fewer of the burdens of kinship activity than women. And particular community institutions may not serve the needs of all community groups equally well, for example denying *racial or religious minorities* rights or opportunities enjoyed by majority communities. Therefore, besides underlying forces that stabilize or destabilize societies, groups who enjoy more of the benefits and shoulder fewer of the burdens of social cooperation *in any sphere* have an interest in acting to preserve the status quo. Groups who suffer more of the burdens and enjoy fewer of the benefits under existing arrangements *in any sphere* can become agents for social change. In this way groups that are either privileged or disadvantaged by the rules of engagement *in any of the four spheres of social life* can become *agents of history*.

The key to understanding the importance of classes without neglecting or underestimating the importance of privileged and disadvantaged groups defined by community, kinship or political relations is to recognize that *only some* agents of history are economic groups, or classes. Racial, gender, and political groups can also be conscious agents working to preserve or change the status quo, which consists not only of the reigning economic relations, but the dominant gender, community, and political relations as well.[3] Pre-Mandela South African society is a useful case to consider. Of course the economy generated privileged and exploited classes – capitalists and workers, landowners and tenants, etc. South African patriarchal gender relations also disadvantaged women compared to men, and undemocratic political institutions empowered a minority and disenfranchised most citizens. But the most important social relations, from which the system derived its name, *apartheid*, were rules for classifying citizens into specific communities – whites, colored, blacks – and defining different rights and obligations for people according to their community status. The community relations of apartheid created oppressor and oppressed *racial community groups* who played the principal roles in the social struggle to preserve or overthrow the status quo in South Africa. This perspective need not deny that classes, or gender groups for that matter, played significant roles as well. But a social theory that recognizes all spheres of social life, and understands that privileged and disadvantaged groups can emerge from any of these areas where the burdens and benefits of social cooperation are not distributed equally, can help us avoid neglecting important agents of history, and help us understand why not all forms of oppression will be redressed by a social revolution in one sphere of social life alone – as important as that change may be.

3. Broadly speaking the term "economism" means attributing greater importance to the economy than is warranted. It can take the form of assuming that dynamics in the economic sphere are more important than dynamics in other spheres when this, in fact, is not the case in some particular society. It can also take the form of assuming that classes are more important agents of social change, and racial, gender or political groups are less important "agents of history" than they actually are in a particular situation.

Hopefully this conception of human beings, human societies, and different spheres of social life in the liberating social theory summarized in this chapter provides a proper setting for our study of "political economy" – one that neither overstates nor understates its role in the social sciences. In chapter 2 we proceed to think about how to evaluate the performance of any economy.

2 What Should We Demand from Our Economy?

It is easy enough to say we want an economy that distributes the burdens and benefits of social labor fairly, that allows people to make the decisions that affect their economic lives, that develops human potentials for creativity, cooperation and empathy, and that utilizes human and natural resources efficiently. It is also easy to say we want "sustainable development." But what does all this mean more precisely?

ECONOMIC JUSTICE

Is it necessarily unfair when some work less or consume more than others? Do those with more productive property deserve to work less or consume more? Do those who are more talented or more educated deserve more? Do those who contribute more, or those who make greater sacrifices, or those who have greater needs deserve more? By what logic are some unequal outcomes fair and others not?

Equity takes a back seat to efficiency for most mainstream economists, while the issue of economic justice has long been a passion of political economists. From Proudhon's provocative quip that "property is theft," to Marx's three volume indictment of capitalism as a system based on the "exploitation of labor," economic justice and injustice has been a major theme in political economy. After briefly reviewing evidence of rising economic inequality within the United States and globally, we compare conservative, liberal and radical views of economic justice, and explain why political economists condemn most of today's growing inequalities as escalating economic injustice.

Increasing inequality of wealth and income

As we begin the twenty-first century, escalating economic inequality makes all other economic changes pale in comparison. The evidence of increasing wealth and income inequality is overwhelming. In a study published in 1995 by the Twentieth Century Fund, Edward Wolff concludes:

> Many people are aware that income inequality has increased over the past twenty years. Upper-income groups have continued to do well while others, particularly those without a college degree and the young have seen their real income decline. The 1994 *Economic Report of the President* refers to the 1979–1990 fall in real income of men with only four years of high school – a 21% decline – as stunning. But the growing divergence evident in income distribution is even starker in wealth distribution. Equalizing trends of the 1930s–1970s reversed sharply in the 1980s. The gap between haves and have-nots is greater now than at any time since 1929.[1]

Chuck Collins and Felice Yeskel report: "In 1976, the wealthiest one percent of the population owned just under 20% of all the private wealth. By 1999, the richest 1 percent's share had increased to over 40% of all wealth." And they calculate that in the twenty-three years between 1976 and 1999 while the top 1% of wealth holders doubled their share of the wealth pie, the bottom 90% saw their share cut almost in half.[2] Between 1983 and 1989 the average financial wealth of households in the United States grew at an annual rate of 4.3% after being adjusted for inflation. But the top 1% of wealth holders captured an astounding 66.2% of the growth in financial wealth, the next 19% of wealth holders captured 36.8%, and the bottom 80% of wealth holders in the US lost 3.0% of their financial wealth. As a result, the top 1% increased their share of total wealth in the US from 31% to 37% in those six years alone, and by 1989 the richest 1% of families held 45% of all nonresidential real estate, 62% of all business assets, 49% of all publicly held stock, and 78% of all bonds.[3] Moreover, "most wealth growth arose from the appreciation (or capital gains) of pre-existing wealth and not savings out of income. Over the 1962 to 1989 period, roughly three-quarters of new wealth

---

1. Edward N. Wolff, *Top Heavy: A Study of the Increasing Inequality of Wealth in America* (The Twentieth Century Fund, 1995): 1–2.
2. Chuck Collins and Felice Yeskel with United for a Fair Economy, *Economic Apartheid in America* (The New Press, 2000): 54–7.
3. *The New Field Guide to the US Economy*, by Nancy Folbre and the Center for Popular Economics (The New Press, 1995).

was generated by increasing the value of initial wealth – much of it inherited."[4] When we look to see who benefitted from the stock market boom between 1989 and 1997 the same pattern emerges. The top 1% of wealth holders captured an astonishing 42.5% of the stock market gains over those years, the next 9% of wealth holders captured an additional 43.3% of the gains, the next 10% captured 3.1%, while the bottom 80% of wealth holders captured only 11% of the stock market gains.[5]

While growing wealth inequality has been more dramatic, income inequality has been growing as well. Real wages have fallen in the US since the mid 1970s to where the average hourly wage adjusted for inflation was lower in 1994 than it had been in 1968. Moreover, this decline in real hourly wages has occurred despite continual increases in labor productivity. Between 1973 and 1998 labor productivity grew 33%. Collins and Yeskel calculate that if hourly wages had grown at the same rate as labor productivity the average hourly wage in 1998 would have been $18.10 rather than $12.77 – a difference of $5.33 an hour, or more than $11,000 per year for a full-time worker.[6] Moreover, the failure of real wages to keep up with labor productivity growth has been worse for those in lower wage brackets. Between 1973 and 1993 workers earning in the 80th percentile gained 2.7% in real wages while workers in the 60th percentile lost 4.9%, workers in the 40th percentile lost 9.0%, and workers in the 20th percentile lost 11.7% – creating much greater inequality of wage income.[7]

In contrast, corporate profit rates in the US in 1996 reached their highest level since these data were first collected in 1959. The Bureau of Economic Analysis reported that the before-tax profit rate rose to 11.4% and the after-tax rate rose to 7.6% in 1996 – yielding an eight-year period of dramatic, sustained increases in corporate profits the Bureau called "unparalleled in US history." Moreover, whereas previous periods of high profits accompanied high rates of investment and economic growth, the average rate of economic growth over these eight years was just 1.9%. Whatever was good for corporate profits was clearly *not* so good for the rest of us.

4. Lawrence Mishel and Jared Bernstein, *The State of Working America 1994–1995* (ME Sharpe, 1994): 246.
5. *The State of Working America 1998–1999*: 271.
6. *Economic Apartheid in America*: 56.
7. *The State of Working America 1994–1995*: 121.

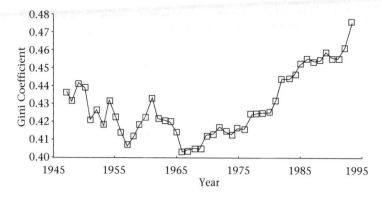

Figure 2.1   Gini Coefficients for US Household Income 1947–93[8]

While there are a number of different ways to measure inequality, the most widely used by economists is a statistic called the Gini coefficient. A value of 0 corresponds to perfect equality and a value of 1 corresponds to perfect inequality. Figure 2.1 plots the Gini coefficient for household income in the United States from 1947 to 1993. The steady increase in the Gini coefficient from a low of 0.405 in 1966 to a high of 0.479 in 1993 represents a remarkable, and historically unprecedented 18.3% increase in income inequality among US households over the time period.

Trends in global inequality are equally, if not more disturbing. Walter Park and David Brat report in a study of gross domestic product per capita in 91 countries that the value of the Gini rose steadily from 0.442 in 1960 to 0.499 in 1988. In other words, between 1960 and 1988 there was an increase in the economic inequality between countries of 13%.[9] All evidence available so far confirms that this trend continued in the 1990s and first two years of the new millennium as neoliberal globalization accelerated.

The facts are clear: We are experiencing increases in economic inequality inside the US reminiscent of the "Robber Baron era" of US capitalism over a hundred years ago, and global inequality is accelerating at an unprecedented pace. But how should we interpret

8. Source: Edward Wolff, *Economics of Poverty, Inequality and Discrimination* (South-Western Publishing, 1997): 75.
9. Walter Park and David Brat, "A Global Kuznets Curve?" *Kylos*, Vol. 48, 1995: 110.

the facts? When are unequal outcomes inequitable and when are they not?

Different conceptions of economic justice

What is an equitable distribution of the burdens and benefits of economic activity? Philosophers, economists, and political scientists have offered three different distributive maxims attempting to capture the essence of economic justice, which we can label the conservative, liberal, and radical definitions of economic justice.

Conservative Maxim 1: *Payment according to the value of one's personal contribution and the contribution of the productive property one owns.*

The rationale behind the conservative maxim is that people should get out of an economy what they and their productive possessions contribute to the economy. If we think of the goods and services, or benefits of an economy, as a giant pot of stew, the idea is that individuals contribute to how big and rich the stew will be by their labor and by the productive assets they bring to the kitchen. If my labor and productive assets make the stew bigger or richer than your labor and assets, then according to maxim 1 it is only fair that I eat more stew, or richer morsels, than you do.

While this rationale has obvious appeal, it has a major problem I call the *Rockefeller grandson problem*. According to maxim 1 the grandson of a Rockefeller with a large inheritance of productive property *should* eat 1000 times as much stew as a highly trained, highly productive, hard working son of a pauper – even if Rockefeller's grandson doesn't work a day in his life and the pauper's son works for fifty years producing goods or providing services of great benefit to others. This will inevitably occur if we count the contribution of productive property people own, and if people own different amounts of machinery and land, or what is the same thing, different amounts of stocks in corporations that own the machinery and land, since bringing a cooking pot or stove to the economy "kitchen" increases the size and quality of the stew we can make just as surely as peeling more potatoes and stirring the pot more does. So anyone who considers it *unfair* when the idle grandson of a Rockefeller consumes more than a hard working, productive son of a pauper cannot accept maxim 1 as the definition of equity.

A second line of defense for the conservative maxim is based on a vision of "free and independent" people, each with his or her own property, who, it is argued, would refuse to voluntarily enter a social contract on any other terms. This view is commonly associated with the writings of John Locke. But while it is clear why those with a great deal of productive property in Locke's "state of nature" would have reason to hold out for a social contract along the lines of maxim 1, why would not those who wander the state of nature with little or no productive property in their backpacks hold out for a very different arrangement? If those with considerable wherewithal can do quite well for themselves in the state of nature, whereas those without cannot, it is not difficult to see how requiring unanimity would drive the bargain in the direction of maxim 1. But then maxim 1 is the result of an unfair bargaining situation in which the rich are better able to tolerate failure to reach an agreement over a fair way to assign the burdens and benefits of economic cooperation than the poor, giving the rich the upper hand in negotiations over the terms of the social contract. In this case the social contract rationale for maxim 1 loses moral force because it results from an unfair bargain.

This suggests that unless those with more productive property acquired it through some greater merit on their part, the income they accrue from this property is unjustifiable, at least on equity grounds. That is, while the unequal outcome might be desirable for some other reason such as improving economic efficiency, it would not be just or fair. In which case maxim 1 must be rejected as a definition of equity if we find that those who own more productive property did not come by it through greater merit. One way people acquire productive property is through inheritance. But it is difficult to see how those who inherit wealth are more deserving than those who don't. It is possible the person making a bequest worked harder or consumed less than others in her generation, and in one of these ways sacrificed more than others. Or it is possible the person making the bequest was more productive than others. And we might decide that greater sacrifice or greater contribution merits greater reward. But in these scenarios it is not the heir who made the greater sacrifice or contribution, it is the person who made the bequest, so the heir would not deserve greater wealth on those grounds. As a matter of fact, if we decide rewards are earned by sacrifice or personal contribution, inherited wealth violates either norm since inheriting wealth is neither a sacrifice nor a personal contribution. A more compelling argument for inheritance is that banning inheritance is unfair to those wishing to make bequests rather than that it is unfair to those who would receive them. One could argue that if wealth is justly acquired it is wrong to prevent anyone from disposing of it as they wish – including bequeathing it to their descendants. However, it should be noted that any "right" of wealthy members of older generations to bequeath their gains to their offspring would have to be weighed against the "right" of people in younger generations to start with "equal economic opportunities."[10] Indeed, these two "rights" are obviously in conflict, and some means of adjudicating between them is required. But no matter how this matter is settled, it appears that those who receive income from inherited wealth benefit from an unfair advantage.

A second way people acquire more productive property than others is through good luck. Working or investing in a rising or declining company or industry constitutes good luck or bad luck. But unequal distributions of productive property that result from differences in luck are not the result of unequal sacrifices, unequal contributions, or any difference in merit between people. Luck, by its very definition is not deserved, and therefore the unequal incomes that result from unequal distributions of productive property due to differences in luck appear to be inequitable as well.

A third way people come to have more productive property is through unfair advantage. Those who are stronger, better connected, have inside information, or are more willing to prey on the misery of others can acquire more productive property through legal and illegal means. Obviously if unequal wealth is the result of someone taking unfair advantage of another it is inequitable.

The last way people might come to have more productive property than others is by using some income they earned fairly to purchase more productive property than others can. What constitutes fairly earned income is the subject of maxims 2 and 3 which are discussed below. But there is a difficult moral issue regarding income from productive property even if the productive property was purchased with income we stipulate was fairly earned in the first place. In chapter 3 we will discover that labor and credit markets allow people

10. We are not talking about willing personal belongings to decedents, which is unobjectionable, but passing on productive property in quantities that significantly skew the economic opportunities of members of the new generation.

with productive wealth to capture part of the increase in productivity of *other people* that results when other people work with the productive wealth. Whether or not, and to what extent, the profit or rent which owners of productive wealth initially receive is merited we will examine very carefully. But even if we stipulate that some compensation is justified by a meritorious action that occurred *once* in the past, it turns out that labor and credit markets allow those who own productive wealth to parlay it into *permanently* higher incomes which *increase* over time with no further meritorious behavior on their parts. This creates the dilemma that ownership of productive property *even if justly acquired* may well give rise to additional income that, while fair initially, becomes unfair after some point, and increasingly so. The simple corn model we explore in chapter 3 illustrates this moral dilemma nicely.

In sum, if unequal accumulations of productive property were the result only of meritorious actions, and if compensation ceased when the social debt was fully repaid, using words like "exploitation" to describe payments to owners of productive property would seem harsh and misleading. On the other hand, if those who own more productive property acquired it through inheritance, luck, unfair advantage – or because once they have more productive property than others they can accumulate even more with no further above-average meritorious behavior through labor or credit markets – then calling the unequal outcomes that result from differences in wealth unfair or exploitative seems perfectly appropriate. Most political economists believe a compelling case can be made that differences in ownership of productive property which accumulate within a single generation due to unequal sacrifices and/or unequal contributions people make themselves are small compared to the differences in wealth that develop due to inheritance, luck, unfair advantage, and accumulation. Edward Bellamy put it this way in *Looking Backward* written at the end of the nineteenth century: "You may set it down as a rule that the rich, the possessors of great wealth, had no moral right to it as based upon desert, for either their fortunes belonged to the class of inherited wealth, or else, when accumulated in a lifetime, necessarily represented chiefly the product of others, more or less forcibly or fraudulently obtained." One hundred years later Lester Thurow estimated that between 50 and 70% of all wealth in the US is inherited. Daphne Greenwood and Edward Wolff estimated that 50 to 70% of the wealth of households under age 50 was inherited. Laurence Kotlikoff and

Lawrence Summers estimated that as much as 80% of personal wealth came either from direct inheritance or the income on inherited wealth.[11] A study published by United for a Fair Economy in 1997 titled "Born on Third Base" found that of the 400 on the 1997 Forbes list of wealthiest individuals and families in the US, 42% inherited their way onto the list; another 6% inherited wealth in excess of $50 million, and another 7% started life with at least $1 million. In any case, presumably what Proudhon was thinking when he coined the phrase "property is theft" was that most large wealth holders acquire their wealth through inheritance, luck, unfair advantage, or unfair accumulation. A less flamboyant radical might have stipulated that he was referring to productive, not personal property, and added the qualification "property is theft – more often than not."

Liberal Maxim 2: *Payment according to the value of one's personal contribution only.*

While those who support the liberal maxim find most property income unjustifiable, advocates of maxim 2 hold that all have a right to the "fruits of their own labor." The rationale for this has a powerful appeal: If my labor contributes more to the social endeavor it is only right that I receive more. Not only am I not exploiting others, they would be exploiting me by paying me less than the value of my personal contribution. But ironically, the same reason for rejecting the conservative maxim applies to the liberal maxim as well.

Economists define the value of the contribution of any input in production as the "marginal revenue product" of that input. In other words, if we add one more unit of the input in question to all of the inputs currently used in a production process, how much would the value of output increase? The answer is defined as the marginal revenue product of the input in question. But mainstream economics teaches us that the marginal productivity, or contribution of an

11. Lester Thurow, *The Future of Capitalism: How Today's Economic Forces Will Shape the Future* (William Morrow, 1996), Daphne Greenwood and Edward Wolff, "Changes in Wealth in the United States 1962–1983," *Journal of Population Economics* 5, 1992, and Laurence Kotlikoff and Lawrence Summers, "The Role of Intergenerational Transfers in Aggregate Capital Accumulation," *Journal of Political Economy* 89, 1981.

input, depends as much on the number of units of that input available, and on the quantity and quality of other, complimentary inputs, as on any intrinsic quality of the input itself – which undermines the moral imperative behind any "contribution based" maxim – that is, maxim 2 as well as maxim 1. But besides the fact that the marginal productivity of different kinds of labor depends mostly on the number of people in each labor category in the first place, and on the quantity and quality of non-labor inputs available for them to use, most of the remaining differences in people's personal productivities are due to personal differences beyond people's control which *cannot* be traced to differential sacrifices. No amount of eating and weight lifting will give an average individual a 6 feet 11 inches frame with 350 plus pounds of muscle. Yet professional football players in the United States receive hundreds of times more than an average salary because those attributes make their contribution outrageously high in the context of US sports culture. The famous British political economist, Joan Robinson, pointed out long ago, that however "productive" a machine or piece of land may be, that hardly constitutes a moral argument for paying anything to its owner. In a similar vein one could argue that however "productive" a high IQ or a 350 pound physique may be, that doesn't mean the owner of this trait deserves more income than someone less gifted who works as hard and sacrifices as much. The bottom line is that the "genetic lottery" greatly influences how valuable a person's contribution will be. Yet the genetic lottery is no more fair than the inheritance lottery – which implies that as a conception of economic justice maxim 2 suffers from a similar flaw as maxim 1.[12]

In defense of maxim 2 it is frequently argued that while talent may not deserve reward, talent requires training, and herein lies the sacrifice that merits reward: Doctor's salaries are compensation for all the extra years of education. But longer training does not necessarily mean greater personal sacrifice. It is important not to confuse the cost of someone's training to society – which consists mostly of the

---

12. Milton Friedman argued this point eloquently in *Capitalism and Freedom* (University of Chicago Press, 1964): chapter 10. However, his conclusion was that since maxim 2 cannot be defended on moral grounds, critics of capitalism, which distributes the burdens and benefits of economic cooperation according to maxim 1, should mute their criticisms. Essentially Friedman reminded critics of capitalism who favor maxim 2 over maxim 1 that those who live in glass houses shouldn't throw stones!

trainer's time and energy, and scarce social resources like books, computers, libraries, and classrooms – with the personal sacrifice of the *trainee*. If teachers and educational facilities are paid for at public expense – that is, if we have a universal public education system – and if students are paid a living stipend – so they forego no income while in school – then the personal sacrifice of the student consists only of their discomfort from time spent in school. But even the personal suffering we endure as students must be properly compared. While many educational programs are less personally enjoyable than time spent in leisure, comparing discomfort during school with comfort during leisure is not the relevant comparison. The relevant comparison is with the discomfort others experience who are working instead of going to school. If our criterion is greater personal sacrifice *than others*, then logic requires comparing the student's discomfort to whatever level of discomfort others are experiencing who work while the student is in school. Only if schooling is more disagreeable than working does it constitute a greater sacrifice than others make, and thereby deserves reward. So to the extent that education is born at public rather than private expense, and the personal discomfort of schooling is no greater than the discomfort others incur while working, extra schooling merits no compensation on moral grounds.

In sum, I call the problem with maxim 2 the *"doctor–garbage collector problem."* If education were free all the way through medical school, how could it be fair to pay a brain surgeon who is on the first tee at his country club golf course by 1 p.m. even on the four days a week he works, ten times more than a garbage collector who works under miserable conditions 40 plus hours a week.

Radical Maxim 3: *Payment according to effort, or the personal sacrifices one makes.*

Which brings us to radical maxim 3. Whereas differences in contribution will be due to differences in talent, training, job assignment, luck, and effort, the only factor that deserves extra compensation according to maxim 3 is extra effort. By "effort" is meant personal sacrifice for the sake of the social endeavor. Of course effort can take many forms. It may be longer work hours, less pleasant work, or more intense, dangerous, unhealthy work. Or, it may consist of undergoing training that is less gratifying than the training experiences of others, or less pleasant than time others spend working who train less. The underlying rationale for maxim 3 is that people should eat from the stew pot according to the sacrifices they made to cook it. According to maxim 3 no other consideration, besides differential sacrifice, can justify one person eating more stew than another.

Even for those who reject contribution-based theories of economic justice like maxims 1 and 2 as inherently flawed because people's abilities to contribute are different through no fault of their own, there is still a problem with maxim 3 from a moral point of view that I call the "*AIDS victim problem.*" Suppose someone has made average sacrifices for 15 years, and consumed an average amount. Suddenly they contract AIDS through no fault of their own. In the early 1990s a medical treatment program for an AIDS victim often cost close to a million dollars. That is, the cost to society of providing humane care for an AIDS victim was roughly a million dollars. If we limit people's consumption to the level warranted by their efforts, we would have to deny AIDS victims humane treatment, which many would find hard to defend on moral grounds.

Of course this is where another maxim comes to mind: *payment according to need.* Whether taking differences in need into consideration is required by economic justice or is required, instead, for an economy to be *humane* is debatable. In my personal view the **humane maxim**, payment according to need, is in a different category than the other three and expresses a commendable value, but a value beyond economic justice. It seems to me that it is one thing for an economy to be an equitable economy – one that is fair and just. It is another thing for an economy also to be humane. While I believe justice requires compensating people according to the sacrifices they make, it seems to me that it is our humanity that compels us to provide for those in need. When considered in this light a just economy is not the last word in morally desirable economies. A just economy that allowed AIDs victims to suffer for lack of proper medical care would, indeed, be morally deficient because it would be inhumane. If thought of in this way, besides striving for economic justice, we must work for a humane economy as well, which entails distribution according to effort or sacrifice, tempered by need.

EFFICIENCY

As long as resources are scarce relative to human needs and socially useful labor is burdensome, in part, efficiency is preferable to wastefulness. Political economists do not have to imitate our mainstream colleagues and concentrate on efficiency to the detriment of other important criteria such as economic justice and democracy in order to recognize that people have every reason to be resentful if their sacrifices are wasted or if limited resources are squandered.

The Pareto Principle

Economists usually define economic efficiency as Pareto optimality – named after the late nineteenth-century Italian economist Wilfredo Pareto. A **Pareto optimal outcome** *is one where it is impossible to make anyone better off without making someone else worse off.* The idea is simply that it would be inefficient or wasteful not to implement *a change that made someone better off and nobody worse off.* Such a change is called a **Pareto improvement**, and another way to define a Pareto optimal, or efficient outcome, is an outcome where there are no further Pareto improvements possible.

This does not mean a Pareto optimal outcome is necessarily wonderful. If I have 10 units of happiness and you have 1, and there is no way for me to have more than 10 unless you have less than 1, and no way for you to have more than 1 unless I have fewer than 10, then me having 10 units of happiness and you having 1 is a Pareto optimal outcome. But you would be right not to regard it very highly, and being a reasonable person, I would even agree with you. Moreover, there are usually *many* Pareto optimal outcomes. For instance, if I have 7 units of happiness and you have 6, and if there is no way for me to have more than 7 unless you have fewer than 6, and no way for you to have more than 6 unless I have fewer than 7, then me having 7 and you having 6 is also a Pareto optimal outcome. And we might both regard this second Pareto optimal outcome as better than the first, even though I am personally better off under the first. So the point is not that being in a Pareto optimal situation is necessarily wonderful – that depends on *which* Pareto optimal situation we're in. Instead the point is that *non*-Pareto optimal outcomes are clearly undesirable because we could make someone better off without making anyone worse off – and it is "inefficient" or wasteful not to do that. In other words, there is something wrong with an economy that systematically yields non-Pareto optimal outcomes, i.e., fails to make some of its participants better off when doing so would make nobody worse off.

It is important to recognize that the Pareto criterion, or definition of efficiency, is not going to settle most of the important economic issues we face. Most policy choices will make some people better off but others worse off, and in these situations the Pareto criterion has nothing to tell us. Consequently, if economists confine themselves to the narrow concept of efficiency as Pareto optimality, and only recommend policies that are, in fact, Pareto improvements, we would be rendered silent on most issues! For example, reducing greenhouse gas emissions makes a lot of sense because the future benefits of stopping global warming and avoiding dramatic climate change far outweigh the present costs of reducing emissions. But since a relatively few people in the present generation will be made somewhat worse off no matter how we go about it, the fact that many more people in future generations will be much better off does not allow us to recommend the policy as a Pareto improvement – that is, on efficiency grounds in the narrow sense.

The efficiency critierion

The usual way around this problem is to broaden the notion of efficiency from Pareto improvements to changes where the benefits to some outweigh the costs to others. This broader notion of efficiency is called the *efficiency criterion* and serves as the basis for *cost benefit analysis*. Simply put, the efficiency criterion says *if the*

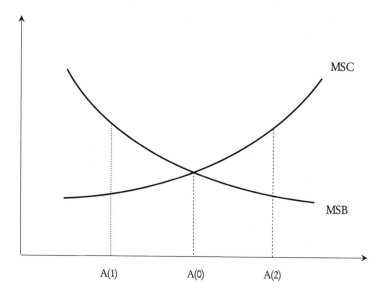

Figure 2.2   The Efficiency Criterion

overall benefits to any and all people of doing something outweigh the overall costs to any and all people, it is "efficient" to do it. Whereas, if the overall costs outweigh the overall benefits of doing something it is "inefficient" to do it.

We can illustrate the efficiency criterion using a very useful graph. Suppose we knew the cost to society of growing each and every apple. That is, suppose we knew how much of society's scarce land, labor, fertilizer, etc. it took to grow each and every apple, and we also knew how much pesticide it took, and how much it "cost" society when more pesticide seeped into our ground water, etc. We call this the "Social Cost" of producing apples, and we call the Social Cost of the last (or next) apple produced the Marginal Social Cost of apples, or MSC for short. Suppose we also knew the benefit to society of having another apple available to consume. The Social Benefit of the last (or next) apple consumed is called the Marginal Social Benefit of apples, or MSB for short. Now let us assume that the more apples we have consumed already the less beneficial an additional apple will be, and the more apples we have produced already the more it costs society to produce another one. In this case if we plot the number of apples on the horizontal axis and measure the Marginal Social Benefit and Marginal Social Cost of apples on the vertical axis, the MSB curve will be downward sloping and the MSC curve will be upward sloping as it is in Figure 2.2. What is incredibly useful about this diagram is it allows us to determine how many apples we *should* produce and consume, i.e. the socially efficient or "optimal" quantity of apples to produce, A(0). It is the amount where the marginal social cost of producing the last apple, MSC, is equal to the marginal social benefit from consuming the last apple, MSB. We can demonstrate that the socially efficient, or optimal level of apple production and consumption is the level below where the MSC and MSB curves cross by showing that any lower or higher level of production and consumption allows for an increase in net social benefits and therefore violates the efficiency criterion.

Suppose someone thought we should produce fewer apples than the level where MSC equals MSB, such as A(1) < A(0). For any level of production less than A(0), such as A(1), what would be the effect of producing one more apple than we are already producing? To see what the additional cost to society would be, we go up from A(1) to the MSC curve. To see what the additional benefit to society would be we go up from A(1) to the MSB curve. But when we produce and consume at A(1) the MSB curve is higher than the MSC curve, indicating that producing and consuming another apple increases social benefits more than it increases social costs. In other words, at A(1) there would be positive net social benefits from expanding production and consumption of apples.

Suppose someone thought we should produce more apples than the level where MSC equals MSB, such as A(2) > A(0). For any level of production greater than A(0), such as A(2), what would be the effect of producing one apple less than we are already producing? To see what the savings in social cost would be we go up from A(2) to the MSC curve. To see what the lost social benefit would be we go up from A(2) to the MSB curve. But when we produce and consume at A(2) the MSC curve is higher than the MSB curve indicating that producing and consuming one apple less reduces social benefits by less than it reduces social costs. In other words, at A(2) there are potential positive net social benefits from reducing production and consumption of apples.

The conclusion is for all A < A(0) we should expand apple production (and consumption), and for all A > A(0) we should reduce apple production (and consumption.) Therefore the only level of apple production that is efficient from society's point of view is the level where the Marginal Social Benefit of the last apple consumed is equal to the Marginal Social Cost of the last apple produced, A(0). In any other case we could increase net social benefits by expanding or reducing apple production and consumption.

Mainstream economists do not like to admit that policies recommended on the basis of the efficiency criterion are usually *not* Pareto improvements since they *do* make some people worse off. The efficiency criterion and all cost benefit analysis necessarily (1) "compares" different people's levels of satisfaction, and (2) attaches "weights" to how important the satisfactions of different people are when we calculate overall, or *social benefits* and *social costs*. Notice that when I stipulated that a few would be worse off in the present generation if we reduce greenhouse gas emissions while many will be benefitted in the future I was attributing greater weight to the gains of the many in the future than the loses of a few in the present. I think it is perfectly reasonable to do this, and do not hesitate to do so. But I am attaching weights to the well being of different people – in this case roughly equal weights, which I also believe is reasonable. If one refuses to attach weights to the well beings of different people the efficiency criterion cannot be used. I also stipulated that the benefits of preventing global warming to people in the future were large compared to the cost of reducing emissions to people in the present. I was willing to compare how large a gain was for one person compared to how small a loss was for a different person. If one refuses to compare the size of benefits and costs to different people, the efficiency criterion cannot be used. Unlike the narrow Pareto principle, the efficiency criterion requires comparing the magnitudes of costs and benefits to *different* people and deciding how much importance to attach to the well being of *different* people.

In other words, the efficiency criterion requires *value judgments* beyond what are required by the Pareto principle. So when mainstream economists pretend they have imposed no value judgments, and have separated efficiency from equity issues when they apply cost benefit analysis and recommend policy based on the *efficiency criterion* they misrepresent themselves. While a Pareto improvement makes some better off at the expense of none – and therefore does not require comparing the sizes of gains and losses to different people or weighing the importance of well being to different people – policies that satisfy the efficiency criterion generally make some better off precisely at the expense of others, which necessarily requires comparing the magnitudes of costs and benefits to different people and making a value judgment regarding how important the interests of the "winners" are compared to the interests of the "losers." Mainstream economists like to point out that if a policy passes the efficiency criterion that means the magnitude of benefits enjoyed by the winners is necessarily larger than the magnitude of costs suffered by the losers, which means it would be *theoretically possible* for the winners to fully compensate the losers and still be better off themselves. But first, this requires a comparison of the magnitude of gains to some compared to the magnitude of losses to others – already a large step beyond the narrow conceptualization of efficiency enshrined in the Pareto principle that does not permit comparing different people's satis-factions. Secondly, either compensation is paid, or it is not paid. If a policy requires winners to fully compensate losers then it *is* a Pareto improvement and we do not need the broader efficiency criterion to recommend it. If, on the other hand, a policy does not require that losers be fully compensated from the gains to winners, then it requires a value judgment that those who win deserve to do so, and those who lose deserve to do so, before it can be recommended – however much economists who claim to forswear "value judgments" may wish otherwise. In the end, the only reason we need the efficiency criterion in the first place is precisely because so many important choices fall outside the purview of the Pareto principle, i.e. cannot be reduced to efficiency defined narrowly.

Seven deadly sins of inefficiency

How might an economy be wasteful in the sense that it fails to achieve a Pareto optimal outcome? It turns out there are seven different ways that any economy might be inefficient. I facetiously call them the seven "deadly sins" of inefficiency.

The production sector of an economy will be inefficient if:

1. It leaves productive resources idle. (Example: unemployed workers, or idle crop land.)
2. It uses inefficient technologies, that is, uses more of some input than necessary to get a given amount of output. (Example: The same number of shoes can be made with less leather by more careful cutting.)
3. It misallocates productive resources so that swapping inputs between two different production units would lead to increases in output in both. (Example: Assigning carpenters to a farm and agronomists to the construction industry.)

The consumption sector will be inefficient if:

4. There are undistributed, or idle consumption goods. (Example: Wheat rotting in silos while people go hungry.)
5. Final goods are misdistributed so that two or more consumers could exchange goods and both be better off than under the original distribution. (Examples: Apples are distributed to orange lovers while oranges are distributed to apple lovers.)

And the production and consumption sectors will be inefficiently integrated if:

6. Goods are misallocated between consumers and producers so it is possible for a producer and consumer to swap goods and have the output of the producer rise and the satisfaction of the consumer increase as well. (Example: Personal computers are distributed to households that suffer for lack of heat while

employees at accounting firms are unproductive in overheated offices without personal computers to work with.)

7. Resources are misallocated to different industries so it is possible to shift productive resources from one industry to another to produce a different mixture of outputs more to consumers' tastes. (Example: Most land suitable for orchards is planted in pear trees even though most consumers prefer apples to pears.)

The seven deadly sins of inefficiency provide an orderly, and not overly intimidating, procedure for checking to see if an economy will be inefficient in the narrow sense of the Pareto principle. All we need to do is check if the economy is prone to "sinning" in any of these seven ways. If not, we can conclude the economy is efficient, or will achieve Pareto optimality, whatever other desirable or undesirable qualities it may posess. Moreover, if the economy is prone to inefficiency we will know what *kind* of inefficiency it suffers from.

Endogenous preferences

There is an important issue traditional treatments ignore which complicates how we should think about efficiency. When people make choices in light of their present preferences, the actions they take not only fulfill their present preferences (to a greater or lesser degree), they also change people's human characteristics to some extent, and thereby change their future needs and desires. In chapter 1 we saw this is what it means to say people have "consciousness" and are "self-creative." While traditional treatments of efficiency take account of the first effect of people's choices – the "preference fulfillment effect" – the second effect – the "preference development effect" – is usually ignored even though evaluating the effect of economic choices and institutions on people's human development patterns may be as important as evaluating how well those choices and institutions succeed in fulfilling their present preferences. However, when economic choices have human development effects that means they also change people's preferences, creating the following dilemma: How are we to judge the efficiency of economic institutions using people's preferences as our yardstick if those preferences are in part a product of those same economic institutions in the first place? While this may appear to be a vicious circle giving rise to a philosophical conundrum that cannot be resolved, it turns out there are some conclusions we can draw about economic efficiency even when we recognize that people's preferences are influenced by the economic institutions that purport to satisfy those preferences.

The view that people are self-conscious agents whose characteristics and therefore preferences develop can be summarized in a model of "endogenous preferences." Using such a model it is possible to demonstrate that if an economy is *biased* against a certain kind of activity – that is, if people must pay more than the true cost to society to engage in the activity:

1. The degree of inefficiency in the economy will be greater than recognized by traditional theory that fails to treat preferences as endogenous, and the inefficiency will increase, or "snowball" over time.
2. Individual human development patterns will be "warped" in the sense that they will not develop in ways that would generate the most fulfillment people could enjoy, and the warping will increase or "snowball" over time.
3. These detrimental, non-traditional effects of the bias in the economy will be disguised to participants who adjust unconsciously, or forget they have adjusted after the fact.

The intuition behind these political economy welfare theorems[13] is that to the extent people recognize the "preference development" as well as the "preference fulfillment" effects of their choices, it is sensible for them to take both effects into account when making decisions. If an economic institution is biased against some activity – charging people more than the true social cost of their engaging in the activity – then rational people will choose activities in part to develop a lower preference for that activity than if they were only charged the true social cost for engaging in it. It follows that the demand for the activity in the future will be less than had people not adjusted their preferences. But this reduced demand implies that even fewer resources will be allocated to supplying the activity than had people not adjusted their preferences. The more time people have to make these individually rational adjustments, the lower demand, and therefore supply of the activity will be, leading to ever greater misallocations of productive resources as time goes on, and

13. For a rigorous derivation of these results see chapter 6 in Robin Hahnel and Michael Albert, *Quiet Revolution in Welfare Economics* (Princeton University Press, 1990).

ever greater deviations of people's human development trajectories from those that would have maximized their well being under a system of unbiased prices. If after the fact people forget that they adjusted their preferences in response to the bias, they will only see themselves as getting what they want.

In other words, if an economic institution introduces a bias in the terms of availability of an activity, the consequence will be a "snowballing" divergence from efficient allocations. This implies *that a major criterion for judging economic institutions should be determining whether they exert any systematic biases on individual choice*, because to the extent that people's preferences are endogenous, any biases will be more detrimental than traditionally recognized.

While traditional economists limit their evaluations of economies to efficiency (without considering the complication of endogenous preferences) and equity (about which they have little to say), political economists have good reason to take other criteria into account as well. Specifically, *how* and *by whom* decisions are made, and the *social effects* of economic activities are important to evaluate and take into account.

SELF-MANAGEMENT

I define **self-management** as *decision making input in proportion to the degree one is affected*, and believe more self-management is desirable, all other things being equal, or as economists like to say, *ceteris paribus*.

The first thing to notice is that defined in this way self-management is seldom equivalent either to individual freedom or majority rule. Only if a single individual were the only person affected by a decision would self-management be the same as individual freedom, i.e. the right of a single individual to decide whatever she pleases. And only if all were equally affected by a decision would self-management be the same as majority rule, i.e. one person one vote. Since most economic decisions affect more than one person, but affect people to different degrees, self-management as I have defined it usually requires that some people have more decision making power while others have less regarding any particular economic decision.

But why is more self-management a good thing? Throughout history most humans have lived in circumstances with few opportunities for economic self-management. So admittedly, most people don't die without it. Political economists contend that just as denial of material means of subsistence conflicts with human "natural" needs for food, shelter, and clothing, denial of self-management opportunities is in conflict with our "species nature." The capacity to analyze and evaluate the consequences of our actions, and choose among alternatives based on our assessments, in conjunction with the need to employ this capacity, is what we called "consciousness." Development of the capacity and desire for self-management is nothing more than development of the capacity to garner satisfaction from this innate human potential. For that reason, economic institutions that satisfy this need and develop this capacity are preferable to economic institutions that stifle self-management. In brief, we human beings have the ability to analyze and evaluate the consequences of our economic actions and choose accordingly, and we garner considerable satisfaction from doing so!

SOLIDARITY

By **solidarity** I simply mean *concern for the well being of others, and granting others the same consideration in their endeavors as we ask for ourselves*. Empathy and respect for others has been formulated as a "golden rule" and "categorical imperative," and outside the economics profession solidarity is widely held to be a powerful creator of well being. Solidarity among family members, between members of the same tribe, or within an ethnic group, frequently generate well being far in excess of what would be possible based on material resources alone. But in mainstream economics concern for others is defined as an "interpersonal externality" – a nasty sounding habit – and justification is demanded for why it is necessarily a good thing.

Besides consciousness, sociability is an important part of human nature. Our desires develop in interaction with others. One of the strongest human drives is the never ending search for respect and esteem from others. All this is a consequence of our innate sociability. Because our lives are to a great extent joint endeavors, it makes sense that we would seek the approval of others for our part in group efforts. Since many of our needs are best filled by what others do for/with us, it makes sense to want to be well regarded by others.

Now compare two different ways in which an individual can gain the esteem and respect of others. One way grants an individual status by elevating her above others, by positioning the person in a status hierarchy that is nothing more than a pyramidal system of relative rankings according to established criteria – whatever they may be. For one individual to gain esteem in this way it is necessary that at least one other – and usually many others – lose esteem. We have at best a zero-sum game, and most often a negative-sum game since losers in pyramidal hierarchies far outnumber winners. The second way grants individuals respect and guarantees that others are concerned for their well being out of group solidarity. Solidarity establishes a predisposition to consider others' needs as if they were one's own, and to recognize the value of others' diverse contributions to the group's social endeavors. Solidarity is a positive-sum game. Any group characteristic that enhances the overall well being that members can obtain from a given set of scarce material resources is obviously advantageous. Solidarity is one such group characteristic. So political economists consider economic institutions that enhance feelings of solidarity preferable to economic institutions that undermine solidarity among participants.

VARIETY

I define **economic variety** as *achieving a diversity of economic lifestyles and outcomes*, and believe it is desirable *ceteris paribus*. The argument for variety as an economic goal is based on the breadth of human potentials, the multiplicity of human natural and species needs and powers, and the fact that people are neither omniscient nor immortal.

First of all, people are very different. The fact that we are all human means we have genetic traits in common, but this does not mean there are not differences between people's genetic endowments. So the best life for one is not necessarily the best life for another. Second, we are each individually too complex to achieve our greatest fulfillment through relatively few activities. Even if every individual were a genetic carbon copy of every other, the complexity of this single human entity, their multiplicity of potential needs and capacities, would require a great variety of different human activities to achieve maximum fulfillment. To generate this variety of activities would in turn require a rich variety of social roles even in a society of genetic clones. And with a variety of social roles we would discover that even genetic clones would develop quite different derived human characteristics and needs.

While the above two arguments for the desirability of a variety of outcomes are "positive," there are "negative" reasons that make variety preferable to conformity as well. Since we are not omniscient nobody can know for sure which development path will be most suitable for her, nor can any group be certain what path is best. John Stuart Mill astutely pointed out long ago in *On Liberty* that this implies the majority should be *thankful*, rather than resentful, to have minorities testing out different lifestyles – because every once in a while every majority is wrong. Therefore, it is in the majority's interest to have minorities testing their dissident notions of "the good life" in case one of them turns out to be a better idea. Finally, since we are not immortal, each of us can only live one life trajectory. Only if others are living differently can each of us vicariously enjoy more than one kind of life.

ENVIRONMENTAL SUSTAINABILITY

It took a massive movement to raise the issue of whether or not modern economies were "environmentally sustainable," or instead, on course to destroy the natural environment upon which they depend. But it sometimes seems there are as many different definitions of "sustainability" and "sustainable development" as people who use the words. There are even some in the environmental movement who, with good reason, have suggested that "sustainable development" has become the enemy, rather than the friend, of the environment. It is also not clear that if we leave aside the political question of how to popularize important ideas, there is anything in the notion of "sustainability" that is not already implicit in the values of efficiency, equity, and variety. If an economy uses up natural resources too quickly, leaving too little or none for later, it has violated the efficiency criterion. If an economy sacrifices the basic needs of future generations to fulfill desires for luxuries of some in the present generation, it has failed to achieve intergenerational equity. If we chop down tropical forests with all their biodiversity and replace them with single species tree plantations, we have destroyed, rather than promoted variety.

Be this as it may, perhaps it is wise to adopt a principle the environmental movement has made popular: the *precautionary principle*. According to the precautionary principle when there is fundamental uncertainty with very large downside potential, it is best to take proactive action. In this case, it is by no means clear that the concepts of efficiency, equity and variety include everything we need to consider regarding relations between the human economy and the natural environment. Since it is riskier to leave out the criterion of environmental sustainability than include it, let us include the goal of sustainability, while recognizing that it can be defined in different ways. (1) *Weak sustainability* requires only leaving future generations a stock of natural and produced capital that is as valuable, in sum total, as that we enjoy today. (2) *Strong sustainability* requires leaving future generations a stock of natural capital that is as valuable as that we enjoy. (3) *Environmental sustainability* requires leaving stocks of each different kind of natural capital that are as large as those we enjoy. Obviously these are different notions of sustainability. The first allows for complete substitution between produced and natural capital. The second allows for substitution between different kinds of natural capital, but not between natural and produced capital. The third does not even permit substitution between different kinds of natural capital.

CONCLUSION

So the criteria political economists should consider when evaluating the performance of an economy, or evaluating the consequences of different economic policies, or comparing the desirability of different kinds of economies are: (1) *equity*, defined as reward according to sacrifice; (2) *efficiency*, defined narrowly as Pareto optimality, and more broadly as the efficiency criterion, but with the preference development effect accounted for rather than ignored; (3) *self-management*, defined as decision making power in proportion to the degree one is affected; (4) *solidarity*, defined as concern for the well being of others; (5) *variety*, defined as achieving a variety of economic life styles and outcomes; and (6) *environmental sustainability* which can be defined in a number of ways.

3   A Simple Corn Model

This is the first of three chapters presenting theoretical models and analyses that are useful for political economists. The simple corn model presented here requires no more sophisticated mathematical skill than arithmetic. Chapter 5 contains some useful micro economic models, and chapter 9 some useful macro economic models. All the models sharpen the logical basis of subjects treated verbally in the eight, non-technical chapters of the book. More importantly, all three technical chapters are well within the grasp of anyone with a high school education, and they permit readers who master them to be "players" rather than "spectators" in the field of political economy. Since the primary purpose of this book is to equip readers to practice political economy on their own, rather than have to rely on someone else's analysis and conclusions, I highly recommend these chapters to readers willing to invest a little extra time to become more intellectually independent.

A SIMPLE CORN ECONOMY

The simple corn economy allows us to explore efficiency, inequality, and the relationship between them in a very simple setting. It allows us to see how economic institutions like labor markets and credit markets which establish relationships between employers and employees, and borrowers and lenders, can affect efficiency and inequality simultaneously. It also provides a convenient context to see how different conceptions of economic justice such as the conservative, liberal, and radical "maxims" discussed in the last chapter give rise to different conclusions about when unequal outcomes are inequitable and when they are not.

Imagine an economy consisting of 1000 members. There is one produced good corn, which all must consume. Corn is produced from inputs of labor and seed corn. All members of this society are equally skilled and productive, and all know how to use the two technologies that exist for producing corn. We assume that each person needs to consume exactly 1 unit of corn per week. After their "necessary consumption" we assume people care about leisure. That is, after consuming 1 unit of corn, people care about working as few days as possible in order to enjoy as many days of the week in leisure activities as possible. Finally, we assume that after consuming 1 unit of corn and minimizing the number of days they have to work, i.e., maximizing their leisure, if people have the chance to accumulate more corn rather than less they will want to do so.[1] There are two ways to make corn: a *labor intensive technique* (LIT) and a *capital intensive technique* (CIT):

Labor Intensive Technique:
6 days of labor + 0 units of seed corn yields 1 unit of corn
Capital Intensive Technique:
1 day of labor + 1 unit of seed corn yields 2 units of corn

In either case the corn produced appears only at the end of the week. That is, if I work Monday through Saturday using the labor intensive technology I will get a yield of 1 unit of corn on Sunday. If I work with a unit of seed corn on Tuesday using the capital intensive technology the unit of seed corn is tied up for the whole week and is gone by Sunday, and I will get a yield of 2 units of corn on Sunday. There is no need to replace seed corn used in the labor intensive process since none is used. On the other hand, if we are to get back to where we started after using the capital intensive process, we need to use 1 of the 2 units of corn produced to replace the unit of seed corn used up. Another way of saying this is that the capital intensive process produces 2 *gross* units of corn but only 1 *net* unit of corn. So each technique produces 1 net unit of corn available at the end of the week. The labor intensive process uses 6 days of labor and requires no seed corn to get 1 unit of corn, net. The capital intensive process uses 1 unit of labor and requires 1 unit of seed corn to get 1 unit of corn, net. Finally, we assume either technique can be used

---

1. Obviously this simple model deviates from real world conditions in many respects. The assumption that people only wish to consume 1 unit of corn, after which they wish to minimize work time, after which they wish to maximize accumulation is convenient for now. We will consider the implications of people's preferences for how they work, and who decides how they work, and discuss the effects of more realistic assumptions about consumption and savings later.

in any "scale" desired. For example, if I work only 1 day in the LIT I will get ⅙ unit of corn on Sunday. If I work half a day in the CIT I will get 1 unit of corn gross, and half a unit of corn net on Sunday.[2]

But why would anyone ever produce corn the labor intensive way? If I work 1 day using the capital intensive technique I can produce 2 units of corn, and after replacing the 1 unit of seed corn I used up I have 1 unit left over. On the other hand, I would have to work 6 days to end up with 1 unit of corn if I used the labor intensive technique. So no one would ever use the labor intensive technique if she could use the capital intensive technique instead.[3] However, a key feature of the model is that you cannot use the capital intensive technology unless you have seed corn to begin with. So if someone does not have access to seed corn, yet needs to produce more corn, they have no choice but to use the labor intensive technology. This is how the model nicely captures one critical feature of modern economies – the role of *capital*, represented in our model by seed corn.

In our simple corn economy there is an easy way to measure economic efficiency. What people want is net corn production. In other words the only benefit people get from the economy is net corn production. On the other hand, what people don't like is working since it detracts from their leisure. In other words the only burden people bear in the economy is the amount of time they have to work. In this simple situation the economy is more efficient the lower the average number of days of work per unit of net corn produced.[4] So *we can measure the **efficiency** of the economy by the average number of days worked per unit of net corn produced.* There is also a simple way to measure the degree of inequality in the economy. Since everyone consumes the same amount of corn, 1 unit, the only difference in outcomes that people care about is the number of days they have to work. So we can define the ***degree of inequality*** in the economy as the

2. In other words, we are assuming what economists call "constant returns to scale."
3. Remember we are assuming for now that people don't care whether they work an hour in the labor intensive process or the capital intensive process.
4. Efficiency means minimizing the ratio of "pain" to "gain." "Pain" in our simple economy has been reduced to total number of days worked, and "gain" has been reduced to the total number of units of net corn produced. So average days worked per unit of net corn, or total days worked divided by total net corn production, is the obvious measure of efficiency in our simple corn economy.

difference between the maximum number of days anyone works and the minimum number of days anyone works.[5]

To explore how the distribution of seed corn and economic institutions like a labor market and credit market affect efficiency and inequality in the economy we explore *two different* **situations** and *three different sets of* **rules** for how people can behave in the economy. In situation 1 we give some people more of the economy's scarce seed corn than others. This situation is obviously most relevant to real world circumstances where some people have more capital than others. In situation 2 we give everyone equal amounts of scarce seed corn. While there has never been a capitalist economy in which everyone started out with the same amount of capital, nonetheless, it is interesting to explore what would happen in this situation as compared to the real world of unequal endowments of scarce capital.[6] In each situation we explore what people would do under three different sets of rules. First *we do not permit people to enter into any kind of economic relationship with each other at all.* That is, we require people to be completely self-sufficient. This rule, or way of running the economy, we call **autarky**. Next *we permit people to enter into an employment relationship where anyone who wishes to hire someone, and anyone who wishes to work for someone else, for a wage the employer and employee both agree to, are free to do so.* In other words, we legalize, or open a **labor market**. Finally, instead of opening a labor market, we open a **credit market**. Under this third set of rules *people are free to borrow corn from others and lend corn to others at a rate of interest both borrower and lender agree to.*

Political economists *define* **classes** *as groups of people who play the same economic role as one another, but enter into economic relationships*

5. Shortly we will discover that our measure of the degree of inequality is imperfect whenever people accumulate different amounts of corn. Our measure also fails to address changes in the degree of inequality between people who are not at the upper and lower extremes. But this imperfect measure is sufficient for our purposes, so we avoid unnecessary complications involved in devising a better measure.

6. What does it mean to say capital is "scarce" in our simple economy? As long as the total amount of seed corn in the economy is insufficient to allow us to produce all of the corn people need to consume using the more efficient, capital intensive technology, and thereby avoid having to use the less efficient labor intensive technology at all, seed corn is "scarce." So as long as we have fewer than 1000 units of seed corn initially, seed corn is scarce in the sense that we could reduce the amount of days people had to work if we had more.

with other groups of people playing a different role, with whom they have conflicting interests of one sort or another. So under the rules of autarky there can be no "classes" because nobody enters into any relationship with anyone else. In autarky it may, or may not be the case that everyone suffers or benefits to the same degree from their economic activity, but any differences that occur cannot be the result of relationships people enter into with one another because under the rules of autarky everyone works for herself using her own seed corn. There are no employers (a class), nor employees (a class) with conflicting interest over how high or low the wage rate will be. Nor are there lenders (a class), nor borrowers (a class) with conflicting interests over how high or low the interest rate will be. Clearly if we open a labor market and some people become employers and others become employees classes will emerge. And if we open a credit market and some become lenders and others borrowers classes will emerge as well.

Finally, political economists distinguish between *outcome* – in our simple model, does one person work more or less than another[7] – and *decision making process* – in our simple model, who decides how the work will be done. *In the simple corn model if I decide what I will do and how I will do it we say my work is **self-managed**. If someone else decides what I will do and how I will do it, we say my labor is other-directed or **alienated**.* Political economists believe being human means being able to make one's own decisions regarding how to use one's productive capabilities. Therefore, irrespective of whether the outcome is deemed fair or unfair, many political economists believe people are being denied a "species right" to exercise their capacity of self-management when their work is other-directed or alienated. Most political economists consider self-managed decision making processes more desirable than other-directed, or alienated decision making processes.

SITUATION 1: INEGALITARIAN DISTRIBUTION OF SCARCE SEED CORN

We begin with a situation that reflects real world conditions, namely that some people begin with more of the economy's scarce capital

---

7. Besides differences in work time, differences in outcome would include differences in consumption, accumulation, or desirability of working with different technologies if we allow for such differences in our model.

than others. We give 100 people 5 units of seed corn each, leaving the other 900 people no seed corn at all,[8] and proceed to analyze what the 100 "seedy" people and 900 "seedless" people would do under three different rules for running the economy.

Autarky

Having no seed corn and needing 1 unit of corn to consume, each of the 900 seedless people have no choice but to work 6 days (Monday through Saturday) for themselves using the labor intensive technology. On the other hand, each of the 100 seedy people have plenty of seed corn and can avoid the less productive labor intensive process. Each seedy person needs only to work 1 day (Monday) using the capital intensive technology, using one of their units of seed corn. This yields 2 units of corn on Sunday. If she uses 1 to replace the unit of seed corn used up, there is 1 unit of corn left over for consumption. How efficient is this outcome? The total number of days worked is 900(6) + 100(1) or 5500 days (of work "pain.") The total amount of net corn produced is 1000 units (of consumption "gain"). So the average days worked (pain) per unit of net corn produced (gain) is 5500/1000 or 5.500 days per unit of net corn. The maximum number of days anyone works is 6 while the minimum number of days anyone works is 1, so the degree of inequality in the economy under autarky would be 6 − 1 or 5 days.

Labor market

If we legalize a labor market the first thing to consider is if people would use it, and if so, what the wage rate would be. If I am one of the 100 seedy people I might consider becoming an employer. If I hire someone to work for me for a day with one of my units of seed corn in the capital intensive process, my employee would produce 2 units of corn on Sunday that would be mine. After using one of those units of corn to replace the one used up in the capital intensive production process, there would still be 1 unit of corn net of replacement. As long as the wage rate were less than 1 unit of corn per day I would have some corn *profit* without having worked myself at all.[9] Provided the daily wage rate were less than a unit of corn I would be

---

8. This is obviously a dramatic degree of inequality in the distribution of capital. However, *qualitatively* none of our results depend on the degree of inequality in the initial distribution of scarce capital.
9. For simplicity we assume that supervisory time is zero for employers.

eager to become an employer. Of course if profits are positive anyone would like to be an employer, including any of the 900 seedless. But having no seed corn, if a seedless person hired an employee they would have to put them to work in the labor intensive process. Since a day's work in the labor intensive process only produces $\frac{1}{6}$ unit of net corn, the daily wage rate would have to be less than $\frac{1}{6}$ unit of corn for it to be profitable for the seedless to become employers.

Who would be willing to be an employee? Since employees work (while employers do not) and receive no profits (which employers do) this appears the less attractive role to play in the labor exchange.[10] Why would anyone agree to be an employee when they have the option of becoming an employer or working for themselves? If the wage rate is sufficiently high it might not be profitable for you to be an employer, and/or you might be able to get more corn for a day's work as someone else's employee than you could working for yourself. How high would the wage rate have to be to make it worthwhile for a seedy person to become an employee? If the daily wage rate is less than 1 unit of corn the seedy will want to be employers, not employees, because they can earn positive profits as employers without working at all. Moreover, for any wage rate less than 1 unit of corn per day the seedy are better off working for themselves using the capital intensive process since they get 1 unit of net corn per day they work for themselves. So unless the daily wage rate were higher than 1 unit of corn the seedy will not willingly become employees. On the other hand, for any wage rate higher than $\frac{1}{6}$ unit of corn per day the seedless are better off becoming employees than they would be becoming either employers or working for themselves. If the daily wage rate, w, is greater than $\frac{1}{6}$ the seedless would receive negative profits as employers since lacking seed corn they can only put their employees to work in the less productive labor intensive process. And if w is greater than $\frac{1}{6}$ the seedless are better off working as someone else's employee than they would be working for themselves since they only get $\frac{1}{6}$ unit of corn under self-employment in the labor intensive process. Another way of summing up the situation is: For any $w < \frac{1}{6}$ neither seedy nor seedless will be willing to be employees. Instead, everyone would want to be an employer. For any $1 \leq w$ neither seedy nor seedless

10. Employees also have to put up with being told how to do their work by their employers. But for now we are assuming that none of our 1000 people care whether they engage in self-managed or alienated labor.

will be willing to be employers. Instead, everyone would want to be an employee. Since we define a labor market to be one in which people agree to be employers and employees voluntarily, only for $\frac{1}{6} \le w < 1$ would the labor market be used.

Consider some daily wage between $\frac{1}{6}$ and 1, say $w = \frac{1}{3}$. Would there be willing employers and willing employees at this wage rate? The seedless would not be willing to be employers since when $w = \frac{1}{3}$ profits are negative for seedless employers who could only put their employees to work in the labor intensive process. But the seedy would gladly be employers since every day of labor a seedy person hired would yield her a profit of $\frac{2}{3}$ units of corn. (One day of labor working with 1 unit of seed corn in the capital intensive process yields 2 units of corn, gross, and 1 unit of corn net, leaving $\frac{2}{3}$ units profits after paying $\frac{1}{3}$ units in wages.) None of the seedy would be willing to be employees for a daily wage of $\frac{1}{3}$ units of corn since they can get 1 unit of corn per day of self-employment in the capital intensive process. But all the seedless would be willing to be employees since a daily wage of $\frac{1}{3}$ is twice as much as the $\frac{1}{6}$ per day they get by self-employment in the labor intensive process. As a matter of fact, for any $\frac{1}{6} \le w < 1$ all the seedy would be willing to be employers and all the seedless would be willing to be employees.

But this does not mean that any daily wage rate higher than $\frac{1}{6}$ and lower than 1 could become the permanent, stable, or what economists call **equilibrium wage** in our economy. As a matter of fact, $\frac{1}{3}$ is not an equilibrium wage. At $w = \frac{1}{3}$ all 900 seedless people would want to work 3 days each as employees. That would be a total supply of labor of $900(3) = 2700$ days. But the total demand for labor would only be 500 days. This is because while each seedless person would like to hire as many days of labor as possible since profits are positive at $w = \frac{1}{3}$, profits are only positive if you put your employees to work in the capital intensive process, and each seedy person only has 5 units of capital, which is only sufficient to put 5 days of labor to work in the CIT. So the maximum possible demand for labor in our economy is 5 days of labor per seedy employer times 100 seedy employers, or 500 days of labor. So if w were equal to $\frac{1}{3}$, the supply of labor (2700 days) would greatly exceed the demand for labor (500 days). In any market where excess supply prevails, all buyers will be able to buy all they want at the going price, but only some of the sellers will succeed in selling all they want to sell at the going price. There is an incentive for frustrated sellers, i.e. those who find they cannot sell all they would like to at the going price, to offer to sell at a lower price in order to move from the group of frustrated sellers who could not find buyers to the group of satisfied sellers who do find buyers. But this will drive the price down.[11] For any daily wage rate higher than ⅙ there will be excess supply in the labor market in our economy, and the self-interested behavior of seedless people who cannot get all the days of work they want, combined with the self-interested behavior of seedy people who see that they could find willing employees at an even lower wage rate, will push the wage rate down. Presumably this would continue until the daily wage was ⅙, at which there would no longer be excess supply in the labor market. We have found the equilibrium wage for our economy. If we legalize a labor market there would be some people willing to become employees and some people willing to be their employers for any wage rate between ⅙ and 1. But for all wage rates higher than ⅙ there would be excess supply in the labor market which would push w down to ⅙ – the equilibrium daily wage rate.

At $w = ⅙$ what will each seedless person do? She will work 6 days and end up with 1 unit of corn to eat. Some may work all 6 days in the capital intensive process as employees. Some may work all 6 days for themselves in the labor intensive process. Some may be self-employed for some days and employees for other days, but all of the seedless will work a total of 6 days each in any case.

At $w = ⅙$ what will each seedy person do? She will hire as many days of labor as she can put to work in the capital intensive process, i.e. 5 days of labor; 5 days of labor working with her 5 units of seed corn in the capital intensive process will produce 10 units of corn, gross, on Sunday. Five of the 10 units will be used to replace the 5 units used up.[12] Since our seedy employer hired 5 days of labor at a daily wage rate of ⅙ she must pay (⅙)(5) = 0.833 units of corn in wages, leaving 5 – 0.833 = 4.167 units of corn in profits. Each seedy person consumes 1 unit out of her profits and therefore will be able to accumulate, or add to her stock of seed corn for the following

11. There is also an incentive for savvy buyers who notice there are more sellers than buyers at the going price to lower the price they are willing to pay. We study the logic of this *micro law of supply and demand* further in chapter 4.
12. We require replacement of seed corn used because we want to explore what economists call "reproducible solutions," i.e. we want outcomes that could be repeated indefinitely, week after week.

week 3.167 units of corn, beginning the second week with 5 + 3.167 = 8.167 units of seed corn.

How has opening up a labor market affected the degree of inequality and efficiency of our economy? The maximum number of days anyone works is still 6. But now the minimum number of days worked is 0, giving a degree of inequality of 6 – 0 = 6 which is greater than 5 under autarky. In fact, opening the labor market has increased the degree of inequality in the economy by more than the difference between 6 and 5 would indicate. The seedless continue to work 6 days and consume 1 unit of corn. But the seedy not only reduce their work time from 1 day to 0 while continuing to consume 1 unit of corn, they each accumulate 3.167 units of corn as well while the seedless accumulate nothing. In other words, a more accurate measure of the degree of inequality in the economy which accounted for differences in accumulation would tell us that the degree of inequality had risen to something greater than the 6 indicated by our imperfect measure.

We calculate the efficiency of the economy as before, dividing the total number of days worked by total net corn production. The seedless work 900(6) days while the seedy work 100(0) days, or 5400 total days worked – 100 less than under autarky because the 100 seedy people no longer work 1 day each. But when counting total net corn production we have to remember that not all net corn produced got consumed this time. Some net corn produced gets consumed. As before, there are 1000 units of net corn consumed since each of the 1000 people consumes one each. But unlike under autarky, the seedy also accumulate corn when we legalize a labor market. Each seedy person accumulates 3.167 units of corn for a total of 100(3.167) = 316.7 units of corn accumulated. So the average number of days worked per unit of net corn produced is now [900(6) + 100(0)], or 5400 total days worked divided by [1000 + 316.7], or 1316.7 units of net corn = 4.101 as our measure of efficiency for the economy.

Credit market

What if wage slavery were made illegal – just as chattel slavery was abolished by law in the United States after the Civil War – but borrowing and lending seed corn were legalized? That is, what if instead of opening a labor market we open a credit market? What does it mean to open, or legalize a credit market, and under what circumstances would people use it? In our simple economy a credit market means that someone lends seed corn to someone else on

Monday morning and the borrower pays the lender back on Sunday not only the amount she borrowed on Monday, i.e. the principal, but some additional amount of corn in interest that the borrower and lender agree to. Are there weekly interest rates per unit of borrowed corn at which we would find some people willing to be lenders and other people willing to be borrowers? Is there an *equilibrium weekly rate of interest*, r, that we might expect to eventually prevail in our simple economy?

The first thing to consider is why anyone would ever want to be a borrower rather than a lender. After all, the lender gets back more than she lent and the borrower has to give back more than she borrowed! The reason to borrow in our economy is to avoid having to work in the less productive, labor intensive process for lack of seed corn. If I have a unit of seed corn I can get 1 unit of corn for a day of self-employed labor in the capital intensive process. Whereas, if I have no seed corn, a day of self-employment in the LIT only yields ⅙ unit of corn. As outrageous as a ⅚ or 83.3% weekly rate of interest may seem, for any r < ⅚ the seedless in our economy are better off borrowing seed corn at the beginning of the week and using it to work for themselves in the capital intensive process instead of working for themselves in the labor intensive process. If a seedless person borrows 1 unit of seed corn and works with it for a day she will get 2 units of corn on Sunday. She can use 1 of the 2 units to pay back the principal and still have 1 unit of corn, net, for 1 day of work. As long as the rate of interest is less than ⅚ she will still have more than ⅙ unit of corn left after paying interest as well as principal – which is better than had she not borrowed at all and worked the day in the labor intensive process instead. So there will be plenty of willing seedless borrowers if r < ⅚. And it is not hard to imagine that the seedy will be willing to lend. As long as r > 0 the seedy do better for themselves by lending and collecting interest for no work on their part.[13] So we will have willing (seedy) lenders and willing (seedless) borrowers for any 0 < r ≤ ⅚.

---

13. If the interest rate became low enough a seedy person would not want to lend out all 5 units of her seed corn. If the interest rate was so low she could not get 1 unit in interest for all 5 units lent, she should keep enough seed corn (something less than 1 unit out of her stock of 5) to do however much work she had to do herself in the capital intensive rather than the labor intensive process. However, we are about to discover that the equilibrium interest rate in our simple economy is high enough, by a considerable margin, to rid our seedy lenders of this technical worry.

But is any of the above interest rates that would yield willing lenders and willing borrowers an equilibrium weekly rate of interest? Suppose $r = \frac{1}{2}$. Each seedless person would want to borrow 2 units of seed corn since they would end up with half a unit of corn after repaying principal and interest for each unit they borrowed and worked with in the capital intensive process for a day, so 2 units of borrowed corn along with 2 days of work would get them the 1 unit of corn they need to consume. That would generate a total demand for seed corn in our Monday morning credit market of 900(2) = 1800 units of corn. But the maximum total supply of seed corn in our Monday morning credit market is only 100(5) = 500 units of seed corn available to be lent. This large excess demand for seed corn at $r = \frac{1}{2}$ would put upward pressure on the interest rate as frustrated (seedless) borrowers unable to borrow all they want would offer to pay a slightly higher rate of interest, and savvy (seedy) lenders who recognized they could get more than half a unit would begin to demand more. At any $r < \frac{5}{6}$ there would be excess demand in our credit market pushing the interest rate up until it reached $\frac{5}{6}$, the equilibrium weekly interest rate.

At $r = \frac{5}{6}$ what will each seedless person do? She will work 6 days and consume 1 unit of corn. Each seedless person will work for herself with borrowed corn using the capital intensive process for up to 6 days and use the labor intensive process for the remainder of the 6 days. Either way a seedless person ends up with $\frac{1}{6}$ unit of corn per day of self-employment no matter if she borrows and pays interest or does not borrow and uses the less productive labor intensive technique. So she must work a total of 6 days. At $r = \frac{5}{6}$ what will each seedy person do? She will lend all 5 units of corn, receive $(\frac{5}{6})(5)$ or 4.167 units of corn in interest in addition to being repaid her 5 units of corn principal, consume 1 unit, and have 3.167 units of corn to add to her stock for the following week.

As in the case of the labor market, the degree of inequality in the economy will be 6 – the seedless work 6 days and the seedy 0 – but this imperfect measure underestimates how much opening the credit market increases the degree of inequality because it does not account for the fact that now the seedy accumulate 3.167 units per week while the seedless accumulate nothing.

Opening a credit market also increases the efficiency of the economy to exactly the same extent as opening a labor market. Total days worked is 900(6) + 100(0), or 5400. Total net corn produced is 1000 for consumption and 100(3.167) or 316.7 for accumulation, or

1316.7. So the average days worked per unit of net corn is 5400/1316.7 = 4.101 once again. Obviously opening a credit market has exactly the same effect as opening a labor market on outcomes, i.e. the efficiency and degree of inequality in our simple economy.[14]

While there is much to consider regarding the explanation and interpretation of these results, before turning to these substantive issues it is instructive to see what the effects of opening a labor or credit market would be if the 500 units of scarce seed corn were distributed equally among people in the first place.

SITUATION 2: AN EGALITARIAN DISTRIBUTION OF SCARCE SEED CORN

In situation 2 we distribute the same 500 units of seed corn in an egalitarian manner. We give each of the 1000 people ½ unit of seed corn and examine what people would do under autarky, with access to a labor market, and with access to a credit market.

Autarky

In autarky each person must work entirely for herself and can only have access to her own half unit of seed corn. What would each of our 1000 people do? As long as you have seed corn you will use the capital intensive process. So the first thing every person would do is work a half day (Monday morning), using their half unit of seed corn in the capital intensive process to produce 1 unit of corn, gross, available on Sunday. After replacing the half unit of seed corn they used up, they would have a half unit of corn left for consumption. But everyone needs 1 unit of corn per week for consumption. Under autarky, to get the other half unit of corn she needs to consume each person would then have to work 3 more days using the labor intensive technology, for a total of 3½ days of work per week. So with an egalitarian distribution of 500 units of scarce seed corn, under autarky the efficiency of the economy – or average number of days

---

14. While credit and labor markets have the same effect on outcomes in our simple economy they do *not* have the same effect on the decision making process. The labor market turns seedless people who were self-employed under autarky into employees who engage in other-directed, or alienated labor. The credit market allows lenders to benefit materially from the increased efficiency that comes from borrowers working in the capital instead of labor intensive process, but leaves borrowers working under their own management.

worked per unit of net corn produced – will be 3.5(1000)/1000 or 3.5, and the degree of inequality in the economy will be 3.5 – 3.5 or zero.

Labor market

The equilibrium wage will be exactly the same if we open a labor market in situation 2 as it was in situation 1. This might seem surprising, but the equilibrium wage does not depend on the distribution of the scarce seed corn but only on the comparative efficiencies of the capital and labor intensive technologies and whether or not seed corn is scarce. Since neither productive technology, nor the scarcity of seed corn has changed between situations 1 and 2, the equilibrium wage will still be ⅙.[15]

Suppose a person decides she wants to be an employer. With only half a unit of seed corn she can only profitably employ somebody for half a day. But her employee working half a day with that half unit of seed corn produces 1 unit of corn on Sunday. Half of that unit must go to replace the half unit used up leaving ½ or $^6/_{12}$ units net of replacement. Since she has only hired half a day of labor she only has to pay half the daily wage rate, or ½(⅙) = $^1/_{12}$ unit of corn in wages. Subtracting $^1/_{12}$ in wages from $^6/_{12}$ leaves $^5/_{12}$ units of corn profits. So far this looks very attractive – $^5/_{12}$ units of corn profits without having to work at all – and we might suspect that all 1000 people will want to be employers. But our employer still needs $^7/_{12}$ more units of corn for her consumption. And the bad news is that she has no alternative but to work in the labor intensive process herself to produce this $^7/_{12}$ because her employee has tied up her half unit of seed corn for the week. How many days will it take working in the labor intensive technology to produce $^7/_{12}$ units of corn? Each day she works she produces ⅙, or $^2/_{12}$. So it will take her 3½ days to produce $^7/_{12}$ units of corn.

If someone decides not to be an employer the first thing she will do is work half a day with her own half unit of seed corn in the capital intensive technology, which we know yields half a unit of corn net of replacement on Sunday. At which point she will still need another half unit for consumption and has two ways to get it: She can work as somebody else's employee or she can work for

---

15. Whether or not seed corn is scarce depends on the productivity of the capital intensive technology, the total amount of seed corn available, and the amount of corn each must consume – none of which has changed between situation 1 and situation 2.

herself in the labor intensive process. With $w = \frac{1}{6}$ it will take her 3 more days of work no matter whether she is self-employed or someone else's employee, or some combination of the two. So under an egalitarian distribution of scarce seed corn, while employers would reap positive profits, surprisingly it turns out that employers and employees would end up working the same number of days, 3.500, and consuming the same amount as one another, 1 unit of corn. This means that under an egalitarian distribution of scarce seed corn the degree of inequality in the economy would remain the same as it was under autarky if we opened a labor market, zero. And the efficiency of the economy would remain the same as well, 3.500 days of work per unit of net corn produced.

Credit market

Just as the equilibrium wage depends only on the relative productivity of the capital and labor intensive technologies and on whether or not capital is scarce, the equilibrium weekly interest rate depends only on these factors, not on the distribution of the scarce seed corn. So if we opened a credit instead of a labor market in situation 2, the interest rate would be $\frac{5}{6}$ just as it was in situation 1. And while it might seem that all would wish to be lenders at this attractive rate of interest it turns out that lenders and borrowers alike would end up having to work the same number of days, $3\frac{1}{2}$ to get their unit of corn to consume.

Anyone who lends her half unit of corn will get $(\frac{1}{2})(\frac{5}{6}) = \frac{5}{12}$ units of corn interest at the end of the week. But to get the other $\frac{7}{12}$ units of corn she needs to consume she will have to work $3\frac{1}{2}$ days using the labor intensive technology. Before anyone would borrow seed corn she will first work with her own half unit for half a day using the capital intensive process, netting half a unit for consumption. Only then would she borrow seed corn in order to work in the more productive, capital intensive process rather than the less productive, labor intensive process. But if the weekly interest rate is $\frac{5}{6}$ she only ends up with $\frac{1}{6}$ unit per day she works with borrowed corn, which is neither better nor worse than the $\frac{1}{6}$ she gets working in the labor intensive process without borrowing corn. In either case, or in any combination, she would have to work 3 more days after working for half a day with her own seed corn, for a total of $3\frac{1}{2}$ days of work. Again, opening a credit market under an egalitarian distribution of scarce seed corn does not change the degree of inequality in the economy from what it was under autarky, zero. Nor does it change the efficiency of the economy which remains 3.500 days of work on average per unit of net corn.

CONCLUSIONS FROM THE SIMPLE CORN MODEL

The main results from the simple corn model are:

1. Under autarky, with a labor market, or with a credit market, as long as there is an unequal distribution of scarce seed corn there will be unequal outcomes. Some will have to work more days than others to consume the same amount of corn. (In situation 1 under autarky the degree of inequality was 5 and with a labor market or credit market it was 6.)
2. With an inegalitarian distribution of scarce seed corn, opening a labor market or a credit market increases the efficiency of the economy but increases the degree of inequality in the economy as well. (In situation 1 opening either a labor or credit market reduced the average number of days of work needed to produce a unit of net corn from 5.500 to 4.101, while it increased the degree of inequality from 5 to 6.)
3. Opening a credit market and opening a labor market have identical effects on efficiency and the degree of inequality in the economy, i.e. on economic outcomes, even if they do not affect decision making processes in the economy in the same way. (In either situation outcomes were the same when we opened a labor market and when we opened a credit market, while only opening a labor market moved some people from self-managed to alienated labor.)

The first result is easy to understand. If seed corn allows people to produce corn with less work, and if seed corn is scarce, having more seed corn than someone else is an advantage under any of our rules for running the economy.

The second result may seem less intuitive. Why would a change in rules that increases the efficiency of the economy also increase the degree of inequality in the economy? In situation 1 much of the scarce seed corn does not get used to put people to work in the more productive, capital intensive process under autarky. This is because there is no incentive for the seedy to work with more than 1 of their 5 units of seed corn themselves under autarky – leaving $100(4) = 400$ of our 500 units of seed corn idle. Opening a labor market creates an incentive for the seedy to use all their seed corn to hire employees at a profit. A side effect of the seedy's search for profit is that all the scarce seed corn in the economy gets used to put people to work in the more productive, capital intensive process rather than the less productive, labor intensive process. Not surprisingly this yields an efficiency gain for the economy. Similarly, opening a credit market creates a different, but equally effective incentive for the seedy to lend all their seed corn for a positive rate of interest which also means that all of the scarce seed corn in the economy will be used to put people who otherwise would have worked in the less productive, labor intensive technology to work instead in the more productive, capital intensive technology. Opening either a labor or credit market yields the same efficiency gain for the economy.

The reason opening a labor or credit market also increases the degree of inequality in the economy is that as long as seed corn is scarce the seedy as the employers (or lenders) will be able to capture the efficiency gain of the increased productivity of their employees (or debtors.) Since the seedy were already better off under autarky – working 1 day instead of 6 – if they capture the efficiency gain from opening a labor or credit market the difference between them and the seedless must increase. In situation 1 the efficiency gain from opening a labor or credit market takes the form of fewer days worked by the seedy – each works 1 day less than under autarky for a total reduction of 100 days of work – and more corn accumulated by the seedy – each accumulates 3.167 units more than under autarky for a total increase of 316.7 units of corn accumulated. Once we realize that the outcome for the seedless is the same under autarky and with a labor or credit market – under all three sets of rules the seedless work 6 days and consume 1 unit of corn – it is obvious that the entire efficiency gain from opening a labor or credit market must have gone to the seedy. And since the seedy were already better off under autarky, the degree of inequality must now be greater.

The reason the seedy capture the entire efficiency gain in our model is because seed corn is scarce, so when the seedless compete among themselves for access to seed corn through a credit market they bid the interest rate up to the point where the lenders capture the entire efficiency gain from opening the credit market. Similarly, when the seedless compete for access to work with scarce seed corn through a labor market they bid the wage rate down to the point where the entire efficiency gain from opening a labor market goes to their employers.[16] In either case it is the labor of the seedless that becomes more efficient when we open a credit or labor market. But as long as seed corn is scarce it will be their creditors or their employers who capture the lion's share of their increased productivity. In our simple model the lenders and employers will capture the entire efficiency gain. But even in more complicated and realistic models it is generally the case that employers and lenders capture the lion's share of efficiency gains from the employment and credit relationships as long as seed corn, or capital, is scarce. As long as the seedy capture more than 50% of the increase in their employees' or creditors' productivity, the degree of inequality in the economy necessarily rises.

The reason there are no efficiency gains from opening a labor or credit market under an egalitarian distribution of scarce seed corn is there is no inefficiency in the first place. In situation 2 all 500 units of seed corn are used to put people to work in the more productive, capital intensive technology under autarky because each person has an incentive to use her half unit of seed corn to work in the capital intensive process before working in the less productive, labor intensive process. The reason the degree of inequality does not rise above zero when we open a labor or credit market in situation 2 even though the equilibrium wage and interest rates are the same as in situation 1 is that everyone is free to walk away from the labor and credit markets if they can do better by themselves. This means no one must accept a worse outcome than they get under autarky. With no efficiency gain, when no one accepts a worse outcome no one can achieve a better outcome.

While the third result may be surprising at first, when properly interpreted it makes intuitive sense. Opening a credit market has

16. In our simple model only if seed corn were in excess supply, and labor were therefore scarce, would the seedless in the economy be able to capture the benefits of the employment and credit relationships. If labor were scarce seedy lenders competing among themselves for borrowers would bid the interest rate down to zero, and seedy employers competing for employees would bid the wage rate up to 1 – in which case their seedless debtors and employees would capture the entire efficiency gain from opening credit and labor markets. But just as there has never been a capitalist economy where capital is distributed equally, there has never been one where capital is not scarce. And as long as more capital can improve the productivity of any working in the economy, capital will remain scarce.

exactly the same effect on outcomes as opening a labor market in our simple economy because we have abstracted from all the factors that make labor and credit markets different in the real world. For example, our model has no economies of scale. One person working 1 day with 1 unit of seed corn in the capital intensive technology produces just as much corn per day worked (and per unit of corn used) as 5 people working 1 day each with 5 units of seed corn in the capital intensive technology. So in our model there is no advantage for an employer gathering 5 employees to work together, compared to 5 borrowers borrowing 1 unit of seed corn each and working in isolation from one another. This is often not the case in the real world where there *are* economies of scale. So whereas labor markets and credit markets do not affect outcomes differently in our model, this is not to say they do not affect outcomes differently in the real world. Our model also abstracts from any differences in the productivity of self-managed and other-directed or alienated labor, and from the supervisory costs of monitoring employees. Consequently the model fails to capture differences in outcomes from labor and credit markets due to these factors. Finally, there is no uncertainty and therefore no risk in our model. Since there are different kinds and degrees of uncertainty and risk in real world labor relations and real world credit relations, our model also fails to capture differences in outcome due to these differences between credit and labor markets.

GENERALIZING CONCLUSIONS

The simple corn model is quite different from the real world. And as we just saw, some results are more extreme in the corn model than would be the case in real world settings. What are the effects of relaxing simplifying assumptions in the model? What conclusions from the corn model *can* we generalize to real world situations?

The assumption that people only want to consume 1 unit of corn per week, after which they want to work as few days as possible, is not critical. We could change the model to allow for the fact that people are happier the more they consume as well as the less they work without changing any of the above conclusions.[17]

17. We have already seen that when people accumulate corn the definition and measure of inequality must be modified to take differences in corn accumulated into account as well as differences in days worked.

We could also allow for many different goods without affecting any conclusions. However, in a multi-good world there would be one interesting new wrinkle. In the simple, one-good corn model one solution is the autarkic solution. The analog to the autarkic solution in a world where people produce and consume many goods, is a solution in which people trade goods but do not trade labor or credit. In this case there *are* relationships people enter into with one another even when they do not employ one another or borrow from one another. They enter into a division of labor where not everyone produces every good she consumes by trading goods with one another. Just as there are unequal outcomes in the one-good model when people start with different amounts of seed corn even under autarkic solutions where people enter into no "relations" with one another at all, it turns out unequal outcomes are possible when people with different initial stocks of goods simply trade goods with one another *even when the markets for all goods are completely competitive*. In the simple corn model with inegalitarian distributions of scarce seed corn unequal outcomes can occur without any institutionalized relationship as a transmission vehicle, i.e. under the rules of autarky. In a more realistic model of a multi-good world, unequal outcomes can occur simply through the exchange of goods in competitive markets when people start with different initial stocks of goods.[18] In any case, all conclusions from the simple corn model do generalize to a multi-good model.

Finally, we could modify the model to include more technologies permitting more continuous substitutions between seed corn and labor in production without affecting the major conclusions drawn from the simple corn model. The effect of more continuous "factor substitution" is to eliminate solutions where one factor or the other is in excess supply. It is because we have only two technologies that the simple model yields the extreme result that all benefits from

18. This result surprised many political economists when it was first pointed out by John Roemer in *A General Theory of Exploitation and Class* (Harvard University Press, 1982). In Appendix B of *Panic Rules! All You Need to Know About the Global Economy* (South End Press, 1999) I add a second good, machines, to the simple corn model in order to demonstrate that international trade, even in competitive markets, is likely to increase global inequality even if it also generates global efficiency gains. The effects of international trade on global efficiency and inequality are discussed in chapter 8 of this book as well.

opening or expanding a relationship rebound entirely to one party. By introducing more technologies in between the labor and capital intensive technologies in the simple model, thereby allowing for a greater degree of "substitution" between seed corn and labor in production, both parties can receive part of the efficiency gains from opening a labor or credit market. But as long as those who were worse off in the first place receive less than half the benefit, the degree of inequality will increase as use of the labor or credit market expands – which will be the case as long as capital is scarce. So the result from the simple model does generalize to more realistic settings where efficiency gains from a labor or credit market are shared by both parties. As long as capital is scarce, i.e. as long as having more capital would allow someone to work more productively, the degree of inequality will increase as those who are worse off to begin with capture a smaller percentage of the efficiency gain made possible by the employment or credit relation than those who were better off in the first place.

To summarize regarding the most crucial issue: How can voluntary, mutually beneficial exchanges aggravate inequalities? Nobody is forcing employees to work for employers when we open up a labor market, or borrowers to strike a deal with lenders when a credit market exists. A new opportunity is there for anyone to avail herself of – or not – as they choose. Moreover, we have assumed competitive interaction in all market exchanges. So any increase in inequality that results is not because a buyer can insist on an unduly large share of the benefit from the exchange because sellers have no other buyers to sell to; or because a seller can insist on an unduly large share of the benefit because buyers have no other sellers to buy from. Not only are all exchanges voluntary, and therefore cannot leave either party worse off than they would have been not making the exchange, the exchanges take place under competitive conditions where both parties not only can opt not to make any exchange at all, but both parties can choose a different exchange partner should they find the one they are dealing with unreasonable. The answer to how rising inequality can result from voluntary, competitive exchanges is ultimately simple, and hopefully now intuitive: If those who are initially better off capture a higher percentage of the increased economic efficiency that results from exchange than those who are initially worse off, although exchange will be voluntary and mutually beneficial, it will also increase the degree of inequality in the economy. Moreover, this can occur through competitive as well as noncompetitive markets, and goods markets as well as labor and credit markets. So despite its simplicity, the model helps explain:

1. How unequal ownership of productive assets, or wealth, leads to inequalities in work time, consumption, and accumulation.
2. How both the employment and credit relationships can be mutually beneficial and lead to increasing inequality at the same time.
3. How economic relationships can simultaneously promote more efficient uses of scarce productive resources *and* be transmission vehicles for increasing economic inequality.
4. Why making markets competitive – be they labor, credit, or goods markets – does *not* prevent them from aggravating economic inequality.
5. Why the employment relation is particularly problematic from the perspective of economic justice since it aggravates inequalities in economic outcomes *and* inequalities in decision making power, i.e. causes alienation.

Political economists believe that understanding these issues is important to understanding what is going on in the real world when some people "choose" to work in other people's factories, when farmers "choose" to mortgage their land to borrow operating funds from banks, when third world nations "choose" to borrow from international banks, when workers in third world countries flock to work for subsidiaries of multinational companies, and when under-developed countries willingly trade raw materials for manufactured goods from more developed countries. Who will be employer and who will be employee; who will lend and who will borrow; and who will sell and who will buy which kinds of goods are not accidents in any of the above situations. Nor is it ignorance or short-sightedness that leads the exploited in these situations to "choose" to participate in their own fleecing. Moreover, the model indicates that while greater inequities can be expected from noncompetitive and coercive conditions, as long as people have different amounts of wealth, or scarce capital, to begin with inequalities would persist even if all the above economic relations were fully informed, strictly voluntary, and took place under perfectly competitive conditions.

ECONOMIC JUSTICE IN THE SIMPLE CORN MODEL

To translate conclusions regarding unequal outcomes into conclusions about economic injustice requires applying an ethical framework to the simple corn model. It is tempting to label unequal outcomes in the corn model exploitative, and to equate increases in the degree of inequality with increasing exploitation. Indeed, in many circumstances we can do this, but it is important to be clear how and why we judge unequal outcomes to be inequitable. In the simple corn model making ethical judgments about unequal outcomes requires focusing on *how* people came to have unequal stocks of seed corn in the first place, since it is the unequal initial distribution of seed corn that gives rise to unequal outcomes.

If the inegalitarian distribution of scarce seed corn is due to unequal inheritances, then supporters of both liberal maxim 2 and radical maxim 3 would judge the unequal outcomes that result to be unfair. In the liberal and radical views nobody should have to work more simply because someone else inherited more seed corn than they did. Only a supporter of conservative maxim 1 would see things differently. In the conservative view calling outcomes where those who inherited seed corn work less than those who did not unfair or "exploitative" is unwarranted because according to maxim 1 those who "contribute" seed corn should not have to "contribute" as much labor as those who "contribute" no seed corn.

What if some have more seed corn than others simply because of luck? In the simple corn model we can imagine that even if people began in situation 2 where everyone has a half unit of seed corn, after a few weeks some would enjoy good luck and produce more than 1 net unit of corn in $3\frac{1}{2}$ days' work, allowing them to accumulate more than half a unit of seed corn, while others would suffer bad luck and produce less than 1 net unit of corn in $3\frac{1}{2}$ days of work. If the unlucky still consumed 1 unit of corn they would be unable to replace their half unit of seed corn and therefore have to work more than the lucky every week subsequently – even if all were equally lucky after the first week. Since good luck entails no greater sacrifice than bad luck, unequal outcomes due to unequal stocks of seed corn resulting from unequal luck in a previous week would be deemed unfair by supporters of radical maxim 3. If supporters of conservative maxim 1 consider acquisition through luck blameless, they would be inclined to view unequal outcomes from this cause perfectly fair and equitable. The attitude of supporters of liberal maxim 2 is not clear cut. During the week when the good or bad luck took place differences in outcome might well be considered as differences in the productivity of people's work which, according to maxim 2 justify different outcomes. But once any initial differences in luck were translated into differences in corn stocks, since liberal maxim 2 gives no moral credit for contributions from productive property, different outcomes in subsequent weeks would be seen as inequitable.

Inequalities due to unfair advantage are also easy to visualize in the simple corn model. Suppose those who are stronger take the land closer to the village where everyone lives by force, allowing them to consistently produce more than 1 unit of corn in 3½ days of work because they don't have to walk as far to get to and from the fields, while the weaker people are forced to walk farther to and from work each day so they consistently produce less than 1 unit of corn in 3½ days of work. The strong will end up with more seed corn than the weak because they used their greater physical strength to achieve an unfair advantage. And as we saw in situation 1, those who begin with more seed corn can easily acquire even more seed corn with no additional work of their own if they can hire others in a "free" labor market or lend to others in a "free" credit market. Not surprisingly in this case, all three maxims condemn unequal outcomes that result from unfair advantage as unfair. Since there is no unequal sacrifice unequal outcomes are unfair according to radical maxim 3. Since the greater productivity of the strong is achieved unfairly, the unequal outcomes are unfair according to liberal maxim 2. And if productive property is unjustly acquired, presumably supporters of conservative maxim 1 would view any rewards to the unfairly acquired property as unjust as well.

But the most difficult scenario from an ethical perspective is the following: What if we start in situation 2, and while most people work 3½ days a week – half a day using the CIT and 3 days using the LIT – 100 enterprising souls work an extra 3 days using the LIT. That is, what if instead of taking 3½ days of leisure like their 900 counterparts, these 100 go-getters use 3 of their leisure days in week one working in the LIT, and add an extra half unit of seed corn to their stock as a result? In this case they would not have acquired their greater stock of seed corn through inheritance, luck, or unfair advantage. Instead, they would have more seed corn than the other 900 people at the start of week two because they made the sacrifice of working longer than others had in week one. Or, the greater sacrifice might take the form of working the same number of days but working harder, with greater intensity in week one. Or, it might take the form of tightening their belt and consuming less than a whole unit of corn, and therefore saving more than others do in week one. In the case of extra seed corn acquired through some greater sacrifice, the fact that the seedy can work fewer than 3½ days in week two would not seem unfair or inequitable from even the radical perspective. Consequently it appears even radicals should refrain from using a word like "exploitation" to characterize the unequal outcome in week two when our industrious (or thrifty) 100 end up working less than their 900 sisters. One could view their shorter work week in week two simply as compensation for their extra days of work in week one. However, three important points need to be borne in mind.

First of all, it is common for defenders of capitalism to rationalize inequalities as being entirely of this nature even though over-whelming evidence suggests this is the *least* important cause of unequal outcomes in capitalist economies. Edward Bellamy put it this way in 1897:

> Why, dear me, there never would have been any possibility of making a great fortune in a lifetime if the maker had confined himself to the product of his own efforts. The whole acknowledged art of wealth-making on a large scale consisted in devices for getting possession of other people's product without too open breach of the law. It was a current and a true saying of the times that nobody could honestly acquire a million dollars. Everybody knew that it was only by extortion, speculation, stock gambling, or some other form of plunder under pretext of law that such a feat could be accomplished. (*Equality*, republished by AMS Press, 1970)

Second, it is not necessarily the case that all 1000 people had an equal opportunity to work more than 3½ days the first week. For example, what if some of the 1000 people are single mothers who are hard pressed to arrange for day care for even 3½ days a week? Would not that change our attitude about whether or not the unequal outcomes in week two were fair?

But the most troubling problem is the following: Suppose all have equal opportunity to work extra days the first week but only 100 choose to do so. On Monday of the second week the industrious 100 who chose to work 3 extra days the first week would have 1 unit of seed corn, while everyone else would still have only a half. Even under the rules of autarky this would permit the industrious to work only 1 day a week, *forever*, while everyone else would continue to have to work 3½ days a week, *forever*. After only two weeks of this the industrious would have worked 5 days fewer than the rest and therefore already have more than "made up" for their extra 3 days work the first week. At what point does their compensation become excessive, and the continued inequality therefore become inequitable? More troubling still is the fact that if there is a labor market or credit market the 100 who were more industrious the first week can soon accumulate enough seed corn to never have to work themselves again, and accumulate ever greater stocks of seed corn to boot – while everyone else continues to work 3½ days every week. The problem is that a small unequal sacrifice in the first week leads to *permanent* inequalities precisely because capital does make labor more productive, and labor and credit markets allow those with more capital to appropriate part of the increased productivity of *others* without working themselves at all. This is not to say we cannot devise rules for where and how to draw the line between just and unjust compensation for sacrifice in early weeks. But it is clear that simply because the initial reason for unequal corn stocks – unequal sacrifice – might warrant a legitimate compensating inequality later, this does not mean that *whatever* compensation results from a greater sacrifice in the first week is necessarily fair and just.

4 Markets: Guided by an Invisible Hand or Foot?

Adam Smith and his disciples today see markets working as if they were guided by a beneficent, invisible hand, allocating scarce productive resources and distributing goods and services efficiently. Critics, on the other hand, see markets working as if they were guided by a malevolent, invisible foot, misrepresenting people's preferences and misallocating resources. After explaining the basic laws of supply and demand on which economists of all stripes more or less agree, this chapter explains the logic behind these opposing views and points out what determines where the truth lies.

HOW DO MARKETS WORK?

If we leave decisions to the market about how much to produce, how to produce it, and how to distribute it, what will happen? Only after we know what markets will do can we decide if they are leading us to do what we would want to, or misleading us to do things we should not want to do.

What is a market?

A market is a social institution in which participants can exchange a good or service with one another on terms they find mutually agreeable. It is part of the institutional boundary of society located in the economic sphere of social life. If a good is exchanged in a "free" market, anyone can play the role of seller by agreeing to provide the good for a particular amount of money. And anyone can play the role of buyer by agreeing to purchase the good for a particular amount of money. The market for the good consists of all the potential buyers and sellers. Our analysis of the market consists of examining all the potential deals these buyers and sellers would be willing to make and predicting which deals will occur and which ones will not. We do this by using four "laws" concerning supply and demand.

The "law" of supply

The first "law" we use to analyze a market is called the **law of supply** which states that in most markets *we expect the number of units of the good suppliers will offer to sell to increase if the price they receive for the good increases*. There are two reasons for this: (1) At higher prices there are likely to be more suppliers. That is, at a low price some potential suppliers may choose not to play the role of seller at all, but at a higher price they may decide it is worth their while to "enter the market." So, at higher prices we might have a greater number of individual suppliers. (2) Individual suppliers who were already selling a certain quantity at the lower price may wish to sell more units at the higher price. If the individual seller produces the good under conditions of rising cost – i.e. the more units they produce the more it costs to produce another unit – a higher price means they can produce more units whose cost will be covered by their selling price. Or, if the seller has a fixed amount of the good in hand they may be induced to part with a larger portion of it once the price is higher. In any case, the "law of supply" tells us to expect the quantity of a good potential suppliers will be willing to supply to be a positive function of price.

The "law" of demand

The second "law" is the **law of demand** which states that in most markets *we expect the number of units of the good demanders will offer to buy to decrease if the price they have to pay increases*. There are two reasons for this as well: (1) At the higher price some who had been buying before may become unable or unwilling to buy any of the good at all, and may therefore "drop out of the market." So at higher prices we may have a smaller number of individual demanders. (2) Individual demanders who continue to buy may wish to buy fewer units at the higher price than they did at the lower price. If the usefulness of the good to a buyer decreases the more units they already have, the number of units whose usefulness outweighs the price the buyer must pay will decrease the higher the price. So the "law of demand" tells us to expect the quantity of a good potential buyers will be willing to buy to be a negative function of price.

It is important to understand that these so-called "laws" should not be interpreted like the laws of physics. No economist believes that the demand of every individual demander in every market decreases as market price rises, or that the amount every seller offers to supply in every market increases as market price rises. In other words, economists recognize that individuals may well "disobey" the "laws" of supply and demand. Moreover, there may be whole markets that disobey these laws at particular times, so that market supply fails to rise, or market demand fails to fall when market price rises. Markets for stocks and markets for currencies, for example, display annoying propensities to violate the "law of supply" and "law of demand." A rise in the price of Amazon.com stock can unleash a rush of new buyers who demand more of the stock anticipating further increases in price, and can shrink the supply of sellers who become even more reluctant to part with Amazon.com while its price is increasing. The "laws" of supply and demand certainly do little to help us understand stock market "bubbles." In 1997 a drop in the price of Thailand's currency, the bhat, triggered the Asian financial crisis when buyers disappeared from the market afraid to buy bhat while its price was falling, and sellers flooded the market hoping to unload their bhat before it fell even farther in value. Clearly the "laws" of supply and demand are not going to help us understand the logic behind currency crises. We will take up these

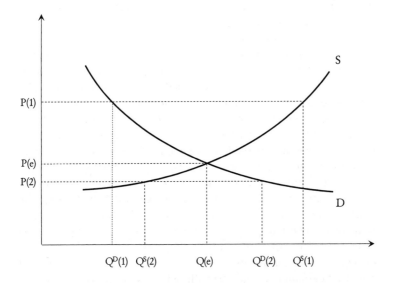

Figure 4.1   Supply and Demand

"annoying" anomalies when market participants interpret changes in market prices as *signals* about what direction a price is moving in when we examine disequilibrating forces than can operate in markets later in this chapter. But for now it is sufficient to note that the "laws" of supply and demand should be interpreted simply as plausible hypotheses about the behavior of buyers and sellers in many markets under many conditions.

At this point economists invariably use a simple graph to illustrate the laws of supply and demand. We plot market price on a vertical axis and the quantity, or number of units all potential suppliers, in sum total, would be willing to supply in a specified time period on the horizontal axis. According to the law of supply as we go up the vertical axis, at ever higher prices, the number of units all potential suppliers would be willing to supply in a given time period, or the "market supply," increases. This gives us an upward sloping market supply curve, or in different words a market supply curve with a positive slope. Similarly, we plot market price on a vertical axis and the quantity, or number of units all potential demanders, in sum total, would be willing to buy in a given time period on the horizontal axis. According to the law of demand as we go up the vertical axis, at ever higher prices, the number of units all potential demanders would be willing to buy, or the "market demand," decreases. This gives us a downward sloping market demand curve, or in different words, a market demand curve with a negative slope. While these are logically two separate graphs illustrating two different "laws" or functional relationships, since the vertical axis is the same in both cases, and the horizontal axis is measured in units of the same good supplied or demanded in the same time period, we can combine the two graphs into one with an upward sloping market supply curve and a downward sloping market demand curve. In this most familiar of all graphs in economics one must remember: (1) the independent variable is price, and this is measured (unconventionally) on the vertical axis, while the dependent variable, quantity supplied or demanded by market participants, is measured (unconventionally) on the horizontal axis. (2) When using the market supply curve the horizontal axis measures the number of units of the good all potential suppliers would be willing to sell at different prices. (3) When using the market demand curve the horizontal axis measures the number of units of the good all potential demanders would be willing to buy at different prices. (4) There is an implicit time period buried in the units of measurement on the horizontal axis. For example, the supply and demand curves and the graph will look different if the horizontal axis is measured in bushels of apples supplied and demanded per week than if it is measured in bushels of apples supplied and demanded per month.

The "law" of uniform price

The **law of uniform price** says that *all units of a good in a market will sell at the same price no matter who are the buyers and sellers.* This might seem surprising since some of the deals struck will be between high cost producers and buyers who are very desirous of the good, and some of the deals will be struck between low cost producers and buyers who are lukewarm about buying at all. Nonetheless, the law of uniform price says a good will tend to sell at the same price no matter who the seller and buyer may be. The logic of this law can be illustrated by asking what would happen if some buyers and sellers were arranging deals at a lower price than others for the same good. In this case it would pay for anyone to enter the part of the market where the good was selling at the lower price as a buyer and buy up all they could, and then enter the part of the market where deals were being struck at the higher price as a seller to re-sell at a profit. This activity is called "arbitrage," and in a free market where any who wish can participate as buyers or sellers the activity of arbitrage should drive all deals to be struck at the same price. Where prices are lower arbitrage increases demand and raises price, and where prices are higher arbitrage increases supply and lowers price – driving divergent prices for the same good in a market closer together. Of course, this assumes that "a rose is a rose is a rose is a rose" in the words of one of the great French *literati*, Gertrude Stein – that is, that there are no qualitative differences between different units of the good. But subject to this assumption, and the energy levels of those who would profit from doing nothing other than buying "cheap" and selling "dear," economists expect all units of a good that is bought and sold in a "well ordered" market to sell more or less at the same price.

The micro "law" of supply and demand

I call the third "law" the **micro law of supply and demand** to distinguish it from a different law we study in chapter 6 that I call the "macro law of supply and demand." The micro law of supply and demand states that *in a free market the uniform market price will adjust until the number of units buyers want to buy is equal to the number of* *units sellers want to sell.* In terms of the supply and demand graph in Figure 4.1, the micro law of supply and demand says that the market will settle at the price across from where the market supply and demand curves cross, and at the quantity bought and sold beneath where the supply and demand curves cross. This price and this quantity bought and sold are called the *equilibrium price* and *equilibrium quantity*, so another way of stating the micro law of supply and demand is: *markets will settle at their equilibrium prices, and if left to the free market the quantity of any good that will be produced and consumed will be the equilibrium quantity.*

The rationale for the micro law of supply and demand is as follows: Suppose the going market price, $P(1)$, is higher than the equilibrium price, $P(e)$. In this case if we read across from this price to find out how much buyers are willing to buy, $Q^D(1)$, as compared to how much suppliers are willing to sell, $Q^S(1)$, we discover from the market demand curve and market supply curve that buyers are not willing to buy all that sellers are willing to sell at this price, $Q^D(1) < Q^S(1)$. In other words, at this price there will be excess supply in the market for the good. What can we expect sellers to do? In conditions of excess supply sellers fall into two groups: those who are happily succeeding in selling their goods at $P(1)$ and those who cannot sell all they want and are therefore frustrated. Those who are not able to sell their goods have an incentive to lower their asking price below the going market price in order to move from the group of frustrated sellers to the group of successful sellers, thereby driving the market price down in the direction of the equilibrium price. Buyers also have an incentive to only agree to buy at a price below the going market price when they notice there is excess supply in the market since they know that there are some frustrated sellers out there who should be willing to accept less than the going market price, providing another reason why market price should start to fall in the direction of the equilibrium price.

On the other hand, suppose the going market price, $P(2)$, is lower than the equilibrium price, $P(e)$. If we read across from this price to find out how much buyers are willing to buy, $Q^D(2)$, as compared to how much suppliers are willing to sell, $Q^S(2)$, we discover from the market demand curve and market supply curve that sellers are not willing to sell all that buyers are willing to buy at this price, $Q^S(2) < Q^D(2)$. In other words, at this price there will be excess demand in the market for the good. What can we expect buyers to do? In conditions of excess demand buyers fall into two groups: those who are happily able to buy all the good they want at P(2), and those who are not able to buy all they want and are therefore frustrated. Those who are not able to buy all they want have an incentive to raise their offer price above the going market price in order to move from the group of frustrated buyers to the group of successful buyers, thereby driving the market price up in the direction of the equilibrium price. Sellers also have an incentive to only agree to sell at a price above the going market price when they notice there is excess demand in the market since they know that there are some frustrated buyers who should be willing to pay more than the going market price, providing another reason why market price should rise in the direction of the equilibrium price.

So for actual market prices above the equilibrium price there are incentives for frustrated sellers to cut their asking price and buyers to offer a lower price, driving the market price down toward the equilibrium price. And as the market price drops the amount of the excess supply will decrease since the law of supply says that supply decreases as price falls and the law of demand says that demand increases as price falls. And for market prices below the equilibrium price there are incentives for frustrated buyers to raise their offer price and for sellers to raise their asking price, driving the market price up toward the equilibrium price. And as the market price rises the excess demand will decrease since the law of demand says that demand decreases as price rises, and the law of supply says that supply increases as price rises. So according to the micro law of supply and demand, the only stable price will be the equilibrium price because self-interested behavior of frustrated sellers or buyers will lead to changes in price under conditions of both excess supply and excess demand, and only at the equilibrium price is there neither excess supply nor excess demand. This particular kind of self-interested behavior of buyers and sellers – individually rational responses to finding oneself unable to sell or buy all one wants at the going market price – can be thought of as "equilibrating forces" that economists expect to operate in markets. So the micro law of supply and demand can be thought of as a "law" explaining why there should be equilibrating forces at work in markets. We will discover below that market enthusiasts and critics disagree about how strong these "equilibrating forces" are compared to "disequilibrating forces" the micro law of supply and demand does not alert us to that sometimes operate alongside equilibrating forces.

There are a few things worth noting at this point:

1. There are different senses in which buyers or sellers are "satisfied." All buyers would always like to pay a lower price, and all sellers would always like to receive a higher price. So in that sense, neither buyers nor sellers are ever "satisfied" no matter what the going price. But when the market price is above the equilibrium price, while successful sellers will be pleased, there will be unsuccessful sellers who will be displeased. Moreover, there is something the non-sellers can do about their frustrations: they can offer to sell at a lower price. Similarly, when the market price is below the equilibrium price, while successful buyers will be pleased, there will be unsuccessful buyers who will be displeased. And what the non-buyers can do about their frustrations is to offer to pay a higher price.

2. It is always the case that the quantity bought will be equal to the quantity sold – whether the market is in equilibrium or not. This follows because every unit that was bought was sold and every unit that was sold was bought! But that is not the same as saying that the quantity demanders *want* to buy is equal to the quantity suppliers *want* to sell. There is only one price at which the quantity demanded will equal the quantity supplied – the equilibrium price. At all other prices there will be either excess supply or excess demand.

3. Since not all markets are always in equilibrium, how much will be bought and sold when a market is out of equilibrium? This is where the assumption of non-coercion in our definition of a market enters in: buyers cannot be forced to buy if they don't want to and sellers can't be forced to sell if they don't want to. When there is excess supply the sellers would like to sell more than the buyers want to buy at the going price. So under conditions of excess supply it is the buyers who have the upper hand, in a sense, and they will determine how much is going to be bought, and therefore sold. In Figure 4.1 when market price is $P(1)$ and there is excess supply buyers will only buy $Q^D(1)$ and therefore, that is all sellers, will be able to sell. When there is excess demand the buyers would like to buy more than the sellers want to sell. So under conditions of excess demand it is the sellers who have the upper hand and will determine how much is going to be sold, and therefore bought. In Figure 4.1 when market price is $P(2)$ and there is excess demand sellers will only sell $Q^S(2)$ and therefore, that is all buyers will be able to buy.

Elasticity of supply and demand

The law of demand just says that as price rises we expect the quantity demanded to fall. It doesn't say whether demand will fall a lot or a little. *If a 1% increase in price leads to more than a 1% fall in quantity demanded, we say that market demand is **elastic**. If a 1% increase in price leads to less than a 1% fall in quantity demanded, we say that market demand is **inelastic**.* Similarly, the law of supply just says that as price rises we expect the quantity supplied to rise; it doesn't say whether supply will rise a lot or a little. If a 1% increase in price leads to more than a 1% rise in quantity supplied, we say that market supply is *elastic*. If a 1% increase in price leads to less than a 1% rise in quantity supplied, we say that market supply is *inelastic*.

The elasticity of supply and demand allows us to predict how much the supply and demand for goods will change when their price changes. Elasticity also holds the key to how revenues of sellers will be affected by changes in supply. For example, the demand for corn is usually elastic. So when a drought hits the corn belt the price will rise and the equilibrium quantity bought and sold will fall. But the percentage fall in sales will be greater than the percentage increase in price because demand for corn is elastic. Since the revenue of corn farmers is simply equal to the market price times the quantity sold, the fact that sales drop by a greater percent than the increase in price means revenues must fall. On the other hand, the demand for oil is usually inelastic. So if war breaks out in the Middle East and a country such as Iraq, Kuwait, Iran, Libya, or Saudi Arabia is temporarily eliminated as a potential supplier the price will rise and the equilibrium quantity bought and sold will fall as before. But because demand for oil is inelastic the percentage fall in sales will be less than the percentage increase in price. In this case the revenue of oil suppliers will increase because the rise in price outweighs the drop in sales when supply decreases.

You can use your understanding of elasticity to predict whether more or less unemployment will result from minimum wage laws, and whether more or fewer shortages will result from price controls. Draw a labor market diagram with one "flat" (elastic) labor demand curve and one "steep" (inelastic) labor demand curve where both demand curves cross the labor supply curve at the same point. Where both demand curves cross the supply curve determines the equilibrium wage rate and the equilibrium level of employment. Now draw in a minimum wage *above* the equilibrium wage and see what happens to employment as buyers (employers) determine the quantity that will be bought and sold in a market with excess supply. Notice that the drop in employment is greater if the demand for labor is more elastic, and smaller if the demand for labor is more inelastic. Draw a diagram for the steel market with one "flat" or elastic supply curve and one "steep" or inelastic supply curve where both supply curves cross the demand curve for steel at the same point. Where both supply curves cross the demand curve determines the equilibrium price of steel and the equilibrium quantity of steel production. Now draw a price ceiling *below* the equilibrium price and see what happens to production when suppliers determine the amount that will be sold and bought in a market with excess demand. Notice that the drop in production and shortage is greater if the supply of steel is more elastic and smaller if the supply of steel is more inelastic.

The principal factors that determine the elasticity of market demand are the availability and closeness of substitutes for the good, and the organization and bargaining power of potential buyers. The principal factors that determine the elasticity of market supply are the mobility of productive factors into and out of the industry and the organization and bargaining power of potential sellers.

THE DREAM OF A BENEFICENT INVISIBLE HAND

Adam Smith noticed something strange but wonderful about free markets. He saw competitive markets as a kind of beneficent, "invisible hand" that guided "the private interests and passions of men" in the direction "which is most agreeable to the interest of the whole society." Smith expressed this view, in perhaps the most widely quoted passage in all of economics in *The Wealth of Nations* published in 1776:

> Every individual necessarily labours to render the annual revenue of the society as great as he can. He generally, indeed, neither intends to promote the public interest, nor knows how much he is promoting it. He intends only his own gain, and he is in this, as in many other cases, led by an *invisible hand* to promote an end which was no part of his intention. Nor is it always the worse for the society that it was no part of it. By pursuing his own interest he frequently promotes that of the society more effectually than

when he really intends to promote it ... It is not from the benevolence of the butcher, the brewer, or the baker that we expect our dinner, but from their regard to their self-interest. We address ourselves, not to their humanity, but to their self-love, and never talk to them of our necessities, but of their advantages.

In the words of Robert Heilbroner: "Adam Smith's laws of the market are basically simple. They show us how the drive of individual self-interest in an environment of similarly motivated individuals will result in competition; and they further demonstrate how competition will result in the provision of those goods that society wants, in the quantities that society desires."[1] But how does this miracle happen?

Suppose consumers' taste for apples increases and their taste for oranges decreases – for whatever reason. Assuming consumers know best what they like, how would we want the economy to respond to this new situation? If there were an omniscient, beneficent God in charge of the economy she would shift some of our scarce productive resources – land, labor, fertilizer, etc. – out of orange production and into apple production. What would a system of free markets do? These changes in consumer tastes would shift the market demand curve for apples out to the right indicating that consumers now would demand more apples at each and every price of apples than before, and the market demand curve for oranges back to the left indicating that consumers would now demand fewer oranges at each and every price than before – leading to excess demand for apples and excess supply of oranges at their old equilibrium prices. The micro law of supply and demand would drive the price of apples up until the excess demand for apples was eliminated and the price of oranges down until the excess supply of oranges was eliminated. At the new higher price of apples, the law of supply tells us that former apple growers, and any new ones drawn into the industry by the higher price of apples, would increase production of apples by purchasing more land, labor, fertilizer, etc. At the new lower price of oranges the law of supply tells us that orange growers would decrease their production of oranges by using less land, labor, and fertilizer, etc. to grow oranges. Bingo! As if guided by an invisible hand, without anyone thinking or planning at all, the free market does what a beneficent God would have done for us!

1. Robert Heilbroner, *The Worldly Philosophers* (Simon and Schuster, 1992): 55.

Or, suppose agronomists develop a new strain of apple that can be grown with less land between trees than before. This is a technical change that reduces the amount of scarce productive resources it takes to grow apples compared to the past. An omniscient, beneficent God would have consumers buy more apples and fewer oranges now that apples are less socially costly. What will free markets do? The cost-reducing change in apple growing technology will shift the market supply curve for apples out to the right because now apple growers can cover the cost of growing more apples than before at each and every price – producing an excess supply of apples at the old equilibrium price. The micro law of supply and demand will lower apple prices until the excess supply is eliminated and we reach the new equilibrium in the apple market. And the law of demand tells us that consumers will buy more apples at the lower price. Meanwhile, over in the orange market, the fall in the price of apples leads some fruit buyers to substitute apples for oranges which shifts the demand curve for oranges back to the left indicating that fewer oranges will be demanded at each and every price of oranges now that the price of apples is lower – creating excess supply in the orange market. This will lead to a fall in the price of oranges and lower levels of orange production. Bingo! The free market will bring about an increase in apple production and consumption and a decrease in orange production and consumption when the social cost of producing apples decreases relative to the social cost of producing oranges – just what we would have wanted to happen.

We can combine Figure 2.2: The Efficiency Criterion (p. 33) and Figure 4.1: Supply and Demand (p. 73) to see what Smith's conclusion that markets harness individually rational behavior to yield socially rational outcomes amounts to. According to the micro law of supply and demand, the market outcome will be the equilibrium outcome, and the number of apples produced and consumed can be found directly below where the market supply curve crosses the market demand curve. According to the efficiency criterion the optimal number of apples to produce and consume can be found directly below where the marginal social cost curve crosses the marginal social benefit curve. So the market outcome will yield the socially efficient outcome if and only if the market supply curve coincides with the MSC curve and the market demand curve coincides with the MSB curve. Another way to put it is that if and only if market supply closely approximates marginal social cost and market demand closely approximates marginal social benefits will free market outcomes be socially efficient outcomes.

But do market supply and demand reasonably express marginal social costs and benefits? That is one way to see the debate between those who see market allocations as being guided by an invisible hand versus those who see them as being misguided by an invisible foot. If market supply and demand closely approximate true marginal social costs and benefits then the individually rational behavior of buyers and sellers and the workings of the micro law of supply and demand would be working in the social interest because they would be driving production and consumption of goods and services toward socially efficient levels. Moreover, whenever conditions changed social costs or benefits these equilibrating forces would move us to the new socially efficient outcome. In other words, markets would yield efficient allocations of scarce productive resources. On the other hand, if there are significant discrepancies between market supply and marginal social costs and/or market demand and marginal social benefits, individually rational behavior of buyers and sellers and the micro law of supply and demand work against the social interest by driving us to produce too little of some goods and too much of others. In other words, by relying on market forces we would consistently get inefficient allocations of productive resources.

Mainstream and political economists agree on one part of the answer before parting company. *They agree that what market supply captures and represents are the costs born by the actual sellers of goods and services; and what market demand represents are the benefits enjoyed by the actual buyers of goods and services.* We call these "private costs" and "private benefits." A rational buyer will keep buying a good as long as the private benefit to her of an additional unit is at least as great as the price she must pay for it. In other words, her marginal private benefit curve is her individual demand curve. Since the market demand curve is simply the summation of all individual demand curves, the market demand curve is simply the sum of all marginal private benefit curves. A rational seller will keep selling as long as the cost to her of producing another unit of output is no greater than the price she will get from selling it. In other words, her marginal private cost curve is her individual supply curve. Since market supply is simply the summation of all individual supply curves, the market supply curve is simply the sum of all marginal private cost curves. So the question becomes: When do private costs and benefits differ from social costs and benefits?

In fairness to Adam Smith, the distinction between private and social costs and benefits was not clear in his lifetime. Smith, and "classical economists" who lived and wrote after him as well, conflated social and private costs and benefits and never asked if anyone other than the seller bore part of the cost of increased production, or anyone other than the buyer enjoyed part of the benefit of increased consumption of different kinds of goods and services. The modern terminology for differences between social and private costs of production is "a production externality." And the name for the difference between social and private benefits from consumption is "a consumption externality." These "external effects" can be negative if someone other than the seller suffers a cost associated with production so social costs exceed private costs, or if someone other than the buyer is adversely affected by the buyer's consumption so private benefits exceed social benefits. Or external effects can be positive if the private costs of production exceed the social costs or social benefits of consumption exceed private benefits. Adam Smith's vision of the market as a mechanism that successfully harnesses individual desires to the social purpose of using scarce productive resources efficiently hinges on the assumption that external effects are insignificant. And, indeed, this is precisely the un-emphasized assumption that lies behind the mainstream conclusion that markets are remarkable efficiency machines that require little social effort on our part. In fact, the mainstream view today is a strident echo of Adam Smith's conclusion that the only "effort" required is the "effort" to resist the temptation to tamper with the free market place and simply: "laissez faire."

THE NIGHTMARE OF A MALEVOLENT INVISIBLE FOOT

Mainstream economic theory teaches that the problem with externalities is that the buyer or seller has no incentive to take the external cost or benefit for others into account when deciding how much of something to supply or demand. And Mainstream theory teaches that the "problem" with public goods is that nobody can be excluded from benefitting from a public good once anyone buys it, and therefore everyone has an incentive to "ride for free" on the purchases of others rather than revealing their true willingness to pay for public goods by purchasing them in the market place. In other words, mainstream economics concedes that the laws of the market place will lead to inefficient allocations of scarce productive resources when public goods and externalities come into play because important benefits or costs go unaccounted for in the market decision making process. If anyone cares to listen, standard economic theory predicts that market forces will lead us to produce too much of goods whose production and/or consumption entail negative externalities, too little of goods whose production and/or consumption entail positive externalities, and much too little, if any, public goods. We can see the problem of negative externalities by looking at the automobile industry, and the problem of public goods by considering pollution reduction.

Externalities: the auto industry

The micro law of supply and demand tells us how many cars will be produced and consumed if we leave the decision to the free market. The price of cars will adjust until there is neither excess supply nor excess demand at which point the "equilibrium" number of cars will be produced and consumed. The question is whether or not this is more, less, or the same number of cars that is socially efficient, or optimal to produce and consume. As we saw, the socially efficient level of auto production and consumption is where the MSB curve crosses the MSC curve. If the market supply curve for cars coincides with the MSC curve for cars, and if the market demand curve for cars coincides with the MSB curve for cars, the market outcome will be the efficient outcome. Otherwise, it will not.

Let us assume that the market supply curve for cars does a reasonably good job of approximating the marginal private costs the makers and sellers of cars incur. That is, we will assume that if car manufacturers can get a price for a car that is something above what it costs them to make it, they will produce and sell the car. In this case the market supply curve, S, closely approximates the marginal private cost (MPC) curve for making cars: S = MPC. But if there are costs to external parties above and beyond the costs of inputs car makers must pay for, there is no reason to expect the car makers to take them into account. So if the corporations making cars in Detroit also pollute the air in ways that cause acid rain, the costs that take the form of lost benefits to those who own, use, or enjoy forests and lakes in Eastern Canada and the United States will not be taken into account by those who make the decisions about how many cars to produce. Nevertheless, along with the cost of steel, rubber and labor needed to make a car – which are costs borne by car manufacturers

– the costs of acid rain are part of the social costs of making cars even if they are not borne by car makers. To the cost of steel, rubber, and labor that comprise the private costs of making a car, must be added the damage from acid rain that occurs when we make a car if we are to have the full cost to society of making another car. In other words, the marginal social cost of making a car, MSC, is equal to the marginal private cost of making the car, MPC, plus the marginal external costs associated with making the car, MEC: MSC = MPC + MEC. Since MEC is positive for automobile production, marginal social cost always exceeds marginal private cost, which means the marginal social cost curve for producing cars lies somewhere above the marginal private cost curve for making cars, which is, in turn, roughly equal to the market supply curve for cars: MSC = MPC + MEC = S + MEC with MEC > 0.

When car buyers consider whether or not to purchase a car they presumably compare the benefit they expect to get in the form of ease and speed of transportation with the price they will have to pay out of their limited income. If the private benefit exceeds the price, they will buy the car, and if it does not, they won't. This means the market demand curve, D, represents the marginal private benefit curve from car consumption, MPB, reasonably well: D = MPB. But I am not the only person affected when I "consume" my car. When I drive my car the exhausts add to the "greenhouse" gases in the atmosphere and contribute to global warming. When I drive from the suburbs through inner city neighborhoods I contribute to urban smog, noise pollution, and congestion. In other words, when I consume a car there are others who suffer negative benefits which means that the social benefit of consuming another car is less than the private benefit of consuming another car. So even if the market demand curve for cars reasonably represents the marginal private benefits of car consumption, it overestimates the marginal social benefits of car consumption because it ignores the negative impact of car consumption on those not driving them. The marginal social benefits from consuming another car, MSB, is equal to the marginal private benefits to the car buyer plus the marginal external benefits to others, MEB: MSB = MPB + MEB. But in the case of car consumption the marginal external "benefits," MEB, are *negative*. This implies that the marginal social benefit curve lies somewhere *below* the market demand curve for automobiles: MSB = MPB + MEB = D + MEB with MEB < 0.

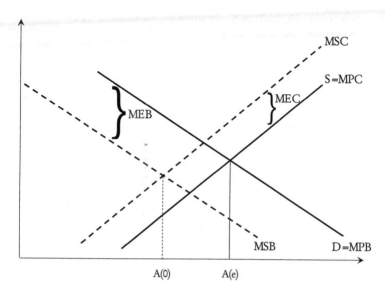

Figure 4.2   Inefficiencies in the Automobile Market

But as can be seen in Figure 4.2, if the MSC curve lies above the market supply curve, and the MSB curve lies below the market demand curve for cars, MSC and MSB will cross to the left of where the market supply and demand curves cross. Therefore the socially efficient, or optimal level of automobile production (and consumption), A(0), will be less than the equilibrium level of production and consumption, A(e), that the micro law of supply and demand will drive us toward. In other words, the market will lead us to produce and consume more cars than is socially efficient, or optimal. The market will lead to too much car production and consumption because sellers and buyers decide how many cars to produce and consume and they have no reason to take anything other than the costs and benefits to them into account. They have no incentive to consider the external costs associated with producing and consuming cars. In fact, they have good reason to ignore these external effects because taking them into account would make them individually worse off. Not surprisingly we discover that if decision makers ignore negative consequences of doing something – in this case the negative external effects of car production and consumption on people *other* than the car producer and buyer – they will decide to do too much of it – in this case they will decide to produce and consume too many cars.[2]

Public goods: pollution reduction

A public good is a good produced by human economic activity that is consumed, to all intents and purposes, by everyone rather than by an individual consumer. Unlike a private good such as underwear that affects only its wearer, public goods like pollution reduction affect most people. In different terms, nobody can be excluded from "consuming" a public good – or benefitting from the existence of the public good. This is not to say that everyone has the same preferences regarding public goods anymore than people have the same preferences for private goods. I happen to prefer apples to oranges, and I value pollution reduction more than I value so-called "national defense." There are others who place greater value on "national defense" than they do on pollution reduction, just as there are others who prefer oranges to apples. But unlike the case of apples and oranges where those who prefer apples can buy more apples and those who like oranges more can buy more oranges, all US citizens have to "consume" the same amount of federal spending on the military and federal spending on pollution reduction. We cannot provide more military spending for the US citizens who value that public good more, and more pollution reduction for the US citizens who value the environment more. Whereas different Americans can consume different amounts of private goods, we all must live in the same "public good world."

What would happen if we left the decision about how much of our scarce productive resources to devote to producing public goods to the free market? Markets only provide goods for which there is what we call "effective demand," that is, buyers willing and able to put their money where their mouth is. But what incentive is there for a buyer to pay for a public good? First of all, no matter how much I

---

2. External effects are notoriously hard to measure in market economies. This is of great significance since their magnitude is critical to how inefficient a market will be, and how large a pollution tax needs to be to correct the inefficiency. In a 1998 report the Center for Technology Assessment estimated that when external effects are taken into account the true social cost of a gallon of gasoline consumed in the US may be as high as $15. I just paid $1.02 a gallon when I filled my car up today in southern Maryland. The $1.02 already includes some hefty taxes, but obviously they are not nearly hefty enough!

value the public good, I only enjoy a tiny fraction of the overall, or social benefit that comes from having more of it since I cannot exclude others who do not pay for it from benefitting as well. In different terms: Social rationality demands that an individual purchase a public good up to the point where the cost of the last unit she purchased is as great as the benefits enjoyed by *all* who benefit, *in sum total*, from her purchase of the good. But it is only rational for an individual to buy a public good up to the point where the cost of the last unit she purchased is as great as the benefit she, herself, enjoys from the good. When individuals buy public goods in a free market they have no incentive to take the benefits others enjoy into account when they decide how much to buy. Consequently they "demand" far less than is socially efficient, if they purchase any at all. In sum, market demand will grossly under-represent the marginal *social* benefit of public goods.

Another way to see the problem is to recognize that each potential buyer of a public good has an incentive to wait and hope that someone else will buy the public good. A patient buyer can "ride for free" on others' purchases since non-payers cannot be excluded from benefitting from public goods. But if everyone is waiting for someone else to plunk down their hard earned income for a public good, nobody will demonstrate "effective demand" for public goods in the market place. "Free riding" is individually rational in the case of public goods – but leads to an "effective demand" for public goods that grossly underestimates their true social benefit. In chapter 5 we explore this logic formally in "the public good game."

What prevents a group of people who will benefit from a public good from banding together to express their demand for the good collectively? The problem is that there is an incentive for people to lie about how much they benefit. If the associations of public good consumers are voluntary, no matter how much I truly benefit from a public good, I am better off pretending I don't benefit at all. Then I can decline membership in the association and avoid paying anything, knowing full well that I will, in fact, benefit from its existence nonetheless. If the associations are not voluntary – i.e., if a government "drafts" people into the public good consuming coalition – there is still an incentive for people to under-represent the degree to which they benefit if assessments are based on degree of benefit. This is where the fact that not all people *do* benefit equally from different kinds of public goods becomes an important part of the problem. If we knew that everyone truly valued a larger military to the same extent, there would be few objections to making everyone contribute the same amount to pay for it. But there is every reason to believe this is *not* the case. In this context, if we believe that payments should be related to the degree to which someone benefits, there is an incentive for everyone to pretend they benefit less than they do. If the effective demand expressed by the non-voluntary consuming coalition is based on these individually rational under-representations, it will still significantly under-represent the true social benefits people enjoy from the public good, and consequently lead to less demand for the public good than is socially efficient, or optimal.

In sum, because of what economists call the "free rider" incentive problem and the "transaction costs" of organizing and managing a coalition of public good consumers, market demand predictably under-represents the true social benefits that come from consumption of public goods. If the production of a public good entails no external effects so the market supply curve accurately represents the marginal social costs of producing the public good, then since market demand will lie considerably under the true marginal social benefit curve for the public good, the market equilibrium level of production and consumption will be significantly less than the socially efficient level. In conclusion, if we left it to the free market and voluntary associations precious little, if any, of our scarce productive resources would be used to produce public goods no matter how valuable they really were. As Robert Heilbroner put it: "The market has a keen ear for private wants, but a deaf ear for public needs."

The fact that pollution reduction is a public good has important implications for *green consumerism* in free market economies. There are a number of cheap detergents that get my wash very white but cause considerable water pollution. "Green" detergents, on the other hand, are more expensive and leave my whites more gray than white, but cause less water pollution. *Whether or not I end up making the socially responsible choice*, because pollution reduction is a public good the market provides *too little incentive* for me to make the socially efficient choice. My own best interests are served by weighing the disadvantage of the extra cost and grayer whites *to me* against the advantage *to me* of the diminution in water pollution that would result if I use the green detergent. But presumably there are many others besides me who also benefit from the cleaner water if I buy the green detergent – which is precisely why we think of "buying green" as socially responsible behavior. Unfortunately the market provides no incentive for me to take *their* benefit into account. Worse still, if I suspect others may consult only their own interests when they choose which detergent to buy, i.e., if I think they will ignore the benefits to me and others if they choose the "green" detergent, by choosing to take their interests into account and consuming green myself I risk not only making a choice that was detrimental to my own interests, I risk being played for a sucker as well.[3]

This is not to say that many people will not choose to "do the right thing" and "consume green" in any case. Moreover, there may be incentives *other than the socially counterproductive market incentives* that may overcome the market disincentive to consume green. The fact that I am a member of the Southern Maryland Green Party and fear I would be ostracized if observed by a fellow party member with a polluting detergent in my shopping basket in the check out line at the supermarket is apparently a powerful enough incentive in my own case to lead me to buy a green detergent despite the market disincentive to do so. (Admittedly I have only a slight preference for white over gray clothes, and who knows how long I will hold out if the price differential increases?) But the point is that because pollution reduction is a public good, market incentives are perverse, i.e. lead people to consume less "green" and more "dirty" than is socially efficient. The extent to which people ignore the perverse market incentives and act on the basis of concern for the environment, concern for others, including future generations, or in response to non-market, social incentives such as fear of ostracism is important for the environment and the social interest, but does not make the market incentives any the less perverse.

The prevalence of external effects

In face of these concessions – markets misallocate resources when there are externalities and public goods – how do market enthusiasts continue to claim that markets allocate resources efficiently – as if guided by a beneficent invisible hand? The answer lies in an assumption that is explicit in the theorems of graduate level micro

3. Most detergents call for a full cup per load of wash. Church & Dwight canceled a ¼ cup laundry detergent product when consumer demand for this "green" product proved insufficient. See Christine Canning, "The Laundry Detergent Market," in *Household and Personal Products Industry*, April 1996.

economic theory texts but only implicit in undergraduate textbooks and in the advice of most economists. The fundamental theorem of welfare economics states that if all markets are in equilibrium the economy will be in a Pareto optimal state *only if there are no external effects or public goods*. The assumption that there are no public goods or external effects is explicit in the statement of the theorem that is the modern incarnation of Adam Smith's 200-year-old vision of an invisible hand – because otherwise the theorem would be false! Since everyone knows there are externalities and public goods in the real world, the conclusion that markets allocate resources reasonably efficiently in the real world rests on the assumption that external effects and public goods are few and far between. This assumption is usually unstated, and its validity has never been demonstrated through empirical research. It is a *pre*sumption implicit in an untested paradigm that lies behind mainstream economic theory – a paradigm that pretends that the choices people make have little effect on the opportunities and well being of others.

If we replace the implicit paradigm at the basis of mainstream economics with one that sees the world as a web of human interaction where people's choices often have far reaching consequences for others, both now and in the future, the presumption that external effects and public goods are the exception rather than the rule is reversed. Since political economists have long seen the world in just this way, and everything we have learned about the relation between human choices and ecological systems over the past 30 years reinforces this vision of interconnectedness, there is every reason for political economists to expect external and public effects to be the rule rather than the exception. What is surprising is that so few political economists have recognized the far reaching implications of their own beliefs when it comes to assessing the efficiency of markets. One stellar exception is E.K. Hunt. In an article "On Lemmings and Other Acquisitive Animals" remarkable for its lack of impact on other political economists when published in June 1973 (*Journal of Economic Issues*), E.K. Hunt stated the "reverse" assumption as follows:

> The Achilles heel of welfare economics [as practiced by mainstream pro-market economists] is its treatment of externalities ... When reference is made to externalities, one usually takes as a typical example an upwind factory that emits large quantities of sulfur oxides and particulate matter inducing rising probabilities of emphysema, lung cancer, and other respiratory diseases to

residents downwind, or a strip-mining operation that leaves an irreparable aesthetic scar on the countryside. The fact is, however, that most of the millions of acts of production and consumption in which we daily engage involve externalities. In a market economy any action of one individual or enterprise which induces pleasure or pain to any other individual or enterprise ... constitutes an externality. Since the vast majority of productive and consumptive acts are social, i.e., to some degree they involve more than one person, it follows that they will involve externalities. Our table manners in a restaurant, the general appearance of our house, our yard or our person, our personal hygiene, the route we pick for a joy ride, the time of day we mow our lawn, or nearly any one of the thousands of ordinary daily acts, all affect, to some degree, the pleasures or happiness of others. *The fact is ... externalities are totally pervasive ...* Only the most extreme bourgeois individualism could have resulted in an economic theory that assumed otherwise.

If the social effects of production and consumption frequently extend beyond the sellers and buyers of those goods and services, as Hunt argues above, and if these external effects are not insignificant, markets will frequently *mis*allocate resources leading us to produce too much of some goods and too little of others. By ignoring negative external effects markets lead us to produce and consume more of goods like automobiles than is socially efficient. By ignoring positive external effects markets lead us to consume less of goods like tropical rain forests that recycle carbon dioxide and thereby reduce global warming than is socially efficient – instead we clear cut them or burn them off to pasture cattle. And while markets provide reasonable opportunities for people to express their preferences for goods and services that can be enjoyed individually with minimal "transaction costs," they do not provide efficient means for expressing desires for goods that are enjoyed, or consumed socially, or collectively – like public space and pollution reduction. Markets create "free rider" disincentives for those who would express their desires for public goods individually, and pose daunting transaction costs for those who attempt to form a coalition of beneficiaries. In other words, *markets have an anti-social bias.*

Worse still, markets provide powerful incentives for actors to take advantage of external effects in socially counterproductive ways, and even to magnify or create new ones. Increasing the value of goods and services produced, and decreasing the unpleasantness of what we have to do to get them, are two ways that producers can increase their profits in a market economy. And competitive pressures will drive producers to do both. But maneuvering to appropriate a greater share of the goods and services produced by externalizing costs and internalizing benefits without compensation are also ways to increase profits. Competitive pressures will drive producers to pursue this route to greater profitability just as assiduously. Of course the problem is, while the first kind of behavior serves the social interest as well as the private interests of producers, the second kind of behavior does not. Instead, when buyers or sellers promote their private interests by externalizing costs onto those not party to the market exchange, or internalizing benefits without compensating external parties, their "rent seeking behavior" introduces inefficiencies that lead to a misallocation of productive resources and consequently decreases the value of all the goods and services produced. Questions market admirers seldom ask are: Where are firms most likely to find the easiest opportunities to expand their profits? How easy is it to increase the quantity or quality of goods produced? How easy is it to reduce the time or discomfort it takes to produce them? Alternatively, how easy is it to enlarge one's slice of the economic pie by externalizing a cost, or by appropriating a benefit without compensation? In sum, why should we assume that it is infinitely easier to expand profits by productive behavior than by rent seeking behavior? Yet this implicit assumption is what lies behind the view of markets as efficiency machines.

Market enthusiasts fail to notice that the same feature of market exchanges primarily responsible for small transaction costs – excluding all affected parties but two from the transaction – is also a major source of potential gain for the buyer and seller. When the buyer and seller of an automobile strike their convenient deal, the size of the benefit they have to divide between them is greatly enlarged by externalizing the costs onto others of the acid rain produced by car production, and the costs of urban smog, noise pollution, traffic congestion, and greenhouse gas emissions caused by car consumption. Those who pay these costs, and thereby enlarge car maker profits and car consumer benefits, are "easy marks" for car sellers and buyers because they are geographically and chronologically dispersed, and because the magnitude of the effect on each of them is small and unequal. Individually they have little incentive to insist on being party to the transaction. Collectively they face transaction cost and free rider obstacles to forming a voluntary coalition to represent a large number of people – each with little, but different, amounts at stake.

Moreover, the opportunity for socially counterproductive rent seeking behavior is not eliminated by making markets perfectly competitive or entry costless, as is commonly assumed. Rent seeking *at the expense of a buyer or seller* may be eliminated by competitive markets, i.e. the presence of innumerable sellers for buyers to choose from and innumerable buyers for sellers to choose from. But even if there were countless perfectly informed sellers and buyers in every market, even if the appearance of the slightest differences in average profit rates in different industries induced instantaneous self-correcting entries and exits of firms, even if every market participant were equally powerful and therefore equally powerless – in other words, even if we embrace the full fantasy of market enthusiasts – as long as there are numerous external parties with small but unequal interests in market transactions, those external parties will face greater transaction cost and free rider obstacles to a full and effective representation of their collective interest than any obstacles faced by the buyer and seller in the exchange. And it is this unavoidable inequality that makes external parties easy prey to rent seeking behavior on the part of buyers and sellers. Even if we could organize a market economy so that buyers and sellers never faced a more or less powerful opponent in a market exchange, this would not change the fact that each of us has smaller interests at stake in many transactions in which we are neither the buyer nor seller. Yet the sum total interest of all external parties can be considerable compared to the interests of the buyer and the seller. It is the transaction cost and free rider problems of those with lesser interests that create an unavoidable inequality in power, which, in turn, gives rise to the opportunity for individually profitable but socially counterproductive rent seeking on the part of buyers and sellers in even the most competitive markets. A sufficient condition for buyers and sellers to profit in socially counterproductive ways from maneuvering, rent seeking, or cost shifting behavior is that each one of us has diffuse interests that make us affected external parties to many exchanges in which we are neither buyer nor seller – no matter how competitive markets may be.

But socially counterproductive rent seeking behavior is not only engaged in at the expense of parties external to market exchanges. The real world bears little resemblance to a game where all buyers and sellers are equally powerful, in which case it would be pointless for sellers or buyers to try to take advantage of one another. In the real world it is often easier for powerful firms to increase profits by lowering the prices they pay less powerful suppliers and raising the prices they charge powerless consumers than it is to search for ways to increase the quality of their products. In the real world there are consumers with little information, time, or means to defend their interests. There are small, capital poor, innovative firms for giants like IBM and Microsoft to buy up instead of tackling the hard work of innovation themselves. There are common property resources whose productivity can be appropriated at little or no cost as they are overexploited at the expense of future generations. And finally, there is a government run by politicians whose careers rely principally on their ability to raise campaign money, begging to be plied for tax dodges and corporate welfare programs financed at taxpayer expense. In other words, in the real world where buyers and sellers are usually not equally powerful, the most effective profit maximizing strategy is often to outmaneuver less powerful market opponents and expand one's slice of the pie at their expense rather than work to expand it.

Snowballing inefficiency

To the extent that consumer preferences are endogenous the degree of misallocation that results from uncorrected external effects in market economies will increase, or "snowball" over time. As people adjust their preferences to the biases created by external effects in the market price system, they will increase their preference and demand for goods whose production and/or consumption entails negative external effects, but whose market prices fail to reflect these costs and are therefore lower than they should be; and they will decrease their preference and demand for goods whose production and/or consumption entails positive external effects, but whose market prices fail to reflect these benefits and are therefore higher than they should be. While this reaction, or adjustment, is individually rational it is socially irrational and inefficient since it leads to even greater demand for the goods that market systems tend to overproduce, and even less demand for the goods that market systems tend to underproduce. As people have greater opportunities to adjust over longer periods of time, the degree of inefficiency in the economy will grow, or "snowball."[4]

Market disequilibria

Nobody knows where the equilibrium price in a market is. What the micro law of supply and demand says is that self-interested behavior on the part of frustrated sellers when there is excess supply because the actual price is higher than the equilibrium price, and self-interested behavior on the part of frustrated buyers when there is excess demand because market price is below the equilibrium price, will tend to move markets toward their equilibria. But as long as a market is out of equilibrium the quantity bought and sold will be less than the quantity that would be bought and sold if the market were in equilibrium. Since the equilibrium quantity is the same as the socially efficient quantity to produce and consume in absence of external effects, this means markets do not yield efficient outcomes when they are out of equilibrium even in absence of external effects. So the first problem is *the slower markets equilibrate the more inefficiency we will endure while they do.*

The second problem is if market participants interpret changes in prices as *signals* about further changes in prices it is *unlikely* they will obey the "laws" of supply and demand. If I believe that even though the price of apples just rose, any further change in the price of apples is just as likely to be down as up, that is, if I do *not* interpret the rise in price as a signal that the price is rising, I will probably demand fewer apples at the new higher price as the law of demand predicts. But if I think that because the price just rose it is more likely to go up than down the next time it changes, I should buy more apples now that I think the chances are greater than I thought before that the price of apples will rise. If I want apples I should buy more apples now before they become even more expensive later. And even if I don't want apples, I should buy more now and sell them tomorrow when the price is even higher. Similarly, if sellers in a market interpret price changes as signals of what direction prices are headed in, they should offer to sell more when the price falls and sell less

---

4. For a rigorous demonstration that endogenous preferences imply snow-balling inefficiency when there are market externalities see theorems 7.1 and 7.2 in Hahnel and Albert, *Quiet Revolution in Welfare Economics*.

when it rises, the law of supply notwithstanding.[5] In this case, when actual buyers' behavior is represented by an upward sloping demand curve and actual sellers' behavior is represented by a downward sloping supply curve, self-interested behavior on the part of frustrated buyers when there is excess demand will raise a price that is higher than the equilibrium price, not lower it. And self-interested behavior on the part of frustrated sellers will lower a price that is lower than the equilibrium price, not raise it. In other words, there will be disequilibrating forces in the market pushing it farther away from equilibrium, not toward it.

A rising price that becomes, at least temporarily, a self-fulfilling prophesy is commonly called a market "bubble," and a falling price that becomes a self-fulfilling prophesy is often called a market "crash." As we will discover in chapter 7 where we study banks and international finance, this kind of disequilibrating dynamic occurs more often than market enthusiasts like to admit, particularly in financial and foreign exchange markets, with disastrous effects on real economies, i.e. on employment, investment, production and consumption. Finally, there can be a different kind of disequilibrating dynamic that operates between markets that are connected in a particular way. When one market is initially out of equilibrium it can cause another market to fall out of equilibrium. When this second market falls out of equilibrium it can push the first market even farther away from equilibrium, which in turn pushes the second market farther out of equilibrium as well. The result can be a "vicious" interaction in which each market pushes the other farther away from its equilibrium, and it is possible for this disequilibrating force to be stronger than the equilibrating forces of price adjustments within markets described in the micro law of supply and demand. In chapter 6 on macro economics we focus on how the market for labor and the market for goods in general interact. One of Keynes' greatest insights was his discovery that disequilibrating

---

5. Mainstream texts persist in treating such behavior as if it was not the obvious violation of the "laws" of supply and demand that it clearly is. Instead of admitting that demand is not always negatively related to market price, and supply is not always positively related to market price, mainstream texts resort to the subterfuge of saying that the change in expectations about the likely direction of future price changes *shifts* demand curves and supply curves that *still do* obey the laws of supply and demand, yielding actual results that contradict what those laws lead us to expect. This is sophistry at its worst.

dynamics that operate between goods and labor markets can push both markets farther away from their equilibrium faster than price and wage adjustments within them push them toward equilibrium. This insight allowed Keynes to explain why production and employment keep dropping in a depression even though there are more and more workers willing to work – if only someone would hire them – and plenty of employers anxious to produce goods – if only someone would buy them.

Conclusion: market failure is significant

In sum, convenient deals with mutual benefits for buyer and seller should not be confused with economic efficiency. When some kinds of preferences are consistently under-represented because of trans-action cost and free rider problems, when consumers adjust their preferences to biases in the market price system and thereby aggravate those biases, and when profits can be increased as often by externalizing costs onto parties external to market exchanges as from productive behavior, theory predicts that free market exchange will often result in a *mis*allocation of scarce productive resources. Theory tells us free market economies will allocate too much of society's resources to goods whose production or consumption entail negative external effects, and too little to goods whose production or consumption entail positive external effects, and there is every reason to believe the misallocations are significant. When markets are less than perfectly competitive – which they almost always are – and fail to equilibrate instantaneously – which they always do – the results are that much worse.

MARKETS UNDERMINE THE TIES THAT BIND US

While political economists criticize market inefficiencies and inequities, many others have complained, in one way or another, that markets are *socially destructive*. In effect markets say to us: You cannot consciously coordinate your economic activities efficiently, so don't even try. You cannot come to efficient and equitable agreements among yourselves, so don't even try. Just thank your lucky stars that even such a hopelessly socially challenged species such as yourselves can still benefit from a division of labor thanks to the miracle of the market system. Markets are a decision to punt in the game of human economic relations, a no-confidence vote on the social capacities of the human species. Samuel Bowles explained markets' antisocial bias eloquently in an essay titled "What Markets Can and Cannot Do" published in *Challenge Magazine* in July 1991:

> Even if market allocations *did* yield Pareto-optimal results, and even if the resulting income distribution *was* thought to be fair (two very big "ifs"), the market would still fail if it supported an undemocratic structure of power or if it rewarded greed, opportunism, political passivity, and indifference toward others. The central idea here is that our evaluation of markets – and with it the concept of market failure – must be expanded to include the effects of markets on both the structure of power and the process of human development. As anthropologists have long stressed, how we regulate our exchanges and coordinate our disparate economic activities influences what kind of people we become. Markets may be considered to be social settings that foster specific types of personal development and penalize others ... The beauty of the market, some would say, is precisely this: It works well even if people *are* indifferent toward one another. And it does not require complex communication or even trust among its participants. But that is also the problem. The economy – its markets, work places and other sites – is a gigantic school. Its rewards encourage the development of particular skills and attitudes while other potentials lay fallow or atrophy. We learn to function in these environments, and in so doing become someone we might not have become in a different setting ... By economizing on valuable traits – feelings of solidarity with others, the ability to empathize, the capacity for complex communication and collective decision making, for example – markets are said to cope with the scarcity of these worthy traits. But in the long run markets contribute to their erosion and even disappearance. What looks like a hardheaded adaptation to the infirmity of human nature may in fact be part of the problem.

Markets and hierarchical decision making economize on the use of valuable but scarce human traits like "feelings of solidarity with others, the ability to empathize, the capacity for complex communication and collective decision making." But more importantly, markets and hierarchical relations contribute to the erosion and disappearance of these worthy traits by rewarding those who ignore democratic and social considerations and penalizing those who try to take them into account. It is no accident that despite a monumental increase in education levels, the work force is less capable of exercising its self-management potential at the end of the twentieth century than it was at the beginning, or that people feel more alone, alienated, suspicious of one another, and rootless than ever before. Robert Bellah, Jean Bethke Elshtain, and Robert Putnam among others have documented the general decay of civic life and weakening of trust and participation across all income and educational levels in the United States. There is no longer any doubt that "the social fabric is becoming visibly thinner, we don't trust one another as much, and we don't know one another as much" in Putnam's words.[6] While it is easier to blame the spread of television than a major economic institution, the atomizing effect of markets as they spread into more and more areas of our lives bears a major responsibility for this trend.

Market prices are systematically biased against social activities in favor of individual activities. Markets make it easier to pursue well being through individual rather than social activity by minimizing the transaction costs associated with the former and maximizing the transaction costs associated with the latter. Private consumption faces no obstacles in market economies where joint, or social consumption runs smack into the free rider problem. Markets harness our creative capacities and energy by arranging for other people to threaten our livelihoods. Markets bribe us with the lure of luxury beyond what others can have and beyond what we know we deserve. Markets reward those who are the most efficient at taking advantage of his or her fellow man or woman, and penalize those who insist, illogically, on pursuing the golden rule – do unto others as you would have them do unto you. A mathematics instructor at a small college in Liaoyang China who had doubled his income running a small fleet of taxis summarized his experience with marketization as follows: "It's really survival of the fittest here. If you have a cutthroat heart, you can make it. If you are a good person, I don't think you can."[7]

6. Putnam made this remark when interviewed at the 1995 annual meeting of the American Association of Political Scientists in Chicago (*Washington Post*, September 3, 1995: A5).
7. Reported in "With Carrots and Sticks, China Quiets Protesters," *Washington Post*, March 22, 2002: A24. John Pomfret covered the downside of China's conversion to a capitalist economy in a series of eye opening articles published in the *Washington Post* during March 2002. Most whom Pomfret interviewed protesting layoffs, lost back pay, and rampant corruption declined to be identified by name, knowing this would almost surely lead

Of course, we are told we can personally benefit in a market system by being of service to others. But we know we can often benefit more easily by tricking others. Mutual concern, empathy, and solidarity are the appendices of human capacities and emotions in market economies – and like the appendix, they continue to atrophy as people respond sensibly to the *rule of the market place – do others in before they do you in.*

---

to their arrest. Pomfret ended the above article with a quote from a rare exception. Wang Bing offered the following assessment of China's conversion to capitalism: "They say the country is heading in the right direction. Maybe. But for the average guy here, things are definitely getting worse. The workers used to be the masters of this country. What are we the masters of now?"

5 Micro Economic Models

This chapter presents some simple micro economic models that illustrate important themes in political economy. While the rest of the book can be read without benefit of the models in this chapter, readers who want to be able to analyze economic problems themselves from a political economy perspective are encouraged to read this chapter.

THE PUBLIC GOOD GAME

The "public good game" illustrates why markets will allocate too few of our scarce productive resources to the production of public, as opposed to private, goods. Assume 0, 1, or 2 units of a **public** good can be produced and the cost to society of producing each unit is $11. Either Ilana or Sara can purchase 1 unit, or none of the public good – each paying $11 if she purchases a unit, and nothing if she does not. Suppose Sara gets $10 of benefit for every unit of a public good that is available and Ilana gets $8 of benefit for every unit available. We fill in a game theory payoff matrix for each woman buying, or not buying, 1 unit of the public good as follows: We calculate the net benefit for each woman by subtracting what she must pay if she purchases a unit of the public good from the benefits she receives from the total number of public goods purchased and therefore available for her to consume. Ilana's "payoff" is listed first, and Sara's second in each "cell." For example, in the case where both Ilana and Sara buy a unit of the public good, and therefore each gets to consume 2 units of the public good, Ilana's net benefit is 2($8) – $11, or $5, and Sara's net benefit is 2($10) – $11, or $9.

		SARA	
		Buy	*Free Ride*
ILANA	*Buy*	($5, $9)	(–3, $10)
	Free Ride	($8, –$1)	($0, $0)

(1) Will Sara buy a unit? No. Sara is better off free riding no matter what Ilana does. If Ilana buys Sara is better off not buying and free riding since $10 > $9. If Ilana does not buy Sara is also better off not buying than buying since $0 > –$1.

(2) Will Ilana buy a unit? No. Ilana is also better off free riding no matter what Sara does since $8 > $5 and $0 > –$3.

(3) Assuming that Sara and Ilana's benefits are of equal importance to society, what is the socially optimal number of units of the public good to produce? 2 units since $5 + $9 = $13 is greater than $10 – $3 = $8 – $1 = $7 which is greater than $0 + $0 = $0.

Suppose the social cost and price a buyer is charged is $5. The game theory payoff matrix for buying or not buying 1 unit of the public good now is:

| | | SARA | |
		Buy	Free Ride
ILANA	Buy	($11, $15)	($3, $10)
	Free Ride	($8, $5)	($0, $0)

(4) Will Sara buy a unit? Yes. Buying is best for Sara no matter what Ilana does since $15 > $10 if Ilana buys, and $5 > $0 if Ilana does not buy.

(5) Will Ilana buy a unit? Yes. Buying is best for Ilana no matter what Sara does since $11 > $8 if Sara buys, and $3 > $0 if Sara does not buy.

(6) Assuming that Sara and Ilana's benefits are of equal importance to society, what is the socially optimal number of units of the public good to produce? Two units yield the largest possible net social benefit of any of the four possible outcomes: $11 + $15 = $26.

Finally, suppose the social cost and price a buyer is charged is $9. Now the game theory payoff matrix for buying or not buying 1 unit of the public good is:

		SARA	
		Buy	*Free Ride*
ILANA	*Buy*	($7, $11)	(–$1, $10)
	Free Ride	($8, $1)	($0, $0)

(7) Will Sara buy a unit? Yes, since Sara is better off buying no matter what Ilana does: $11 > $10 when Ilana buys, and $1 > $0 when Ilana does not buy.

(8) Will Ilana buy a unit? No, since Ilana is better off free riding no matter what Sara does: $8 > $7 when Sara buys, and $0 > –$1 when Sara does not buy.

(9) Assuming that Sara and Ilana's benefits are of equal importance to society, what is the socially optimal number of units of the public good to produce? It is 2 units since $7 + $11 = $18 is greater than $8 + $1 = $10 – $1 = $9, which is greater than $0 + $0 = $0.

What the "public good game" demonstrates is the following conclusion: Unless the private benefit to each consumer of a unit of a public good exceeds the entire social cost of producing a unit, the free rider problem will lead to underproduction of the public good. When the cost is $11 the private benefit for both Sara and Ilana is less than the social cost, and neither buys – although buying and consuming 2 units is socially beneficial. When the cost is $9 the private benefit for Ilana is still less than the social cost so she does not buy, and only 1 unit is bought (by Sara) and consumed (by both women) – although producing and consuming 2 units would be more efficient. Only when the cost is $5 is the private benefit to both Sara and Ilana sufficient to induce each to buy, and *then and only then* do we get the socially efficient level of public good production. Obviously for most public goods the private benefit to most individual buyers will not outweigh the entire social cost of producing the public good, and we will therefore get significant "underproduction" of public goods if resource allocation is left to the free market.

THE PRICE OF POWER GAME

When people in an economic relationship have unequal power the logic of preserving a power advantage can lead to a loss of economic efficiency. This dynamic is illustrated by the "Price of Power Game" which helps explain phenomena as diverse as why employers sometimes choose a less efficient technology over a more efficient one, and why patriarchal husbands sometimes bar their wives from working outside the home even when household well being would be increased if the wife did work outside.

Assume P and W combine to produce an economic value and divide the benefit between them. They have been producing a value of 15, but because P has a power advantage in the relationship P has been getting twice as much as W. So initially P and W jointly produce 15, P gets 10 and W gets 5. A new possibility arises that would allow them to produce a greater value. Assume it increases the value of what they jointly produce by 20%, i.e. by 3, raising the value of their combined production from 15 to 18. But taking advantage of the new, more productive possibility also has the effect of increasing W's power relative to P. Assume the effect of producing the greater value renders W as powerful as P eliminating P's power advantage. The obvious intuition is that if P stands to lose more from receiving a smaller slice than P stands to gain from having a larger pie to divide with W, it will be in P's interest to block the efficiency gain. We can call this efficiency loss "the price of power." But constructing a simple "game tree" helps us understand the obstacles that prevent untying this Gordian knot as well as the logic leading to the unfortunate result.

As the player with the power advantage P gets to make the first move at the first "node." P has two choices at node 1: P can reject the new, more productive possibility and end the game. We call this choice R (for "right" in the game tree diagram in Figure 5.1), and the payoff for P is 10 (listed on top) and the payoff for W is 5 (listed on the bottom) if P chooses R. Or, P can defer to W allowing W to choose whether or not they will adopt the new possibility. We call this choice L (for "left" in the game tree diagram in Figure 5.1), and the payoffs for P and W in this case depend on what W chooses at the second node. If the game gets to the second node because P deferred to W at the first node, W has three choices at node 2: Choice R1 is for W to reject the new possibility and of course the payoffs remain 10 for P and 5 for W as before. Choice L1 is for W to

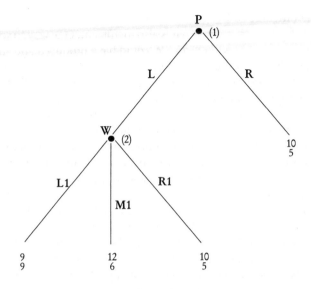

Figure 5.1   Price of Power Game

choose the new, more productive possibility and insist on dividing
the larger value of 18 equally between them since the new process
empowers W to the extent that P no longer has a power advantage
in their relationship, and therefore W can command an equal share
with P. If W chooses L1 the payoff for P is therefore 9 and the payoff
for W is also 9. Finally, choice M1 (for "middle" in the game tree in
Figure 5.1) is for W to choose the new, more productive possibility
but to offer to continue to split the pie as before, with P receiving
twice as much as W. In other words in M1 W promises P not to take
advantage of her new power, which means that P still gets twice as
much as W, but since the pie is larger now P's payoff is 12 and W's
payoff is 6 if W chooses M1 at node 2.

   We solve this simple dynamic game by backwards induction. If
given the opportunity, W should choose L1 at node 2 since W
receives 9 for choice L1 and only 5 for choice R1 and only 6 for
choice M1. Knowing that W will choose L1 if the game goes to node
2, P compares a payoff of 10 by choosing R with an expected payoff
of 9 if P chooses L and W subsequently chooses L1 as P has every
reason to believe she will. Consequently P chooses R at node 1
ending the game and effectively "blocking" the new, more
productive possibility.

The outcome of the game is not only unequal – P continues to receive twice as much as W – it is also inefficient. One way to see the inefficiency is that while P and W could have produced and shared a total value of 18 they end up only producing and sharing a total value of 15. Another way to see the inefficiency is to note that there is a Pareto superior outcome to (R). (L,M1) is technically possible and has a payoff of 12 for P and 6 for W, compared to the payoff of 10 for P and 5 for W that is the "equilibrium outcome" of the game.

It is the existence of L1 as an option for W at node 2 that forces P to choose R at node 1. Notice that if L1 were eliminated so that W had only two choices at node 2, R1 and M1, W would choose M1 in this new game, in which case P would choose L instead of R at node 1. While this outcome would remain unequal it would not be inefficient. So one could say the inefficiency of the outcome to the original game is because W cannot make a *credible* promise to P to reject option L1 if the game gets to node 2. Since there is no reason for P to believe W would actually choose M1 over L1 if the game gets to node 2, P chooses R at node 1. In effect P will block an efficiency gain whenever it diminishes P's power advantage sufficiently. If P stands to lose more from a loss of power than he gains from a bigger pie to divide, P will use his power advantage to block an efficiency gain.

If we turn our attention to how the efficiency loss might be avoided, two possibilities arise. The most straightforward solution, that not only avoids the efficiency loss but generates equal instead of unequal outcomes for P and W, is to eliminate P's power advantage. If P and W have equal power and divide the value of their joint production equally they will always choose to produce the larger pie and there will never be any efficiency losses. The more convoluted solution is to accept P's power advantage as a given, and search for ways to make *credible* a promise from W not to take advantage of her enhanced power. Is there some way to transform the initial game so that a promise from P not to choose L1 is credible?

What if W offered P 2 units of "value" to choose L rather than R at node 1? If a contract could be devised in which W had to pay P 2 units, if and only if P chose L at node 1, then the new game would have the following payoffs at node 2: If W chose R1' P would get 10 + 2 =12 instead of 10, and W would get 5 – 2 = 3 instead of 5. If W chose M1' P would get 12 + 2 = 14 instead of 12 and W would get 6 – 2 = 4 instead of 6. Finally, if W chose L1' P would get 9 + 2 = 11 instead of 9 and W would get 9 – 2 = 7 instead of 9. Under these circumstances, in the Transformed Price of Power Game illustrated in

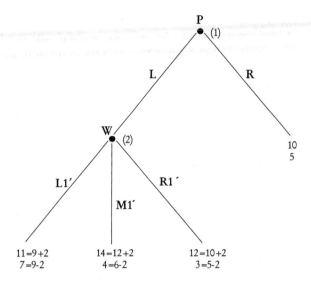

Figure 5.2   Transformed Price of Power Game

Figure 5.2 W would choose L1' since 7 is greater than both 4 and 3. But when W chooses L1' at node 2 that gives P 11 which is more than P gets by choosing R at node 1. Therefore a bribe of 2 paid by W to P if and only if P chooses R over L would give us an efficient but unequal outcome. It is efficient because P and W produce 18 instead of 15 and because (L,L1') is Pareto superior to (R). It is still unequal because P receives 11 while W receives only 7.

There are many economic situations where implementing an efficiency gain changes the bargaining power between collaborators and therefore the Price of Power Game can help illustrate aspects of what transpires. Below are two interesting applications.

The price of patriarchy

If P is a patriarchal head of household and W is his wife, the game illustrates one reason why the husband might refuse to permit his wife to work outside the home even though net benefits for the household would be greater if she did.[1] Patriarchal power within the household can be modeled as giving the husband the "first mover

---

1. I do not mean to imply that there are not many *other* reasons husbands behave in this way. Nor am I suggesting that *any* of the reasons are morally justifiable, including the reason this model explains.

advantage" in our model. Patriarchal power in the economy can be modeled as a gender-based wage gap for women with no labor market experience. If we assume that as long as the wife has not worked outside the home she cannot command as high a wage as her husband in the labor market, her exit option is worse than her husband's should the marriage dissolve. This unequal exit option makes it possible for a patriarchal husband to insist on a greater share of the household benefits than the wife as long as she has no outside work experience.[2] But after she works outside the home for some time the unequal exit option can dissipate, and with it the husband's power advantage within the home.

The obstacles to eliminating efficiency losses in this situation by eliminating patriarchal advantages are not economic. Gender-based wage discrimination can be eliminated through effective enforcement of laws outlawing discrimination in employment such as those in the US Civil Rights Act. The psychological dynamics that give "first mover" advantages to husbands within marriages requires changes in the attitudes and values of both men and women about gender relations. Of course eliminating the efficiency loss due to patriarchal power by eliminating patriarchal power has the supreme advantage of improving economic justice as well as efficiency.

Trying to eliminate the efficiency loss by making the wife's promise not to exercise the power advantage she gets by working outside the home credible has a number of disadvantages. Most importantly it is grossly unfair. The bribe the wife must pay her husband to be "allowed" to work outside the home is obviously the result of the disadvantages she suffers from having to negotiate under conditions of unequal and inequitable bargaining power in the first place. Second, it may not be as "practical" as it first appears. Those who believe this solution is more "achievable' or "practical" than reducing patriarchal privilege should bear in mind how unlikely it is that wives with no labor market credentials could obtain what would amount to an unsecured loan against their future expected productivity gain! Nor could their husbands co-sign for the

2. I am not suggesting that the wife's lack of work experience in the formal labor market makes her a less productive employee than her husband. If employers do not evaluate the productivity enhancing effects of household work fairly, or use previous employment in the formal sector as a screening device, the effect is the same as if lack of formal sector work experience did, in fact, mean lower productivity. The husband enjoys a power advantage no matter what the reason his wife is paid less than he is initially.

loan without effectively changing the payoff numbers in our revised game. Third, even if wives obtained loans from some outside agent – presumably an institution like the Grameen Bank in Bangladesh that gives loans to women without collateral but holds an entire group of women responsible for non-payment of any of the individual loans – there would have to be a binding legal contract that prevented husbands from taking the bribe and reneging on their promise to allow their wives to work outside the home. Notice that if P can keep the bribe and still choose R he gets $10 + 2 = 12$ which is greater than the 11 he gets if he keeps his promise to choose L.

Finally, notice that any bribe between 1 and 4 would successfully transform the game from an inefficient power game to a conceivably efficient, but nonetheless inequitable power game. If W paid P a bribe of 4 the entire efficiency gain would go to her husband. But even if W paid P only a bribe of 1 and kept the entire efficiency gain for herself, she would still end up with less than her husband. In that case W would get $9 - 1 = 8$ compared to $9 + 1 = 10$ for P. So even if we conjure up a Grameen Bank to give never employed women unsecured loans, even if we ignore all problems and costs of enforcement, there is no way to transform our power game into a game that would deliver equal and equitable outcomes for husbands and wives as well as efficient outcomes. Since P gets 10 by choosing R and ending the game, he must receive at least 10 in order to choose L. But if the productivity gain is only 3 when both work outside, and therefore total household net benefits are only 18, W can receive no more than 8 if P must have at least 10, and no transformation of the game that preserves patriarchal power will produce equitable results. Whether or not this morally inferior solution is actually easier to achieve than reducing patriarchal privilege also seems to be an open question.

Conflict theory of the firm

If P is an employer, or "*p*atron," and W are his employees or "*w*orkers" the Price of Power Game illustrates why an employer might fail to implement a new, more productive technology if that technology is also "employee empowering." In chapter 10 we consider factors that influence the bargaining power between employers and employees, and therefore the wages employees will receive and the efforts they will have to exert to get them. But one factor that can affect bargaining power in the capitalist firm is the technology used. For example, if an assembly line technology is used and employees are physically separated from one another and unable to communicate during work, it may be more difficult for employees to develop solidarity that would empower them in negotiations with their employer, as compared to a technology that requires workers to work in teams with constant communication between them. Or it may be that one technology requires employees themselves to have a great deal of know-how to carry out their tasks, while another technology concentrates crucial productive knowledge in the hands of a few engineers or supervisors, rendering most employees easily replaceable and therefore less powerful. If the technology that is more productive is also "worker empowering," employers face the dilemma illustrated by our Price of Power Game and may have reason to choose an inefficient technology over a more efficient one that is less worker empowering.

When we consider possible solutions in this application the situation is somewhat different than in the patriarchal household application. In capitalism there is inevitably a conflict between employers and employees over wages and effort levels. If new technologies not only affect economic efficiency but the relative bargaining power of employers and employees as well, we cannot "trust" the choice of technology to *either* interested party without running the risk that a more productive technology might be blocked due to detrimental bargaining power effects for whomever has the power to choose. I pointed out above how P might block a more efficient technology if it were sufficiently employee empowering, so we cannot trust employers to choose between technologies. But if W had the power to do so, W might block a more efficient technology if it were sufficiently employer empowering, so we cannot resolve the dilemma by giving unions the say over technology in capitalism either. The solution seems to lie in eliminating the conflict between employers and employees. This can only happen in economies where there are no employers and employees and no division between profits and wages, that is, in economies where employees manage and pay themselves. We consider economies of this kind in chapter 11.

INCOME DISTRIBUTION, PRICES AND TECHNICAL CHANGE

Mainstream economic theory explains the prices of goods and services in terms of consumer preferences, production technologies, and the relative scarcities of different productive resources. Political economists, on the other hand, have long insisted that wages, profits and rents are determined by power relations among classes in addition to factors mainstream economic theory takes into account, and therefore that the relative prices of goods in capitalist economies depend on power relations between classes as well as on consumer preferences and production technologies.

The labor theory of value Karl Marx developed in *Das Kapital* was the first political economy explanation of "wage, price and profit"[3] determination. In *Production of Commodities by Means of Commodities* (Cambridge University Press, 1960) Piero Sraffa presented an alternative political economy explanation that avoided logical inconsistencies and anomalies in the labor theory of value, and extends easily to include different wage rates for different kinds of labor and rents on different kinds of natural resources – which the labor theory of value could not. The model below is based on Sraffa's theory, and is often called "the modern surplus approach."[4]

3. Karl Marx wrote a pamphlet under this title in which he presented a popularized version of the labor theory of value from *Das Kapital*.
4. The "surplus approach" is only one part of a political economy explanation of the determination of wages, profits, rents, and prices. The surplus approach does *not* explain why consumers come to have the preferences they do, *nor* what determines the relative power of employers, workers, and resource owners. Instead the surplus approach takes consumer demand and the power relationships between workers, employers, and resource owners as givens, and seeks to explain what prices will result under those conditions. While it does not explain what causes changes in the power relations between workers, employers, and resource owners, the surplus approach does explain how any changes in power between them will affect prices as well as income distribution. And while it does not explain what causes technological innovations, it does explain which new technologies will be chosen, and how their implementation will affect wages, profits, rents, prices, and economic efficiency. Logically, the surplus approach is the *last* part of a micro political economy. Other political economy theories must explain the factors that influence preference formation and power relations between different classes. In chapter 4 the effect of market bias on preference formation was treated briefly. In chapter 10 factors affecting the bargaining power of workers and capitalists are explored. For a more rigorous political economy theory of "endogenous preferences" see chapter 6 in Hahnel and Albert, *Quiet Revolution in Welfare Economics*. See chapters 2 and 8 for a more thorough presentation and defense of the "conflict theory of the firm" and a more thorough examination of the factors that influence the bargaining power of capitalists and workers. But once consumer demand and the bargaining power between classes is given, the "surplus approach," or Sraffa model, provides a rigorous explanation of price formation and income distribution in capitalism.

The Sraffa model

Assume a two sector economy defined by the technology below where $a(ij)$ is the number of units of good i needed to produce 1 unit of good j, and $L(j)$ is the number of hours of labor needed to produce 1 unit of good j. Suppose:

$$a(11) = 0.3 \qquad a(12) = 0.2$$
$$a(21) = 0.2 \qquad a(22) = 0.4$$
$$L(1) = 0.1 \qquad L(2) = 0.2$$

The first column can be read as a "recipe" for making 1 unit of good 1: It takes 0.3 units of good 1 itself, 0.2 units of good 2, and 0.1 hour of labor to "stir" these ingredients to get 1 unit of good 1 as output. Similarly, the second column is a recipe for making 1 unit of good 2: It takes 0.2 units of good 1, 0.4 units of good 2 itself, and 0.2 hours of labor to make 1 unit of good 2.

Let $p(i)$ be the price of a unit of good i, w be the hourly wage rate, and $r(i)$ be the rate of profit received by capitalists in sector i. The first step is to write down an equation for each industry that expresses the truism that revenue minus cost for the industry is, by definition, equal to industry profit. If we divide both sides of this equation by the number of units of output the industry produces we get the truism that revenue per unit of output minus cost per unit of output must equal profit per unit of output. Another way of saying this is: cost per unit of output plus profit per unit of output must equal revenue per unit of output. This is the equation we want to write for each industry.

The second step is to write down what cost per unit of output and revenue per unit of output will be for each industry. For industry 1 it takes $a(11)$ units of good 1 itself to make a unit of output of good 1. That will cost $p(1)a(11)$. It also takes $a(21)$ units of good 2 to make a unit of output of good 1. That will cost $p(2)a(21)$. So $[p(1)a(11) + p(2)a(21)]$ are the non-labor costs of making 1 unit of good 1. Since it takes $L(1)$ hours of labor to make a unit of good 1 and the wage per hour is w, the labor cost of making a unit of good 1 is $wL(1)$. Revenue per unit of output of good 1 is simply $p(1)$.

What is profit per unit of output in industry 1? By definition profits are revenues minus costs, so profits per unit of output must be equal to revenues per unit of output minus cost per unit of output. Also by definition the rate of profit is profits divided by whatever part of costs a capitalist must pay for in advance. Dividing both the numerator and denominator by the number of units of output in industry 1 gives us the truism that the rate of profit in industry 1 is equal to the profit per unit of output in industry 1 divided by whatever part of costs per unit of output capitalists must advance in industry 1. Therefore, the profit per unit of output in industry 1 must be equal to the rate of profit for industry 1 times the cost per unit of output capitalists must advance in industry 1.

We will assume (with Sraffa) that capitalists must pay for non-labor costs in advance but can pay their employees after the production period is over out of revenues from the sale of the goods produced. So the cost per unit of output capitalists must advance in industry 1 is only the non-labor costs per unit, or $[p(1)a(11) + p(2)a(21)]$. We will also assume (with Sraffa) that the rate of profit capitalists receive is the same in both industries, r.[5] Therefore:

profit per unit of output in industry $1 = r[p(1)a(11) + p(2)a(21)]$

And we are ready to write the accounting identity, or truism, that cost per unit of output plus profit per unit of output equals revenue per unit of output in industry 1:

$$[p(1)a(11) + p(2)a(21)] + wL(1) + r[p(1)a(11) + p(2)a(21)] = p(1)$$

Which can be rewritten for convenience as:

(1) $(1+r) [p(1)a(11) + p(2)a(21)] + wL(1) = p(1)$

Similarly for industry 2:

(2) $(1+r) [p(1)a(12) + p(2)a(22)] + wL(2) = p(2)$

5. These assumptions are both convenient because they simplify the analysis. However, they are not necessary, and one of the strengths of the surplus approach is we could change them and still solve the model. In particular, if capitalists in different industries had different bargaining power, or if some industries were more competitive and others less so, or if there were barriers to entry in some industries so capitalists were not free to flee low profit industries and enter high profit ones until profit rates were equal everywhere, we could easily complicate our model and stipulate different rates of profit $r(1)$ and $r(2)$ for the two industries.

We call equations (1) and (2) the "price equations" for the economy. They are 2 equations with 4 unknowns: w, r, p(1), and p(2). (The a(ij) and L(j) are technological "givens.") But we are only interested in relative prices, i.e. how many units of one good trade for how many units of another good. If we set the price of good 2 equal to 1, p(2) = 1, then p(1) tells us how many units of good 2 a unit of good 1 exchanges for, and w tells us how many units of good 2 a worker can buy with her hourly wage. So we now have 2 equations in 3 unknowns: w, r, and p(1), the price of good 1 *relative* to the price of good 2. We proceed to discover: (1) that the wage rate and profit rate must be negatively related, (2) that the relative prices of goods can change even when there are no changes in consumer preferences, productive technologies, or the relative scarcities of resources, (3) which new technologies will be adopted and which will not be, (4) when the adoption or rejection of a new technology will be socially productive or counterproductive, and (5) how the adoption of new technologies will affect the rate of profit in the economy.

(1) What would the wage rate be in this economy if the rate of profit were zero? We simply substitute r = 0, p(2) = 1, and the values representing our technologies (or recipes) for producing the two goods, the a(ij)'s and L(j)'s, into the two price equations and solve for p(1) and w:

$$(1+0)[0.3p(1) + 0.2(1)] + 0.1w = p(1); \quad 0.3p(1) + 0.2 + 0.1w = p(1)$$
$$(1+0)[0.2p(1) + 0.4(1)] + 0.2w = 1; \quad 0.2p(1) + 0.4 + 0.2w = 1$$
$$0.1w = 0.7p(1) - 0.2; \quad w = 7p(1) - 2$$
$$0.2w = 0.6 - 0.2p(1); \quad w = 3 - p(1)$$
$$7p(1) - 2 = w = 3 - p(1); 8p(1) = 5; \quad p(1) = 5/8; p(1) = 0.625$$
$$w = 3 - p(1) = 3 - 0.625; \quad w = 2.375.$$

(2) Suppose the actual conditions of class struggle are such that capitalists receive a 10% rate of profit. Again, with p(2) = 1, what will the wage rate be under these socio-economic conditions?

$$(1 + 0.10)[0.3p(1) + 0.2(1)] + 0.1w = p(1)$$
$$(1 + 0.10)[0.2p(1) + 0.4(1)] + 0.2w = 1$$

Solving these two equations as we did above yields: p(1) = 0.649 and w = 2.086

(3) Suppose the actual conditions of class struggle are such that capitalists receive a 20% rate of profit. Again, with $p(2) = 1$, what will the wage rate be under these socio-economic conditions?

$$(1 + 0.20)[0.3p(1) + 0.2(1)] + 0.1w = p(1)$$
$$(1 + 0.20)[0.2p(1) + 0.4(1)] + 0.2w = 1$$

Solving these two equations as we did above yields: $p(1) = 0.658$ and $w = 1.811$

The answers to the first three questions reveal an interesting relationship between the rate of profit and the wage rate in a capitalist economy. As the rate of profit rises from 0% to 10% to 20% the wage rate falls from 2.375 to 2.086 to 1.811 units of good 2 per hour.[6] Moreover, the change in r and w is not due to changes in the productivity of either "factor of production" since productive technology did not change in either industry. It is possible the fall in w (and consequent rise in r) was caused by an increase in the supply of labor making it less scarce relative to capital – which mainstream micro economic models do recognize as a reason there would be a change in returns to the two "factors." But this is by no means the only reason wage rates fall and profit rates rise in capitalist economies. A decline in union membership, a decrease in worker solidarity, a change in workers' attitudes about how much they "deserve," or an increase in capitalist "monopoly power" leading to a higher "mark up" over costs of production on goods workers buy are also reasons real wages fall and profit rates rise in capitalist economies. Political economy theories like the "conflict theory of the firm" explore how changes in the human characteristics of employees affect wage rates (and consequently profit rates), and how employer choices regarding technologies and reward structures affect their employees' characteristics. Political economy theories like "monopoly capital theory" explore factors that influence the size of mark ups in different industries and the economy as a whole.

The answers to the first three questions also reveal something interesting about relative prices in a capitalist economy. As we

6. This negative relationship between w and r holds in more sophisticated versions of the model and appears again in our long run political economy macro model in chapter 9.

changed from one possible combination of (r,w) to another – from (0, 2.375) to (0.10, 2.086) to (0.20, 1.8106) – p(1), the price of good 1 relative to good 2, changed from 0.625 to 0.649 to 0.658 even though there were no changes in productive technologies (or consumer preferences for that matter). In other words, the relative prices of goods are *not* determined solely by preferences, technologies, and "factor" supplies. Relative prices are also the product of power relationships between capitalists and workers (and owners of natural resources in an extended version of the model).

Technical change in the Sraffa model

One of the conveniences of a Sraffian model is that it allows us to determine when capitalists will implement new technologies and when they will not, and what the long run effects of their decisions on the economy will be.

(4) Under the conditions of question one, [r = 0%, w = 2.375, p(1) = 0.625, and p(2) = 1], suppose capitalists in sector 1 discover the following new capital-using but labor-saving technique:

a'(11) = 0.3
a'(21) = 0.3
L'(1) = 0.05

Will capitalists in sector 1 replace their old technique with this new one?

The new technique is capital-using since a'(21) = 0.3 > 0.2 = a(21). But it is labor-saving since L'(1) = 0.05 < 0.10 = L(1). The extra capital raises the private cost of making a unit of good 1 by: (0.3 – 0.2)p(2), or (0.3 – 0.2)(1) = 0.1. The labor saving lowers the private cost of making a unit of good 1 by: (0.1 – 0.05)w, or (0.1 – 0.05)(2.375) = 0.119. Which means that when the rate of profit in the economy is zero and therefore w = 2.375, this new capital-using, labor-saving technology lowers the private cost of producing good 1 and would be adopted by profit maximizing capitalists in sector 1.

(5) Under the conditions in question three, [r = 20%, w = 1.811, p(1) = 0.658, and p(2) = 1], suppose capitalists in sector 1 discover the *same* new technique: Will they replace their old technique with this new one?

As before the extra capital raises the private cost of making a unit of good 1 by: (0.3 − 0.2)p(2), or (0.3 − 0.2)(1) = 0.1. But now the labor savings lowers the private cost of making a unit of good 1 by: (0.1 − 0.05)w, or (0.1 − 0.05)(1.8106) = 0.091. Which means the new technique now raises rather than lowers the private cost of making a unit of good 1, and would not be adopted by profit maximizing capitalists.

The model permits us to easily deduce what new technologies would be adopted by profit maximizing capitalists. And if a new technology is adopted we can use the model to calculate how the new technology will affect wages, profits and prices in a very straightforward way – as we do below. But the answers to questions four and five reveal a surprising conundrum worth considering before we proceed. The new technique either improves economic efficiency, and is therefore socially productive, or it is not. If it improves economic efficiency, capitalists in industry 1 serve the social interest by adopting it, as we discovered they would under the conditions stipulated in question four. But then, capitalists will obstruct the social interest by *not* adopting the new, more efficient technique, as we discovered they will *not* under the conditions stipulated in question five. On the other hand, if the new technique reduces economic efficiency, capitalists will serve the social interest by *not* adopting it, as we discovered they will *not* under the conditions stipulated in question 5, but will obstruct the social interest by adopting it, as we discovered they will under the conditions stipulated in question 4. In other words, no matter whether the new technique is, or is not more efficient, capitalists will act contrary to the social interest in one of the two sets of socio-economic circumstances above!

Adam Smith actually envisioned *two*, not one, invisible hands at work in capitalist economies: One invisible hand promoted *static* efficiency, and the other one promoted *dynamic* efficiency. He not only hypothesized that the micro law of supply and demand would lead us to allocate scarce productive resources to the production of different goods and services efficiently at any point in time, he also believed that competition would drive capitalists to search for and implement new, socially productive technologies thereby raising economic efficiency over time. Smith assumed that *all* new technology that reduced capitalists' costs of production – and *only* technologies that reduced capitalists' production costs – improved the economy's efficiency. We have just discovered that apparently Smith's second "invisible hand" is imperfect, just like his first! In some circumstances capitalists will serve the social interest by adopting new, more productive technologies that lower their costs of production, but in some circumstances they will not. And in some circumstances capitalists will serve the social interest by rejecting new, less efficient technologies that lower their costs of production, but in some circumstances they will not.

To sort out the logic of when the first invisible hand works, and when it does not, we needed to be able to identify the socially efficient level of output for any good. We used the "efficiency criterion" to do that: The socially efficient amount of anything to produce is the amount where the marginal social benefit of the last unit consumed is equal to the marginal social cost of the last unit produced. To sort out the logic of when the second invisible hand works, and when it does not, we need to be able to identify when a new production technology is more efficient, or socially productive. The surplus approach proves remarkably adept at helping us identify when a new technology improves economic efficiency and is therefore socially productive, and when it reduces economic efficiency, and is therefore socially counterproductive. The only thing we care about in the simple economy in this model is how many hours of labor it takes to get a unit of a good. There is only one primary input to "economize on" in the simple version of the model – labor. Moreover, as long as labor is less pleasurable than leisure, being able to get a unit of a good with less work is socially productive. Whereas any new technology that meant we had to work more hours to get a unit of a good would be socially counterproductive.

It may seem that we have the answers ready made in L(1) and L(2). Since $L'(1) < L(1)$ it may appear that the new technique is obviously socially productive. But unfortunately L(1) is *not* the amount of labor it takes us to get a unit of good 1. L(1) is the number of hours of labor it takes to make a unit of good 1 *once you already have a(11) units of good 1 and a(21) units of good 2*. But since it takes some labor to get a(11) units of good 1 and a(21) units of good 2, it takes more labor than L(1) to produce a unit of good 1. We call L(1) the amount of labor it takes "directly" to get a unit of good 1 – once we have a(11) units of 1 and a(21) units of 2 for L(1) to work with. The amount of labor it took to get a(11) units of 1 and a(21) units of 2 is called the amount of labor needed "indirectly" to produce a unit of good 1. The total amount of labor it takes society to produce a unit of good 1 is the amount of labor necessary directly *and* indirectly. And while the new technique in question reduces direct labor needed to make a unit of good 1, i.e. is "labor-saving," it unfortunately increases the amount of indirect labor it takes to make a unit of good 1, i.e. is "capital-using."

Fortunately it is not terribly complicated to calculate the amount of labor, directly and indirectly necessary to produce a unit of good 1 and a unit of good 2 in our simple model. Let v(1) represent the total amount of labor needed directly and indirectly to make a unit of good 1, and v(2) represent the total amount of labor needed directly and indirectly to make a unit of good 2. Since v(i)a(ij) represents the amount of labor it takes to produce a(ij) units of good i we can write the following equations for the total amount of labor needed both directly and indirectly to make each good:

(3) $v(1) = v(1)a(11) + v(2)a(21) + L(1)$
(4) $v(2) = v(1)a(12) + v(2)a(22) + L(2)$

These are two equations in two unknowns, so v(1) and v(2) can be solved for as soon as we know the technology, or "recipe" for production in each industry. All we have to do is solve for the original values for the initial technologies – v(1) and v(2) – solve for the new values with the new technologies – v'(1) and v'(2) – and compare them. If v'(1) < v(1) and v'(2) < v(2) the new technology is socially productive. If v'(1) > v(1) and v'(2) > v(2) the new technology is socially counterproductive.[7]

7. It is obvious why the new technology for industry 1 will change v(1) since it changes L(1) and a(21). But even though there is no change in technology in industry 2, *since good 1 is an input used to produce good 2 and since v(1) will change, v(2) will also change*. This also resolves another potential concern.

For the old technologies we write:

$$v(1) = 0.3v(1) + 0.2v(2) + 0.1$$
$$v(2) = 0.2v(1) + 0.4v(2) + 0.2$$

Which can be solved to give: $v(1) = 0.2632$ and $v(2) = 0.4211$

For the new technologies we write:

$$v'(1) = 0.3v'(1) + 0.3v'(2) + 0.05$$
$$v'(2) = 0.2v'(1) + 0.4v'(2) + 0.2$$

Which can be solved to give: $v'(1) = 0.2500$ and $v'(2) = 0.4167$ – revealing that the new technology *is* truly more efficient, or socially productive, because it lowers the amount we have to work to get a unit of either good to consume. Why is it capitalists will serve the social interest by adopting the new, more efficient technology when $w = 2.375$ and $r = 0\%$, but obstruct the social interest by rejecting this technology that would make the economy more efficient when $w = 1.811$ and $r = 20\%$?

To solve this puzzle we start with what we know: We know that the new technology made the economy more efficient. We know that the new technology was capital-using and labor-saving. And we know capitalists in industry 1 embraced it when the wage rate was 2.375 (and the rate of profit was zero), but rejected it when the wage rate was 1.811 (and the rate of profit was 20%). The reason for the capitalists' seemingly contradictory behavior is clear: When the wage rate was higher the savings in labor costs because the new technology is labor-saving was greater – and great enough to outweigh the increase in non-labor costs because the new technology was capital-using. But when the wage rate was lower the savings in labor costs were less and no longer outweighed the increase in non-labor costs. Apparently the price signals [p(1), p(2), w, and r] in the economy in the first case led capitalists to make the socially productive choice to adopt the technology, whereas different

---

If the new technology lowers v(1) then it necessarily lowers v(2), whereas if it raises v(1) it necessarily raises v(2). We will never face the dilemma that a new technology in one industry will lower v in one industry but raise v in others – and thereby make it impossible for us to conclude whether or not the technology was socially productive or counterproductive.

price signals in the second case led capitalists to make the socially counterproductive choice to reject the technology.

No matter how efficient, or socially productive a new capital-using, labor-saving technology may be, it is clear that if the wage rate gets low enough (because the rate of profit gets high enough) the efficient technology will become cost-increasing, rather than cost-reducing, and capitalists will reject it. Similarly, no matter how inefficient, or socially counterproductive a new capital-saving, labor-using technology may be, if the wage rate gets low enough (because the rate of profit gets high enough) the inefficient technology will become cost-reducing, rather than cost-increasing, and capitalists will embrace it.[8] In other words, Adam Smith's second invisible hand works perfectly when the rate of profit is zero but cannot be relied on when the rate of profit is greater than zero. Moreover, as the rate of profit rises from zero (and consequently the wage rate falls), the likelihood that socially efficient capital-using, labor-saving technologies will be rejected, and the likelihood that socially counterproductive capital-saving, labor-using technologies will be adopted by profit maximizing capitalists increases.

Technical change and the rate of profit

In any case, clearly it is cost-reducing technological changes that a capitalist will adopt – whether they be capital-using and labor-saving or capital-saving and labor-saving, and whether they be socially productive or counterproductive. Can we conclude anything definitive about the effect of any cost-reducing technical change on the rate of profit, prices, and the wage rate in the economy? Marx hypothesized that capitalist development would entail capital-using, labor-saving changes more often than capital-saving, labor-using changes, and that this would eventually produce a tendency for the rate of profit to fall in capitalist economies in the long run since Marx's labor theory of value led him to believe that profits came only from exploiting "living labor," not "dead labor." For over a hundred years some Marxist political economists

8. For proof that in a simple, static Sraffa model *if and only if* the rate of profit is zero will there be a *one-to-one correspondence* between efficient, or socially productive, and cost-reducing technological changes see theorem 4.9 in John Roemer, *Analytical Foundations of Marxian Economic Theory* (Cambridge University Press, 1981).

explored this area looking for explanations of crises in real world capitalist economies. But in 1961 a Japanese political economist, Nobuo Okishio, published a theorem proving that if the wage rate did not fall, no cost-reducing technical change could lower the rate of profit in the Sraffa model. Instead, cost-reducing changes, *including capital-using, labor-saving changes*, would raise the rate of profit, or leave it unchanged – contrary to the expectations of generations of Marxist theorists. We can see these results even in our simple numerical example.

Let the economy be in the "equilibrium" described in question two, i.e. the rate of profit is 10%, and consequently the wage rate is 2.086, and $p(1)$ is 0.649 if $p(2) = 1$ – as we calculated. Under these conditions the capital-using, labor-saving technical change in industry 1 we have been analyzing is cost-reducing, and will be adopted. Non-labor costs increase by: $(0.3–0.2)(1) = 0.1$ as before, while labor costs decrease by $(0.1–0.05)(2.086) = 0.104$, which is greater, making the technology cost-reducing. The question is *not* if the capitalist in industry 1 who discovers the new technique will get a higher rate of profit than before right after she adopts it. Clearly she will since she was previously getting 10% and now will have lower costs than all her competitors, yet still receive the same price for her output as they and she did before, $p(1) = 0.649$. *Nor* is the question if all capitalists in industry 1 will receive a higher rate of profit if they copy the innovator as long as $p(1)$ holds steady at 0.649. Clearly, as long as prices and the wage rate stay the same, all those who implement the change will have lower costs per unit than before and therefore a higher rate of profit than before. *Instead*, the question is what will happen to the rate of profit in the economy after capitalists from industry 2 move their investments to industry 1 because the profit rate is temporarily higher there, until the profit rates are once again the same in both industries? As long as $r(1) > r(2)$ capitalists will move from industry 2 to industry 1, thereby decreasing the supply of good 2 and driving $p(2)$ up, and increasing the supply of good 1 and driving $p(1)$ down until $r(1) = r(2) = r'$, the new, uniform rate of profit in the economy. We want to know if the *new uniform rate of profit* in the economy with the *new equilibrium prices* will be higher or lower than the old rate of profit, r – assuming the real wage rate stays the same. To answer this question we simply substitute in the new technology for industry 1, set the wage rate equal to the old wage rate, $w = 2.086$, set $p(2) = 1$, as always, and solve for the new equilibrium price of good 1, p'(1), and the new uniform rate of profit in the economy, r'.

$$(1 + r')[0.3p'(1) + 0.3(1)] + (0.05)(2.086) = p'(1)$$
$$(1 + r')[0.2p'(1) + 0.4(1)] + (0.2)(2.086) = 1$$

Solving these two equations in two unknowns yields p'(1) = 0.644 and r' = 0.102. So when the economy reaches its new equilibrium after the introduction of the cost-reducing new technology in industry 1, the price of good 1 relative to the price of good 2 is slightly *lower* (0.644 < 0.649) as we would expect since the cost-reducing change took place in industry 1, and the uniform rate of profit in the economy is slightly *higher* (10.2% > 10%.) Since the change was capital-using and labor-saving this is contrary to Marx's prediction but consistent with what Okishio proved would always be the case for any cost-reducing technical change as long as (1) the real wage stayed constant, and (2) good 1 entered into the production of both itself and good 2.

A note of caution

Micro economic models are notorious for implicitly assuming all macro economic problems away. This means conclusions drawn from micro economic models can be misleading when macro economic problems exist – which is the case with Sraffa models of wage, price, and profit determination as well. Just because the rate of profit cannot go up unless the wage rate goes down in the simple Sraffa model does not mean this is always true in the real world. If an economy is in a recession an increase in the wage rate, by increasing the demand for goods, often leads to an increase in the rate of profit in the short run. We study how increasing wages can increase the demand for goods and services, and thereby lead to increases in business production, sales, and profits in the short run in chapter 6. If an economy has a long run tendency to produce at less than full capacity, increasing the real wage may move the economy closer to full capacity utilization by shifting income from capitalists who save more to workers who save less and consume more. Because the redistribution of income from capitalists to workers increases demand for goods, and therefore capacity utiliza-tion, it can increase the rate of profit for capitalists even in the long run. We study the possibility of "wage-led growth" in a long run political economy macro model in chapter 9. The reason the Sraffa model insists that wage income and profit income are negatively related is that it assumes total income is fixed, because it implicitly assumes the economy is always producing at full capacity levels of output, which means it is always generating the highest level of total income possible. But if this assumption is not warranted – if an increase in the wage rate would change the level of capacity utilization and output – then the Sraffian conclusion that the rate of profit must fall need not follow. Even so, the simple Sraffa model we have explored does capture an important aspect of the relation between the wage rate and rate of profit: *If production and therefore income is held constant* (whether at full capacity levels, or below), the rate of profit and wage rate must be negatively related.

This same important conclusion applies in an extended version of the Sraffa model. If we include a number of other primary inputs to production besides labor, i.e. inputs like land, oil, and minerals that are not produced, if we allow for the fact that there are different kinds of labor, i.e. welders, carpenters, computer programmers, etc. with different wage rates, and if we allow for different rates of profits to capitalists in different industries, a general Sraffa model yields the conclusion that *if the rate of pay to any group in the economy is increased, the rate of pay to all other groups **as a whole** must fall.* Again, this more general conclusion only holds if production and therefore income is held constant – as is implicitly done in Sraffa models. But this conclusion can be easily misinterpreted for yet another reason. Even if production, and therefore income, is held constant, the above conclusion does *not* imply that if the wage rate for one group of workers goes up the wage rates for other workers *must* go down. It is possible that if mine workers, for example, get a wage increase, this will raise the cost of coal and all goods coal is used to produce, and thereby lower the real wage of all other workers who do not get a money wage increase. Certainly this is the possibility that capitalists, and mainstream economists and politicians who favor capitalists over workers, emphasize. But it is also possible for the mine workers to get a wage increase and for other workers to get wage *increases* as well – even if production and therefore income remains constant, *provided the rate of profit of capitalists and/or the returns to owners of natural resources decline.* In other words, the generalized Sraffa theorem that returns to factors are inversely related when production and income are held constant, does not deny the important possibility that when one group of workers gets a wage increase this helps others get wage increases as well by increasing their bargaining power. In essence this is the material basis for solidarity between different groups of workers in capitalist economies and one reason labor union confederations have found it in their interest to support one another when any one of them goes out on strike. When the united mine workers got a substantial wage increase in 1975 it *did* help the steel workers and automobile workers get wage increases as well over the next 12 months, even though the gross domestic product, and therefore gross domestic income, was essentially stagnant. This was possible because rates of profit and rents to resource owners declined – just as their supporters in the Ford Administration feared they would when President Ford tried unsuccessfully to block the mine workers' new contract in 1975.

6   Macro Economics: Aggregate Demand as Leading Lady

Before the Great Depression of the 1930s there was only "economic theory." Thanks to the Great Depression and John Maynard Keynes we now have "micro economics" *and* "macro economics." Economic theory bifurcated because some in the mainstream of the profession finally recognized that standard economic theory shed little light on either the cause of, or cure for the Great Depression. The old theory was relabeled "micro economics" and preserved as the centerpiece of the traditional paradigm, and a new theory called macro economics was created to explain the causes and remedies for unemployment and inflation.

The leading lady in Keynes' new drama was *aggregate demand, the demand for all final goods and services in general.* By focusing on aggregated demand Keynes not only was able to explain why economic downturns can be self-reinforcing, he was able to explain demand pull inflation and how government fiscal and monetary policies could be used to combat unemployment and inflation. Short run macro economics can be understood using one new "law," one "truism," and simple theories of household consumption and business investment behavior.

THE MACRO "LAW" OF SUPPLY AND DEMAND

The new "law" is the macro law of supply and demand. It is the macro analogue of the micro law of supply and demand which is the key to understanding how markets for particular goods and services work. The macro law of supply and demand is the key to understanding how much goods and services in general the economy will produce, that is, whether we will employ our available resources fully and produce up to our potential, or we will have unemployed labor, resources, and factory capacity and consequently produce less than we are capable of. The macro law of supply and demand is also the key to understanding whether or not we will have inflation because the demand for goods and services in general exceeds the supply of goods and services the economy is capable of producing, resulting in excess demand which "pulls" up the prices of all goods and services.

The macro law of supply and demand says: *aggregate supply will follow aggregate demand if it can.* Aggregate supply is simply the supply of all final goods and services produced as a whole, or in the aggregate. It includes all the shirts and shoes produced, all the drill presses and conveyor belts produced, and all the MX missiles and swing sets for parks produced. Aggregate demand is the demand for all final goods and services as a whole. It includes the demand from all the **households** for shirts and shoes, the demand from all **businesses** for drill presses and conveyor belts, and the demand from every level of *government* for missiles and swings sets for parks. The rationale behind the macro law of supply and demand is as follows: The business sector is not clairvoyant and cannot know in advance what demand will be for its products. Of course individual businesses spend considerable time, energy, and money trying to estimate what the demand for their particular good or service will be, but in the end they produce what amounts to their best guess of what they will be able to sell. The business sector as a whole produces as much as it thinks it will be able to sell at prices it finds acceptable. Businesses don't produce more because they wouldn't want to produce goods and services they don't expect to be able to sell. And they don't produce less because this would mean foregoing profitable opportunities.

What if the business community is overly optimistic. That is, what will happen if the business sector produces more than it turns out it is able to sell? This does not mean that every business, or every industry, is producing more than it can sell. No doubt some businesses, and maybe even entire industries, will have underestimated the demand for their product. But what if, on average, or as a whole, businesses overestimate what they will be able to sell? Most businesses will find they are selling less from their warehouse inventories than they are producing and adding to those inventories each month. While a business may decide this is a temporary aberration and continue at current levels of production for a time, if inventories continue to pile up in warehouses businesses will eventually cut back on production rates. When that occurs the supply of goods and services in the aggregate will fall to meet the lower level of aggregate demand – aggregate supply will follow aggregate demand down.

What if businesses are overly pessimistic? That is, what will happen if the business sector produces less than it turns out it is able to sell? Businesses will discover their error soon enough because sales rates will be higher than production rates, and inventories in warehouses will be depleted. So even if they initially underestimate the demand for their products, businesses will increase production when they discover their error, and therefore production, or aggregate supply, will rise to meet aggregate demand – aggregate supply will follow aggregate demand up.

But there might be circumstances under which the business sector won't be able to increase production. What if all the productive resources in the economy are already fully and efficiently employed? In this case the increased labor and resources necessary for one business to increase its production would have to come from some other business where they were already employed, so the increased production of one business would be matched by a decrease in the production of some other business, and production as a whole, or aggregate supply, could not increase. This is why the macro law of supply and demand says that aggregate supply will follow aggregate demand *if it can*. If the economy is already producing the most it can, if it is already producing what we call **potential**, or **full employment gross domestic product**, aggregate supply will not be able to follow aggregate demand should the aggregate demand for goods and services exceed potential GDP.

Like the micro "law" of supply and demand, the macro "law" of supply and demand should be interpreted as the *usual* results of sensible choices people make in particular circumstances, rather than like the law of gravity that applies exactly to every mass in the presence of every gravitational force. The macro law of supply and demand derives from the common-sense observation that, on average, when businesses find their inventories being depleted because sales are outstripping production they will increase production rates if they can; while if they find their inventories increasing because sales rates are less than production rates, they will decrease production.

Notice how this simple, common-sense law provides powerful insights about what level of production an economy will settle on, and whether or not the labor, resources, and productive capacities of the economy will or will not be fully utilized. And notice how the answer to the question: "How much will we produce?" is not necessarily: "As much as we can." If the demand for goods and services in the aggregate is equal to potential GDP, then when aggregate supply follows aggregate demand we will indeed produce up to our capability. But if aggregate demand is less than potential GDP, then when aggregate supply follows aggregate demand, production will be less than the amount we are capable of producing, and consequently, there will be unemployed labor and resources, and idle productive capacity. This does not happen because the business community wants to produce less than it can. It is because it is not in its interest to produce more than it can sell. And while it is true that the owners of the businesses in a capitalist economy are the ones who decide how much we will produce, there is no point in blaming them for lack of economic patriotism when they decide to produce less than we are capable of, because any "patriotic" business that persisted in producing more than it could sell would be rewarded by being competed out of business by less "gung-ho" competitors.

The size and skill level of the labor force, the amount of resources and productive capacity we have, and the level of productive knowledge we have achieved, determine what we *can* produce. We call this level of output potential, or full employment GDP. But whether or not we *will* produce up to our capacities depends on whether there is sufficient aggregate demand for goods and services to induce businesses to employ all the productive resources available. If they have good reason to think they wouldn't be able to sell all they could produce, they won't produce it, and actual GDP will fall short of potential GDP. Any changes in the size or skill of the labor force, quantity or quality of productive resources, size or quality of the capital stock, or state of productive knowledge will change the amount of goods and services we *can* produce, i.e. the level of potential GDP. But what will determine the amount we *will* produce is the level of aggregate demand, and only changes in aggregate demand will lead to changes in what we *do* produce.

In sum: If aggregate demand is equal to potential GDP, actual GDP will be equal to potential GDP. But if aggregate demand is less than potential GDP, actual GDP will be equal to the level of aggregate demand and less than potential GDP. If aggregate demand is greater than potential GDP businesses will try to increase production levels to take advantage of favorable sales opportunities. But once the economy has reached potential GDP, as much as businesses might want to increase production further they won't be able to. Instead, frustrated employers will try to outbid one another for fewer employees and resources than there is demand for – pulling up wages and resource prices. And frustrated consumers will try to outbid one another for fewer final goods and services than there is demand for, pulling up prices in what we call "demand pull inflation" – a rise in the general level of prices caused by demand for goods and services in excess of the maximum level of production we are capable of.

AGGREGATE DEMAND

Aggregate demand, AD, is composed of the consumption demand of all the households in the economy, or what we call aggregate, or *private consumption*, C; the demand for investment, or capital goods by all businesses in the economy, or what we call *investment demand*, I; and the demand for public goods and services by local, state, and federal governments, or what we loosely call *government spending*, G.

One of Keynes' greatest insights was that the forces determining the level of consumer, business, and government demand are substantially independent from the forces determining the level of potential production or output. He also pointed out that even though businesses would try to adjust to discrepancies between aggregate demand and supply when they arose, that in addition to the *equilibrating* forces described in the micro law of supply and demand, *disequilibrating* forces could operate in the macro economy as well. In particular, Keynes pointed out that weak demand for goods and services leading to downward pressure on wages and layoffs was likely to further weaken aggregate demand by reducing the buying power of the majority of consumers. He pointed out that this would in turn lead to more downward pressure on wages and more layoffs, which would reduce the demand for goods even further. The logical result was a downward spiral in which aggregate demand, and therefore production, moved farther and farther away from potential GDP. Keynes ridiculed his contemporaries' faith that excess supply of labor during the depression would prove self-eliminating as wages fell. He quipped that no matter how cheap employees became, employers were not likely to hire workers when they had no reason to believe they could sell the goods those workers would make. Keynes pointed out that the demand reducing effect of falling wages on employment could outweigh the cost reducing effect of lower labor costs on employment – particularly during a recession when finding buyers, not lowering production costs, was the chief concern of businesses. As a result Keynes rejected the complacency of his colleagues in face of high and rising levels of unemployment based on what he considered to be unwarranted faith that (1) demand should be sufficient to buy full employment levels of output, and (2) unemployment should be eliminated by falling wages.

Consumption demand

Keynes reasoned that the largest component of aggregate demand, household consumption, was determined for the most part by the size of the household sector's disposable, or after tax income. He postulated that household consumption: (1) depended positively on disposable income, (2) that only part of any new or additional disposable income would be consumed because part of additional income would be saved, (3) that even should disposable income sink to zero consumption would be positive as people dipped into savings or borrowed against future income prospects to finance necessary consumption. No economic relationship has been more empirically tested and validated than the consumption–income relationship. Countless "cross section studies" using data from samples of households with different levels of income and consumption in the same year, as well as "time series studies" using data for national income and aggregate consumption over a number of years in hundreds of different countries, all invariably confirm Keynes' bold hypothesis and intuition. The "consumption function" is far and away the most accurate indicator of economic behavior in the macro economist's arsenal. In its simplest (linear) form: $C = a + MPC(Y–T)$ where C stands for aggregate consumption, Y stands for gross domestic income, GDI, T stands for taxes which are the part of income households can neither consume nor save since they are obligated to taxes, "a" is a positive number called "autonomous consumption" representing the amount the household sector would consume even if disposable income were zero, and MPC stands for the "**m**arginal **p**ropensity to **c**onsume out of disposable income," that is, the fraction of each additional dollar in disposable income that will go into consumption rather than saving.

Investment demand

The most volatile and difficult part of aggregate demand to predict is business investment demand. First, note that in short run macro models investment is treated as part of the aggregate demand for goods and services because what happens when businesses decide to undertake an investment project is they *first* must buy the machinery and equipment necessary to carry it out. That is, the first effect of investment is to increase the demand for what we call capital or investment goods. This is not to deny that the *purpose* of investment is to increase the ability of businesses to produce more goods and services. But while investment eventually increases potential GDP, and may lead to an increase in the actual supply of goods and services in the future, its immediate effect is to increase the demand for investment goods. Second, Keynes himself had a very eclectic theory of investment behavior emphasizing the importance of psychological factors on business expectations and the rate of change of output as an indicator of future demand conditions. Moreover, political economists emphasize the importance of the rate of profit and capacity utilization in determining the level of investment as we see in a long run political economy macro model studied in chapter 9. But a simple relationship between investment demand and the rate of interest in the economy is sufficient to understand the logic of monetary policy, and all we need for the present.

Businesses divide their after tax profits between *dividends*, paid to stockholders and *retained earnings*, income available for the corporation to use as it sees fit. If a business wants to finance an investment project the first thing it usually does is pay for it out of retained earnings. But often retained earnings are not sufficient to finance a major investment project, and therefore a business must borrow money to add to its retained earnings to purchase all the investment goods a major project requires. A company can borrow from a bank or can borrow from the public by selling corporate bonds, but no matter how it decides to borrow it will have to pay interest. If interest rates in the economy are high, the cost of borrowing will be high. When the cost of borrowing is high the rate of return on an investment project will have to be high to warrant undertaking it given the high cost of borrowing required to carry it out. Presumably fewer investment projects will have this high rate of return, and therefore businesses will want to undertake fewer investment projects when interest rates in the economy are high.[1]

1. Even if a company can finance the entire investment project out of its retained earnings, the opportunity cost of the project is high when interest rates are high because if the retained earnings were not used to finance the project they could be deposited in a savings account paying a high rate of interest. So whether or not a company borrows or finances an investment project entirely out of retained earnings, it is less likely to invest when interest rates are high, and more likely to invest when interest rates are low.

Another way to see why there should be a negative relationship between interest rates and investment demand is to ask when a business is most likely to want to engage in investment. When interest rates are low it is cheaper to finance investment projects. When they are high it is more expensive. As much as possible it makes sense for businesses to refrain from investing when interest rates are high, and wait until interest rates are low to do their investing. We can express this negative relation between the rate of interest and investment demand most simply in a linear investment function such as: $I = b - 1000r$, where I is investment demand measured in billions of dollars, b is the amount of investment the business sector would undertake if the real rate of interest in the economy were zero, and r is the real rate of interest in the economy, expressed as a decimal. While primitive, this investment function is sufficient to illustrate the logic of monetary policy we explore in chapter 7. It says that whenever interest rates rise by 1% investment demand will fall by 10 billion dollars, and whenever interest rates fall by 1% investment demand will increase by 10 billion dollars.

Government spending

If we ignore the foreign sector for the moment, the only other source of demand for final goods and services besides the household and business sectors is the government sector. We call the final goods and services demanded by national, state, and local governments G. While some state and local governments face restrictions on whether or not they can run a deficit, it is possible for the federal government to spend either more or less than it collects in taxes.[2] If the government spends less than it collects in taxes we say the government is running a budget surplus. If it spends more we say it is running a budget deficit. And if it spends exactly as much as it collects in taxes during a year we say the budget is balanced. Any individual or business can spend more than its income in a year if it can convince someone to lend it additional money, and the government can spend more than it collects in taxes by borrowing

2. There are two easy ways to remind yourself that the federal government *can* spend more than it collects in taxes: First, it did so, in fact, every year from 1970 until 1998. Second, were it not possible for the government to spend more than it collects, politicians and economists would not bother debating the wisdom of passing a "balanced budget amendment" to the Constitution outlawing such behavior!

as well. The federal government usually borrows directly from the citizenry by selling treasury bonds to the general public.

So aggregate demand, AD, will be the sum of household consumption demand, C, business investment demand, I, and government spending, G. Household consumption will be determined by household income and personal taxes. Business investment will be determined by interest rates in the economy, among other things we ignore for the time being. And the government can decide to spend whatever it wants independent of how much taxes it decides to collect, since the government can finance deficits by selling treasury bonds. If AD ends up higher than current levels of production there will be excess demand for goods and services and businesses will try to increase production – successfully if current production is below potential GDP, but unsuccessfully if current production is already equal to potential GDP in which case the excess demand will lead to demand pull inflation. If aggregate demand is below current levels of production there will be excess supply, businesses will reduce production to avoid accumulating unsellable inventories, and the economy will produce less than its potential and fail to employ all its productive resources.

THE PIE PRINCIPLE

But one piece of the puzzle is still missing. How much income will there be in the economy? Just as we have to know the rate of interest before we can determine investment demand, we have to know the level of income before we can determine consumption demand. We can wait to see how interest rates are determined in chapter 7 when we study money, banks, and monetary policy. But we cannot wait any longer to know what income will be if we want to know what equilibrium GDP will be in the economy. The answer is given by a simple truism I call *the pie principle*: *The size of the pie we can eat is equal to the size of the pie we baked.* If we produced X billion dollars worth of goods and services during the year, then we have X billion dollars worth of goods and services available to use. Not a dollar more nor a dollar less. Income is just a name for the right to use goods and services. So if we produced X billion dollars of goods and services, i.e., if gross domestic product or GDP is X billion dollars, then we also distributed X billion dollars of income to the actors in the economy, all told, i.e., gross domestic income or GDI is exactly X billion dollars as well.

This truism is easiest to see if we pretend for a moment that the economy only produces one kind of good. Suppose we produce only shmoos – which we eat, wear, live in, and use (like machines) to produce more shmoos. If a shmoo factory produces 100 shmoos what can happen to them? Some will be used to pay the workers' wages. However many are left over will belong to the factory owners as profits. How much did our shmoo factory contribute to gross domestic product? 100 shmoos. How much income was generated and distributed at the same time by our shmoo factory? 100 shmoos no matter how that income was divided between wages and profits. Suppose the workers were powerful and succeeded in getting paid 95 shmoos in wages. Then profits would be 100 – 95 = 5 shmoos. Wages, 95 shmoos, plus profits, 5 shmoos, add up to 95 + 5 = 100 shmoos of total income. On the other hand, suppose employers were powerful and only paid out 60 shmoos in wages. Then employers' profits would be 100 – 60 = 40 shmoos. And wages, 60 shmoos, plus profits, 40 shmoos, add up to 60 + 40 = 100 shmoos of total income again. The sum of the workers' wages and owners' profits cannot exceed 100 shmoos, nor can it be less than 100 shmoos. Since the same will hold for every shmoo factory, gross domestic product, measured in shmoos, and gross domestic income, measured in shmoos, have to be the same in an economy producing one good.

This conclusion extends to an economy that produces many different goods and services where we use some kind of money, like the dollar, to measure both the value of all the goods and services produced and the value of all the income generated and distributed in the process. The level of income in the economy will always be equal to the value of goods and services produced in the economy because the size of the pie we can eat is always equal to the size of the pie we baked. Which is why we don't need two different symbols for GDP and GDI in our model and equations. We can use the letter Y to stand for the value of all final goods and services produced, GDP, *and* for the value of all income paid out, GDI, since they always have the same value.

THE SIMPLE KEYNESIAN CLOSED ECONOMY MACRO MODEL

We are ready to summarize our simple, Keynesian, short-run macro model of an economy "closed off" from international trade and investment with the following equations:

(1) $Y = C + I + G$; (2) $C = a + MPC(Y-T)$; (3) $I = b - 1000r$; (4) $G = G^*$; (5) $T = T^*$

Equations (4) and (5) simply state what the chosen levels of government spending and tax collection are, allowing for the fact that they need not be equal to one another. Equation (3) tells us what investment demand will be, depending on the interest rate in the economy. Equation (2) tells us what household consumption demand will be depending on income and taxes. And equation (1) is what we call the macro economic equilibrium condition. The Y on the left side of (1) is interpreted as GDP, or the aggregate supply of goods and services. The right side of equation (1) is the sum total aggregate demand we will have in the economy. So equation (1) says that Aggregate Supply, AS, equals aggregate demand, AD.

The macro law of supply and demand says that the business sector will increase or decrease production (aggregate supply) until it is equal to the level of aggregate demand – if it can. We define *equilibrium GDP*, or **Y(e)**, to be *the level of production at which aggregate supply **would** be equal to aggregate demand.* Depending on how great aggregate demand is, it may be possible for the business sector to produce equilibrium GDP or it may not be. If AD is less than or equal to potential GDP, which we now call Y(f) for "full employment GDP", it is possible for the economy to produce Y(e), and the macro law predicts that actual GDP will eventually become equal to Y(e). But if AD is greater than potential GDP actual production cannot equal Y(e) but must stop short at Y(f). However, we can still ask: How high *would* GDP have to be in order for aggregate supply to equal aggregate demand? And the answer, Y(e), has great significance because when the business sector produces all it can, Y(f), Y(e) – Y(f) will be the amount of excess demand for final goods and services in the economy giving us a measure of how much "demand pull" inflation to expect.

For any given r*, G*, and T* we can use the equations in our simple model to find the equilibrium level of GDP. All we do is substitute equations (2), (3), and (4) into equation (1). If we use equation (1) we have stipulated that AS = AD. Therefore the Y we calculate when we use equation (1) is Y(e). Moreover, even though Y represents production, or aggregate supply on the left side of the equation, and Y represents income in the expression for disposable income in the consumption function on the right side of the equation, the pie principle assures us that Y as production and Y as income must have the same value on both sides of the equation. Substituting we get:

$$Y(e) = a + MPC(Y(e) - T^*) + b - 1000r^* + G^*$$

Which is a single equation in a single unknown, Y(e). Multiplying MPC through the parenthesis gives:

$$Y(e) = a + MPCY(e) - MPCT^* + b - 1000r^* + G^*$$

Subtracting MPCY(e) from both sides of the equation gives:

$$Y(e) - MPCY(e) = a - MPCT^* + b - 1000r^* + G^*$$

Factoring Y(e) out of each term on the left side of the equation gives:

$$Y(e)(1 - MPC) = a - MPCT^* + b - 1000r^* + G^*$$

Dividing both sides of this equation by (1 – MPC) gives a "solution" for Y(e):

$$Y(e) = [a - MPCT^* + b - 1000r^* + G^*]/(1 - MPC)$$

If we know MPC, T*, a, b, r* and G* we can calculate Y(e). If Y(e) is less than potential GDP, the macro law of supply and demand tells us the economy will settle at a level of production less than potential GDP equal to Y(e). If Y(e) is greater than potential GDP the macro law tells us that the economy will produce up to potential GDP, or Y(f), but the supply of goods and services will still fall short of the demand so we will have demand pull inflation. If Y(e) = Y(f) we will have neither unemployed labor and resources nor demand pull inflation, and we will produce all we are capable of given our present level of resources and productive know how without inflationary pressure.

After "solving" for Y(e) we can compare it with potential GDP, Y(f), to see if we will have an unemployment problem, an inflation problem, or neither. If Y(f) – Y(e) is positive, we say we have an "unemployment gap" in the economy of that many billions of dollars. The size of the unemployment gap represents the value of the goods and services that we could have made but did not make because there wasn't sufficient demand for goods and services to warrant hiring all of the labor force and using all the available resources and productive capacity. Another way of interpreting the size of an unemployment gap is as the value of the goods and services that those unemployed workers and resources could have produced but didn't because they were unemployed. If $Y(f) - Y(e)$ is negative, we have an "inflation gap" in the economy because the level of aggregate demand, which is equal to $Y(e)$, is that many billions of dollars greater than the maximum value of goods and services the economy is presently capable of producing, $Y(f)$.[3]

FISCAL POLICY

We are now ready to understand the logic of *fiscal policy* defined *as any changes in government spending and/or taxes.* The micro economic perspective on fiscal policy is that because of the free rider problem the government must step in and provide public goods since otherwise the economy will produce and consume too few public goods relative to private goods. In this view, according to the efficiency criterion the government should buy an amount of each public good up to the point where the marginal social benefit of another unit, MSB, is equal to the marginal social cost of producing another unit, MSC. Then the government simply collects enough taxes to pay for the public goods the government buys and makes available to the citizenry. But the macro economic perspective focuses on the fact that government spending and taxation affect aggregate demand, and therefore, by changing spending or taxes the government can change the level of aggregate demand in the economy.

If the economy is suffering from an unemployment gap – if there are people willing and able to work who can't find jobs and we are

3. For example, suppose $a = 90$, MPC = $\frac{3}{4}$, $b = 200$, $r^* = 0.10$ (or 10%), $T^* = 40$, $G^* = 40$, and $Y(f) = 900$: $Y(e) = 90 + \frac{3}{4}(Y(e)-40) + 200 - 1000 (0.10) + 40$; $Y(e) - \frac{3}{4}Y(e) = 90 - 30 + 100 + 40$; $\frac{1}{4}Y(e) = 200$; $Y(e) = 800$. The business sector will eventually produce 800 billion dollars worth of goods and services. Since the economy is capable of producing 900 billion dollars worth of goods and services ($Y(f) = 900$) we will fall short of "baking" as big a pie as we could have by 100 billion dollars. We will have unemployed labor and resources that *would* have produced an additional 100 billion *had* they been employed – but they won't be because aggregate demand is only 800 billion so that's all the business sector can sell. For what it's worth the government budget is balanced ($T^* - G^* = 40 - 40 = 0$), but the economy is in a recession only producing 800/900 = 0.89, or 89% of all it is capable of.

therefore producing (and consuming) less than we could – by increasing G* the government could increase aggregate demand and thereby reduce the unemployment gap. Or, by reducing spending the government could decrease aggregate demand and reduce the size of any inflation gap in the economy. Changing taxes will also have a predictable effect on aggregate demand. If the government increases taxes disposable income will fall and household consumption demand will fall. This would be helpful if the economy is suffering from demand pull inflation. If the economy has an unemployment gap, reducing taxes would be helpful because it would increase households' disposable income and induce them to consume more, raising aggregate demand and equilibrium GDP. However, before proceeding to analyze the macro economic effects of three different fiscal policies – changing only G, changing only T, or changing G and T by the same amount in the same direction – we stop to ask why most economists before Keynes were unable to see something that seems so straightforward and simple in retrospect. And we pause to unravel something surprising about the workings of the economy – the *multiplier effect*.

THE FALLACY OF SAY'S LAW

Despite objections from a few non-mainstream economists like Thomas Malthus and Karl Marx, most economists prior to the "Keynesian revolution" labored under an illusion regarding the relation between the level of production of goods and services in general and demand for goods and services in general. The misconception that undermined the ability of most economists before Keynes to understand the macro law of supply and demand, and therefore to understand depressions, recessions, and unemployment, went under the name of "Say's Law," named after the nineteenth-century French economist Jean Baptiste Say. According to *Say's Law*, *in the aggregate, supply creates its own demand* – exactly the opposite of what Keynes' maco law of supply and demand says. Moreover, Say's Law implies there can never be insufficient demand for goods in general, and governments therefore need not concern themselves with recessions which should cure themselves.

The rationale for Say's Law was best explained by the famous British economist and banker David Ricardo. In a series of famous letters to a concerned friend, Thomas Malthus, Ricardo explained that there was no cause for alarm nor need for the government to do anything about a serious recession in Great Britain at the time. Ricardo began by explaining the pie principle to Malthus, namely that every dollar of goods produced generated exactly a dollar of income, or purchasing power. When Malthus pointed out that people generally save part of their income, and therefore consumption demand must inevitably fall short of the value of goods produced, Ricardo pointed out that savings earned interest only if deposited in a bank, such as his, and that he, like all bankers, was always at great pains to lend those deposits to business borrowers since otherwise his bank could make no profits. Ricardo pointed out that his business loan customers borrowed in order to invest, i.e. buy investment or capital goods, which meant that whatever consumption goods households failed to buy because they saved was made up for by business investment demand for capital goods. As long as the interest rate were left free to equilibrate the credit market, Ricardo concluded that any shortfall in aggregate demand due to household savings would be made up for by an exactly equal amount of business investment demand.

Ricardo's explanation of Say's Law was appealing, so appealing in fact that it persuaded generations of economists who subscribed to it. But it contains a fallacy that fell to Keynes to point out. While it is true that every dollar's worth of production generates exactly a dollar's worth of income or potential purchasing power, it is not necessarily true that a dollar's worth of income always generates a dollar's worth of demand for goods and services. Aggregate demand can be greater than income if all actors in the economy as a whole use previous savings, or wealth, to spend more than their current income, or if actors in the economy as a whole borrow against future income. And aggregate demand can be less than income if actors in the aggregate spend less than current income, saving and adding part of current income to their stock of wealth.

What deceived Ricardo (and many others) was that just because the supply of loans is equal to the demand for loans at the equilibrium rate of interest, this does not mean that business demand for investment goods will necessarily be equal to household savings. The easiest way to see this is to recognize that not all loans to businesses are used to buy investment, or capital goods. Sometimes businesses use borrowed funds to buy government bonds, or shares of stocks in other businesses. When they do this they are borrowing someone else's savings only to "save" in a different form. For example, at the time it was made, a loan to USX Steel Company in the early 1980s was the largest bank loan in US history. But USX didn't use a penny of the loan to buy new steel making equipment to replace obsolete equipment in its US plants because USX had decided that producing more steel in the US was no longer profitable. Instead it used the "borrowed savings" to buy a controlling interest in Marathon Oil Company. This was a wise business decision, no doubt appreciated by USX stockholders. But buying all those shares of stock in Marathon Oil did not add a single dollar to the demand for investment goods, or therefore for the aggregate demand for goods and services in general. So even though the interest rate may have equilibrated the market for lending and borrowing in this case, that did not mean the savings of households who did not buy consumer goods was translated into spending on investment goods by business. As Keynes put it, while the interest rate may equilibrate the market for borrowing and lending, this does not necessarily equilibrate savings and investment, and thereby guarantee that in the aggregate, supply will create its own demand. A given value of production *does* generate an equal value of income. But *when* that income gets used to demand goods and services can make a great deal of difference. If less income is used to demand goods and services in a year than were produced in that year, aggregate demand will fall short of aggregate supply, and production will fall as the macro law of supply and demand teaches. If the sum total of household, business, and government demand is greater than production during a year, production will rise (if it can), as Keynes' macro law teaches. It is simply not true that however much businesses decide to produce, exactly that much aggregate demand will necessarily appear to buy it. In any given year there may be either more or less demand for goods than are produced since opportunities exist for whole economies to save and dis-save for months or years.

INCOME EXPENDITURE MULTIPLIERS

Since G is part of aggregate demand one would think that if the government increased G by, say $10 billion, aggregate demand would increase by $10 billion. Or if the government decreased G by $10 billion, aggregate demand would fall by $10 billion. But sur-prisingly, this is not the case. If G increases by $10 billion, aggregate demand will usually increase by a *multiple* of $10 billion dollars.

Let's see how it would happen. Suppose the government increases spending by buying $10 billion more bombers from McDonell

Douglas. Assuming aggregate demand were equal to aggregate supply in the first place, as soon as the government buys $10 billion worth of bombers aggregate demand will be $10 billion larger than aggregate supply. But the macro law of supply and demand tells us that production, or supply will rise to meet the new demand, i.e. McDonell Douglas will produce $10 billion more bombers. But because the size of the pie we can eat is equal to the size of the pie we baked, income, or GDI, will now be $10 billion bigger than it was initially. McDonell Douglas will pay out more wages to its employees who made the new bombers, and more dividends to its stockholders. And since households consume more when their income is higher according to our theory of consumption, household consumption demand will rise once income has risen. This is a second increase in aggregate demand above and beyond the original increase in government spending. This second increase in aggregate demand will take the form of an increased demand for shirts and beer by McDonell Douglas employees, and for sail boats and champagne by McDonell Douglas stockholders, whereas the first increase in aggregate demand was an increased demand for bombers. It is an *additional* increase in aggregate demand, induced by, but clearly different from, the initial increase in government spending.

How much will consumer demand increase? Since production and income have risen by $10 billion, according to our consumption function households will consume MPC times $10 billion more than before. If the MPC were ¾, then household consumption would rise by (¾)$10 billion or $7.5 billion when income rose by $10 billion. But once again, the economy is out of equilibrium. When production rose by $10 billion to meet the new government demand for $10 billion new bombers, we were back to where aggregate supply equaled aggregate demand. But now that consumer demand has risen by an additional $7.5 billion, aggregate demand is, once again, higher than aggregate supply. The macro law of supply and demand tells us that production will again rise to meet this demand, if it can. But when production of shirts, beer, sail boats, and champagne rises by $7.5 billion to meet this new demand, income will rise again, this time by $7.5 billion. And when income rises by $7.5 billion household consumption will rise again, this time by MPC times $7.5 billion, and production will have to rise a third time for aggregate supply to again equal aggregate demand.

This *"multiplier"* chain of events goes on forever, but each additional increase in aggregate demand, and induced increase in production, or aggregate supply, is smaller than the last. Infinitely long series of positive terms can add up to infinity. After all, each term is positive and there is an infinite number of these positive terms. But if the terms diminish in size sufficiently, even though there is an infinite number of them, the sum total need not be infinite. It can, instead, be some finite number. Our government spending multiplier chain is of this second kind.

The government spending multiplier just described is: $10B + MPC($10B) + MPC^2($10B) + ... which can be rewritten: $10B[1 + MPC + MPC^2 ...]. The multiplier chain in brackets will sum to less than infinity as long as the MPC is a positive fraction – which it is as long as people save any of their new income. In high school algebra one proves that $[1 + d + d^2 + ...]$ is simply equal to $[1/(1-d)]$ provided $0 < d < 1$, which means our multiplier chain neatly sums to $[1/(1-MPC)]$, and the overall increase in aggregate demand that would result from an initial increase of $10 billion in government spending is $10B[1/(1-MPC)]. For MPC = $\frac{3}{4}$, $10B[1/(1-(\frac{3}{4}))]$ = $10B[4] = $40B. In other words, when the government raises spending by $10 billion, aggregate demand eventually rises by a multiple of $10 billion, a multiple of 4 if MPC = $\frac{3}{4}$. Hardly what one would have guessed at first glance. But this surprising *government spending multiplier* is a logical necessity of: (1) the macro law of supply and demand that says if aggregate demand increases then production, or aggregate supply will rise to meet it if it can; (2) the fact that the size of the pie we can eat is equal to the size of the pie we baked, meaning that if production increases income will increase by exactly the same amount; and (3) our theory of consumption behavior that says when income rises household consumption demand will rise by a fraction, MPC, of that increase in income. Which leaves us with our first fiscal policy multiplier formula. If we let ΔY represent the change in equilibrium GDP, or Y(e), and ΔG represent the change in government spending, then: $\Delta Y = [1/(1-MPC)] \Delta G$ and the expression in brackets, $[1/(1-MPC)]$ is called the government spending multiplier. It is what we have to multiply any change in government spending by to find out what the overall change in aggregate demand, and therefore equilibrium GDP will be.

If instead of changing G, the government chose to change T instead by ΔT, this would lead to an initial change in consumption demand of $-MPC\Delta T$. But this initial change in consumption demand would unleash the same multiplier process unleashed by the above change in government spending. The macro economy is an "equal opportunity respondent" – reacting to all initial changes in aggregate demand in the same way, irrespective of the source or nature of the initial change. So the overall change in aggregate demand from a change in taxes, ΔT, would eventually be $[1/(1–MPC)]$ times $–MPC\Delta T$, or $\Delta Y = [–MPC/(1–MPC)]\ \Delta T$; where $[–MPC/(1–MPC)]$ is our second fiscal policy multiplier, the tax multiplier.

Finally, if the government did change both spending and taxes at the same time, and if it changed them both by the same amount and in the same direction so that $\Delta G = \Delta T$, the government would be changing both sides of the budget by the same amount, $\Delta BB = \Delta G = \Delta T$. Under these conditions when we add the initial and induced effects of the two changes together we get:

$$\Delta Y = [1/(1 – MPC)]\ \Delta BB + [–MPC/(1 – MPC)]\ \Delta BB =$$
$$(\Delta BB – MPC\Delta BB]/(1–MPC) = \Delta BB(1 – MPC)/(1 – MPC) = [1]\ \Delta BB$$

which gives us the third "fiscal policy" multiplier: if G and T are changed by the same amount in the same direction, aggregate demand and therefore equilibrium GDP will be changed by one times the change in both sides of the government budget. So we have three fiscal policy "tools": change government spending alone, change tax collections alone, and change both spending and taxes by the same amount in the same direction. Any of the three fiscal policies can be used to increase aggregate demand to combat an unemployment gap, or decrease aggregate demand to combat an inflation gap. "Deflationary policies" reduce demand and inflationary pressures. "Expansionary policies" increase demand and raise production closer to potential GDP, i.e. increase the size of the pie we bake. But besides changing the size of the pie we bake, different fiscal policies also have different effects on how the pie is sliced, that is, *the proportion of output that goes to private consumption, the proportion that goes to public goods, and the proportion that goes to investment goods*, or what economists call the composition of output. Economists define **equivalent macro economic policies** as *policies that change aggregate demand, and therefore equilibrium GDP, by the same amount*. So by definition equivalent fiscal policies have the same effect on the size of the pie we bake or on inflationary pressures. But different equivalent fiscal policies have different effects on how the pie we eat is sliced, i.e. the composition of output. Moreover, different equivalent fiscal policies have different effects on the size of a government budget deficit or surplus. So besides looking at *who* gets a tax cut or pays for a tax increase, or whether it is human welfare or corporate welfare programs that are being increased or cut, it is important to consider the effects of different equivalent fiscal policies on the composition of output and the budget deficit when deciding which fiscal policy tool to use. Different classes and interest groups have different interests in these regards and therefore fiscal policy is always about more than simply the most effective way to combat unemployment or inflation. We explore the effects of different equivalent fiscal policies on the composition of output and the budget deficit in a simple closed economy macro model in chapter 9.

OTHER CAUSES OF UNEMPLOYMENT AND INFLATION

While the simple Keynesian macro model is helpful for under-standing *demand pull inflation* and unemployment caused by insufficient aggregate demand for goods and services, commonly called *cyclical unemployment*, there are other kinds of unemploy-ment and inflation the Keynesian model does not explain. Beside cyclical unemployment there is *structural unemployment* and *frictional unemployment*. Cyclical unemployment is caused when low aggregate demand for goods leads employers to provide fewer jobs than the number of people willing and able to work. Structural unemployment results when the skills and training of people in the labor force do not match the requirements of the jobs available. In this case the problem is not too few jobs, but people who are suited to jobs that no longer exist but not to the ones now available. Changes in the international division of labor, rapid technical changes in methods of production, and educational systems that are slow to adapt to new economic conditions are the most important causes of structural unemployment. But even if there were a suitable job for every worker there would be some unemployment. Frictional unemployment is the result of the fact that people do not stay in the same job all their lives, and changing jobs takes time, so when we "take a picture" of the economy the photo will show some people without jobs because we have caught them moving from one job to another even when there are enough jobs for everyone and people's skills match job requirements perfectly.

From a policy perspective it is important to realize that increasing aggregate demand for goods, and thereby labor, adds jobs, but mostly jobs like the ones that already exist. If the unemployment is largely structural, expansionary macro economic policy may not put much of a dent in it while increasing inflationary pressures. Instead, changes in the educational system, and retraining and relocation programs are called for to combat structural unemployment. The true level of frictional unemployment, or what is sometimes called the "natural rate of unemployment," can have important implications for policy. If unemployment is only frictional, there is no need or purpose for government intervention. Adding more jobs or training people to better fit the jobs we have will not reduce frictional unemployment that results from the simple fact that people change jobs from time to time. Conservative economists argued that the rate of frictional unemployment in the US rose from 3–4% in the middle of the twentieth century to 5–6% by the beginning of this century. If this were true, it would imply that strong policy intervention is not warranted until unemployment reaches 7% in today's economy, even though all conceded that intervention was called for when the unemployment rate reached 5% in the past. But why should the rate of frictional unemployment have changed? Are job search methods *less* efficient than before? Are people *less* anxious to start their new jobs than before? Conservatives allude to changes in the composition and motivations of the US labor force insinuating that new entrants into the labor force – primarily women and minorities – have characteristics that lead them to have higher rates of frictional unemployment. But there is little scientific evidence to support the conservative claim which reduces to little more than prejudice and a strong wish to curb government initiatives aimed at reducing unemployment.

The important point is that employers benefit from unemployment. Employer bargaining power *vis-à-vis* their employees over wages, effort levels, and working conditions is enhanced when the unemployment rate is higher and there are more people willing and able to replace those working. Since capitalism relies on fear and greed as its primary means of motivation, a permanently low level of unemployment would reduce employees' fear and thereby pose serious motivational and distributional problems for employers. So it is hardly surprising that there is a "market" for economists who invent rationales to convince the government and the public to accept higher levels of unemployment as unavoidable. There is little more than this to the "debate" over postulated changes in the "natural rate of unemployment."

Just as there are different kinds of unemployment there are also other causes of inflation beside excess demand for goods and services in general. Besides demand pull the most important kind of inflation is cost push. Imagine the following scenario. Employers and employees sit down to negotiate wage increases. At current price levels, employees need a 10% wage increase to get 80% of the value added in the production process – which is the least they think they deserve. Initially, employers resist these demands because they believe they deserve at least 30% of value added which cannot be achieved at current prices if wages rise at all. But faced with potential losses from a strike, employers finally agree to the 10% wage increase, only to turn around and "trump" the workers' play by raising prices 10%. Now that both wages and prices have risen by 10% the distribution of output is exactly what it was initially – 30% to the employers and 70% to the workers. Of course the workers cry "foul" and demand another 10% wage increase "to keep pace with the 10% inflation." If employers give in, only to increase prices again, we have a "wage-price spiral" and inflation as well. Notice that the cause of this inflation is not excess aggregate demand. The cause is an unresolved difference of opinion between employers and employees over who deserves what part of output that plays out in a way that causes wages and prices to keep rising. Whether we call this "cost push inflation" – wages and profits are "pushing" up prices – "wage push" or "profit push" depends on whose view we agree with regarding the distribution of output. If one agrees with labor that workers deserve 80% of output and employers only 20%, the process would logically be called "profit push inflation" since the problem is obviously that employers keep trying to get more than they deserve by raising prices and voiding a non-inflationary and just wage settlement. If one agreed that owners deserved 30% and therefore workers only deserved 70% of output, the process would logically be called "wage push inflation" since the problem is that workers disrupt a non-inflationary, just settlement by insisting on a 10% raise.[4]

It is important to note that structural unemployment can exist in the presence of adequate aggregate demand for goods and services,

4. Mainstream economists usually try to label inflation "wage push" or "profit push" based on whether wages or prices rose first. But arguing over who hit who first is usually a pointless way to settle an ongoing conflict. More logically, it comes down to who one thinks has "right" on their side in the underlying disagreement.

and cost push inflation can exist even when aggregate demand does not exceed aggregate supply. There is no doubt that an increasing tendency toward *stagflation* – defined as *simultaneously increasing rates of unemployment and inflation* – plagued the US economy from the mid-1970s through the mid-1980s. Our Keynesian macro model does *not* help us understand how this is possible. According to this simple model the economy has *either* an unemployment gap, *or* an inflation gap – or neither. It cannot simultaneously have both too little aggregate demand – yielding cyclical unemployment – and too much aggregate demand – yielding demand pull inflation. But demand pull inflation can coexist with rising structural unemployment. And cyclical unemployment can coexist with increasing cost push inflation. Often conflicts over distribution, changes in the international division of labor, and rapid technological changes generate significant amounts of structural unemployment and cost push inflation to go along with the cyclical unemployment and demand pull inflation the simple Keynesian macro model explains.

MYTHS ABOUT INFLATION

Most Americans think inflation is bad for everyone while unemployment is bad only for the unemployed. In reality, the reverse is more the case – unemployment hurts us all and inflation hurts some but helps others. "Okun's Law" estimates that every 1% increase in the US unemployment rate reduces real output by 2%. That is, the pie we all have to eat shrinks by 2% when 1% of the labor force loses their jobs. Moreover, a study of the social effects of unemployment prepared for the Joint Economic Committee of Congress in 1976 – back when Congress still cared about such things – estimated that a 1% increase in the unemployment rate led to, on average: 920 suicides, 648 homicides, 20,240 fatal heart attacks or strokes, 495 deaths from liver cirrhosis, 4227 admissions to mental hospitals, and 3340 admissions to state prisons – each tragedy impacting a network of connected lives.

On the other hand, for every buyer "hurt" by paying a higher price due to inflation, there was a seller who, logically, must have been equally "helped" by receiving a higher price because of inflation. Moreover, we are all *both* sellers *and* buyers in market economies. How could you buy something unless you had already sold something else? But many people think of themselves only as buyers when they think about inflation, forgetting for example that they *sell* their labor, and therefore erroneously conclude that inflation necessarily hurts them – and everyone else who they think of only as buyers.

This is how it really works: ***Inflation means*** *that prices are going up* ***on average***. But in any inflation some prices will go up faster than others. If the prices of the things you buy are rising faster than the prices of the things you sell, you will be "hurt" by inflation. That is, your real buying power, or real income, will fall. But if the prices of the things you sell are rising faster than the prices of the things you buy, your real income will increase. So for the most part, what inflation does is rob Peters to pay Pauls. That is, inflation redistributes real income.

I might object to inflation on grounds that it reduced *my* real income – that I happened to be one of the losers. More importantly, we might find inflation objectionable because those whose real income was reduced were groups we believe are deserving of having higher incomes, while those whose real incomes rose we consider less deserving. And this is often the case, because inflationary redistribution is essentially determined by changes in relative bargaining power between actors in the economy. If corporations and the wealthy are becoming more powerful and employees and the poor are becoming less powerful, as has been the case for the most part over the past quarter-century, inflation will be one mechanism whereby the redistribution of real income becomes more inequitable. But this needn't be the case. Between 1971 and 1973 there was inflation in both the US and Chile. Yet wages rose faster than prices in Chile under the socialist government of Salvador Allende, while prices rose faster than wages in the US under Republican Richard Nixon. The redistributive effects of inflation *can* promote either greater equity or inequity.

Is the conclusion that inflation hurts us all totally misguided? Not exactly. We are all hurt whenever the production of real goods and services is less than it might otherwise have been. So if inflation makes the GDP pie smaller than it would have been had there been less inflation, it would hurt us all. This can happen if inflation increases uncertainty about the terms of exchange to the point that businesses invest less and people work and produce less than they otherwise would have. When actors in the economy find inflation unpredictable and troubling this *can* happen. But to the extent that inflation is predictable and actors can therefore take it into account when they contract with one another there is little reason to believe it reduces real production and income. On the other hand, if the government responds to fears of inflation with deflationary fiscal or monetary policy this *will* reduce production and output, and the government reaction to inflation will "hurt us all." In sum, if the redistributive consequences of inflation aggravate inequities it is lamentable. Or, if inflation is so unpredictable and unsettling that real production falls it is a problem. Otherwise, most of us should think long and hard before joining corporations and the wealthy who put fighting inflation at the top of their list of problems they want the government to prioritize. The wealthy rationally fear that inflation can reduce the real value of their assets. And employers have an interest in prioritizing the fight against inflation over the fight against unemployment because periodic bouts of unemployment reduce labor's bargaining power. But when the rest of the American public routinely joins the predictable outcry of corporations and the wealthy against inflation, it usually does so contrary to its own economic interests.

MYTHS ABOUT DEFICITS AND THE NATIONAL DEBT

Much popular thinking about federal government debt and deficits is based on the following analogy: "If I kept borrowing, going farther and farther into debt, I would eventually go bankrupt. Therefore, if the federal government keeps borrowing, i.e. running deficits, going farther and farther into debt, it will eventually go bankrupt too." But the analogy is false.

There is an important difference between the federal government and private citizens – or other levels of governments and businesses for that matter. If anyone other than the federal government cannot get someone to loan them more money, they can't spend more than their income. But if the federal government's financial credibility bottoms out, and buyers in the market for new treasury bonds dry up, the federal government has one last resort. Unlike the rest of us who can be arrested and sent to jail for counterfeiting if we print up money to finance our deficits, the federal government could print up money in a pinch to pay for any spending in excess of tax revenues. And that is surely what the government would do rather than declare bankruptcy, since the disastrous consequences of federal bankruptcy would be far worse than the inflationary effects of running the printing presses for a while. What's more, since big lenders are sophisticated enough to know the government will never default, even if the general public is not, there are always big money people willing to buy new US Treasury bonds, so the government can always "roll over the debt" rather than running the printing presses anyway.[5]

In any case, the national debt declined from a peak of almost 130% of GDP at the end of World War II to under 35% by 1980. But the Reagan era tax cuts and military spending increases raised the national debt from under 35% to over 75% of GDP between 1981 and 1991. This was totally unprecedented. Previously, the debt/GDP ratio had risen significantly only during major wars and the Great Depression. The Reagan era saw an unprecedented increase in the national debt during peace time and prosperity. It took nearly a century for the national debt to reach $1 trillion. Then the debt tripled in a mere decade in which there was neither war nor depression. The beneficiaries were the wealthy and corporations who saw their taxes cut dramatically, and the military industrial complex who fed at the Pentagon budget trough throughout the 1980s. Those paying the consequences are the beneficiaries of social programs that were cut in the 1990s and those whose taxes were increased to reduce the deficit from $290 billion in 1992 to $161 billion in 1995, to zero in 1998.

But it is important to remember who owns the debt. In 1999 only 22% of the national debt was held by foreigners. So, for the most part "we owe the debt to ourselves." Moreover, the Federal Reserve Bank owned 8%, Federal Agencies owned 19%, the Social Security

5. This is not necessarily true for *all* sovereign governments. Governments of small third world countries often rely on wealthy foreigners to buy their bonds. These lenders will not be satisfied with domestic currency if it cannot be translated into foreign currencies. So gold or foreign currency reserves can become necessary if these governments are to roll over their debt. The US government was once such a government. In 1777 the Continental Congress had to secretly borrow $8 million from France and a quarter million from Spain to buy food, tents, guns, and ammunition for the Revolutionary Army since it could neither raise enough taxes nor convince US merchants to accept more Continental dollars. During the Civil War the Confederate government was forced to resort to printing more and more Confederate currency when they could no longer sell Confederate bonds – both of which became worthless when the South lost the war. But currently less than a quarter of the US national debt is held by foreigners, and there is no concern in financial circles that the US government might default in the foreseeable future.

fund owned 13%, and state and local governments owned another 8%. So broadly speaking, the government owed 48%, or almost half the debt, to itself! US banks, corporations and insurance companies owned 23% and individuals owned the remaining 7%. The problem is *not* that the federal government might go bankrupt, *nor* that we are hopelessly in hock to foreigners. The problem is that interest payments on the debt now take up a lot of our tax dollars every year. There are some eye opening revelations about federal government income and outlays on the last page of the booklet many of us use to fill out our income taxes. In the 1996 1040 Instruction Booklet we were told that personal income taxes were $590 billion in 1995 and net interest payments were $232. One way to read that is that before the government could buy *anything* with our tax dollars, it had to spend 40% of them to finance the debt. Since we were also told defense spending was $326 billion in 1995, after paying the interest on the debt and the defense bill, only $32 billion out of $590 billion in personal taxes was left to buy anything useful in 1995! In the 2001 1040 Instruction Booklet we were told that interest payments on the national debt were 11% of all federal outlays while spending on all social programs was only 16% of outlays.

The problem is that our ability to spend on social programs, and on physical, human, and community development is now severely constrained not only by an absurdly unnecessary, obscene military budget, but by debt service that is the legacy of the banquette President Reagan threw for his supporters in the 1980s – for which he and they refused to pick up the tab. And the problem is that since the average bond holder is a lot wealthier than the average taxpayer, the escalating interest payments on the national debt are an increasingly regressive transfer of income from the have-less taxpayers to the have-more bond owners.

THE BALANCED BUDGET PLOY

In an op-ed piece published in the *Washington Post* on January 8, 1997 Robert Kuttner explained the "either/or budget fallacy" as follows:

> How should the federal budget be balanced? By cutting aid to the poor? Or by reducing entitlements for the middle class? These, of course, are trick questions, since they leave out several options not on the menu: reducing defense spending; rejecting tax cuts which

make budget-balance more difficult; cutting "corporate welfare;" or, not insisting on budget balance at all. But if you fell for the premise that poor *versus* the middle class is the main budget choice for 1997, you are not alone. Both the nominally Democratic Clinton administration and the fervently Republican majority in Congress accept this framing of the choice, as do leading commentators who denounce "entitlements" as budget busters.

In the February 1996 issue of *Z Magazine* Ed Herman called it the balanced budget ploy: "The real aims of the push for a balanced budget are two-fold: to constrain macro-policy and prevent its use in ways that would increase pressures on the labor market and threaten inflation, and to scale back the welfare state." The Full Employment Act of 1947 and the Humphrey–Hawkins Bill of 1975 nominally commit the federal government to whatever policies are necessary to provide jobs for all. And in the past when unemployment rose above 5% public pressure mounted for the government to do something about it. Of course, Republicans and those who spoke for Wall Street always whined that any efforts to decrease unemployment would kindle the fires of inflation. Moreover amending the Full Employment Act to be consistent with price stability, and fanning the public's irrational fear of inflation has long been a top business priority. But after the national debt ballooned in the Reagan era, there was a more effective argument against expansionary fiscal policy: *the budget must be balanced.* Since Americans are even more easily convinced that budget deficits lead to disgrace and disaster than that the bonfires of inflation will consume us all, the "balanced budget ploy" has proved quite effective.

Monetary policy at the Federal Reserve Bank has long been controlled by Wall Street. Now, whenever Main Street pressures Congress or the White House to use fiscal policy to battle joblessness, those elected officials point out – quite logically – that to do so would conflict with the goal of balancing the budget. In effect, the "balanced budget ploy" means that elected politicians can no longer be punished by discontented voters for "presiding" over a listless economy and joblessness. Budget balancing politicians from both the Republican and Democratic Parties now wrap themselves in the patriotic banner of deficit reduction.

The lines of interest are relatively simple: Those who work for a living have greater bargaining power over wages and working conditions the "tighter" the labor market – because the more unemployed workers there are the more vulnerable are the employed. Employers benefit from a "lose" labor market because they can find willing and capable workers more easily and they can threaten employees with replacement should they prove demanding. This is not to say that employers do not suffer as well if a recession gets out of hand and sales fall too far, for too long. But employers have good reason to fear a successful application of Keynesian policies that stabilize the business cycle and keep labor markets permanently "tight." In an economy like Sweden, where labor was powerful between 1945 and 1975, active and successful stabilization policies were more prominent. In the US where labor has always been weaker, the business cycle was never tamed – despite the availability of the same policy tools and know-how for "fine tuning the economy." In the US from 1945 to roughly 1975 the ideological battle was over prioritizing the fight against unemployment or the fight against inflation, because, as we saw, demand management policies cannot battle one without aggravating the other. Politically, business was more influential at the Fed where monetary policy is made, while labor was relatively more influential with the Democratic controlled Congress and with Democratic presidents. But now that inflation has been well under 5% for every year for more than a decade, the ideological battle has shifted to fighting joblessness versus balancing the budget, and those who fear tight labor markets have the ear of not only Republicans but "New" Democrats as well.

Similarly, the more humane and generous the welfare system, the more reasonable employers must be to induce people to work for them. The less safe the welfare "safety net" the more powerful the weapon of fear employers can wield. In the 1990s because Democrats joined Republicans in refusing to deliver our "Peace Dividend" despite the demise of the "Evil Empire," because Democrats vied with Republicans to curry political favor with alternative tax cut schemes for the super wealthy and upper middle class, and because of rising interest payments on the national debt, spending on welfare and social programs had to be savagely cut if deficits were to be eliminated. Democratic President Bill Clinton and Republican House Speaker Newt Gingrich postured over how much and where to make the cuts, but the important point was they agreed that federal deficits had to be eliminated and therefore substantial cuts had to be made in welfare and social programs benefitting the poor. Robert Borsage marveled that "austerity and deficit reduction should be the core domestic economic strategy, despite the fact that the US deficit is smaller, as a proportion of its economy, than that of any other industrial nation."[6]

The importance of the balanced budget ploy is highlighted by the fact that every poll reveals that an overwhelming majority of Americans do *not* want cuts in specific welfare programs or in Medicare or Social Security benefits. If politicians are going to make the cuts regardless, it is important to them to have the fig leaf of the balanced budget to hide behind.

WAGE-LED GROWTH

Mainstream macro economic theories invariably lead their users to expect a negative relationship between wage rates and the rate of economic growth in the long run. Even the few mainstream macro economists who still recommend aggressive expansionary fiscal and monetary policies to increase production in the short run, see higher wage rates as an impediment to capital accumulation and therefore long run economic growth. So how do political economists maintain that it is possible to choose a "high road" to higher rates of economic growth through higher wages, instead of the "low road" of increasing capital accumulation by suppressing wages?

Everyone recognizes that technical change that makes either capital or labor more productive increases potential GDP. So mainstream theorists admit that if wage rates increase because of increases in labor productivity they are compatible with higher rates of economic growth. The dispute is over whether an increase in worker bargaining power that *raises wages more than increases in labor productivity* has a negative or positive effect on long run economic growth. Mainstream economists reason that wage increases in excess of labor productivity increases will squeeze profits and redistribute income from capital to labor. Since capitalists save more of their income than workers this will increase the proportion of output that goes to consumption, decrease the proportion available for accumulation, and thereby drive the growth rate down. Conversely, to increase growth, mainstream economists argue that we must increase capital accumulation by suppressing wages. Political economists like

6. Robert Borsage, "Suffocating in a Consensus Budget," *The Nation*, December 11, 1995.

Michael Kalecki and Josef Steindl argued that even in the long run the relationship between wages and growth is complicated by demand considerations, and consequently it was not necessarily true that higher wages and higher growth rates were always at odds.

The rate of growth of GDP depends not only on the rate of growth of potential GDP but also on how close actual GDP is to potential GDP over the long run. If we hold technology constant, assume no increase in the size of the labor force, and assume no improvements in the *quality* of either capital or labor inputs, the rate of growth of potential GDP is determined entirely by the rate of capital accumulation. But for a given increase in the growth rate of potential GDP, the rate of growth of *actual* GDP will depend on the level of capacity utilization over the long run. For example, if potential GDP grows at 3%, but capacity utilization drops by 3%, actual GDP will not grow at all. Depressing wages, and thereby consumption, does leave more output available for capital accumulation, but by lowering the demand for goods and services it also decreases capacity utilization. Kalecki pointed out that depressing wages may allow for greater capital accumulation, but it also may lead us to use less of the capital we have. He argued that if depressing wages lowered capacity utilization sufficiently it could lower the rate of growth of actual GDP even while increasing the rate of growth of potential GDP. Steindl pointed out that as corporations become larger and increase their monopoly power in the markets where they sell their goods to consumers, they can increase their "mark ups" over costs, raising prices and thereby diminishing the real wage. In other words, Steindl pointed out that real wages can be driven down when corporate power increases over consumers, not only when corporate power increases over workers.

In chapter 9 we study a formal, political economy, long run macro model that captures the insights of Kalecki and Steindl, incorporates Keynes' insights about the effects of capacity utilization and the rate of profit on business investment demand, and allows class struggle as well as labor productivity to affect wage rates, as Marx insisted it would. The model demonstrates how depressing wages can retard the rate of economic growth through its negative effect on long run capacity utilization, and conversely why raising wages can increase the rate of economic growth through its positive effect on capacity utilization. In other words, the model demonstrates the logical possibility of "wage-led growth" even in the long run. In mainstream long run models, where actual production is assumed always to be equal to potential output, there is a "zero sum game" between consumption and growth and between the wage rate and profit rate. By allowing capacity utilization to vary the political economy model allows for "win–win" scenarios and "lose–lose" scenarios as well. Anything that increases capacity utilization over the long run will increase actual production and income over the long run as well. This makes it possible to have more consumption goods *and* more investment goods, and have a higher real wage rate *and* a higher rate of profit. Anything that decreases capacity utilization, output, and income means that *both* consumption and growth, and *both* the wage rate and profit rate might fall.

One of the distinguishing features of capitalism in the advanced economies over the last 20 years has been the dramatic increase in corporate power. At the same time we have witnessed lower rates of economic growth in the advanced economies than during the first 30 years after World War II. The work of Michael Kalecki and Josef Steindl exploring the effects of income distribution on aggregate demand, and incorporating Keynes' insights about the importance of aggregate demand into long run models, provides a plausible explanation of declining growth rates in the advanced economies worthy of consideration: As corporations have increased their power *vis-à-vis* both their employees and their customers they have been able to drive real wages down over the past 30 years. This has prevented aggregate demand from increasing as fast as potential production and led to falling rates of capacity utilization and lower rates of economic growth. The work of Keynes, Kalecki and Steindl and the model we study in chapter 9 might also help explain how the Scandinavian economies could have had higher rates of economic growth than most other advanced economies for over 50 years, *despite* higher tax rates and lower rates of technological innovation than many less successful advanced economies. Could it be that strong unions, high real wages, and high taxes to finance high levels of public spending are not detrimental to long run growth at all, but quite the opposite?

7   Money, Banks, and Finance

> A bank is a place where they lend you an umbrella in fair weather and ask for it back when it begins to rain.
>
> Robert Frost

It is ironic that money and banks top the list of economic subjects that most baffle and bore students. Money is just a clever invention to save time, and bankers, contrary to their stodgy reputations, substitute bigamy for proper marriages between borrowers and lenders – with predictably disastrous consequences when both wives press their legal claims. Once finance is understood, the Savings and Loan crisis of the 1980s, international financial crises of the 1990s and early twenty-first century, and the logic of monetary policy all fall quickly into place.

MONEY: A PROBLEMATIC CONVENIENCE

It is possible to have exchange, or market economies, without money. A barter exchange economy is one in which people exchange one kind of good directly for another kind of good. For instance, I grow potatoes because my land is best suited to that crop. My neighbor grows carrots because her land is better for carrots. But if we both like our stew with potatoes *and* carrots, we can accomplish this through barter exchange. On Saturday I take some of my potatoes to town, she takes some of her carrots, and we exchange a certain number of pounds of potatoes for a certain number of pounds of carrots. No money is involved as goods are exchanged directly for other goods.

Notice that in barter exchange the act of supplying is inextricably linked to an equivalent act of demanding. I cannot supply potatoes in the farmer's market without simultaneously demanding carrots. And my neighbor cannot supply carrots without simultaneously demanding potatoes. Having learned how recessions and inflation can arise because aggregate demand is less or greater than aggregate supply, it is interesting to note that in a barter exchange economy these difficulties would not occur. If every act of supplying is also an act of demanding an equivalent value, then when we add up the value of all the goods and services supplied in a barter exchange economy, and we add up the value of all the goods and services demanded, they will always be exactly the same! No depressions or recessions. No demand pull inflation. It's enough to make one wonder who was the idiot who dreamed up the idea of money!

Sometimes ideas that seem good at the time turn out to cause more trouble than they're worth. Maybe finding some object that everyone agrees to accept in exchange for goods and services was just one of those lousy ideas that looked good until it was too late to do anything about it. But let's think more before jumping to conclusions. Barter exchange seemed to do the job well enough in the example we considered. But what if I want potatoes and carrots in my stew, as before, but my carrot growing neighbor wants carrots and onions in her stew, and my onion growing neighbor wants onions and potatoes in her stew? We would have to arrange some kind of three-cornered trade. I could not trade potatoes for carrots because my carrot growing neighbor doesn't want potatoes. My carrot growing neighbor could not trade carrots for onions because the onion grower doesn't want carrots. And the onion growing neighbor could not trade her onions for my potatoes because I don't want onions. I could trade potatoes for onions which I don't really want – except to trade the onions for carrots. Or, my carrot growing neighbor could trade carrots for potatoes she doesn't want – except to trade the potatoes for onions. Or, my onion growing neighbor could trade onions for carrots she doesn't want – except to trade for potatoes. But arranging mutually beneficial deals obviously becomes more problematic when there are even three goods, much less thousands.

There are two obvious problems with barter exchange when there are more than two goods: (1) Not all the mutually beneficial, multiparty deals might be "discovered" – which would be a shame since it means people wouldn't always get to eat their stew the way they want it. And, (2) even if a mutually beneficial multiparty deal is discovered and struck, the "transaction costs" in time, guarantees, and assurances might be considerable. Money eliminates both these problems. As long as all three of us agree to exchange vegetables for money there is no need to work out complicated three-cornered trades. Each of us simply sells our vegetable for money to whomever wants to buy it, and then uses the money we received to buy whatever we want.

Simple. No complicated contracts. No lawyers needed. But notice that now it *is* possible to supply without simultaneously demanding an equivalent value. When I sell my potatoes for money I have contributed to supply without contributing to demand. Of course, if I turn around and use all the money I got from selling my potatoes to buy carrots for my stew I will have contributed as much to demand as I did to supply when you consider the two transactions together. But money separates the acts of supplying and demanding making it *possible* to do one without doing the other. Suppose I come and sell my potatoes for money and then my six-year-old breaks his arm running around underneath the vegetable stands, I take him to the emergency room, and by the time we get back to the vegetable market it is closed. In this case I will have added to the supply in the Saturday vegetable market without adding to the demand. Nobody is seriously concerned about this problem in simple vegetable markets, but in large capitalist economies the fact that monetized exchange makes possible discrepancies between supply and demand in the aggregate can be problematic. Once a business has paid for inputs and hired labor it has every incentive to sell its product. But if the price it must settle for leaves a profit that is negative, unacceptable, or just disappointing, the business may well wait for better market conditions before purchasing more inputs and labor to produce again. The specter of workers anxious to work going without jobs because employers don't believe they will be able to sell what those workers would produce is a self-fulfilling prophesy that tens of millions of victims of the Great Depression can attest is no mere theoretical concern!

BANKS: BIGAMY NOT A PROPER MARRIAGE

What if there were no banks? How would people who wanted to spend more than their income meet people who wished to spend less? How would businesses with profitable investment opportunities in excess of their retained earnings meet households willing to loan them their savings?

If banks did not exist there would be sections in the classified ads in newspapers titled "loan wanted" and "willing to loan." But beside the cost of cutting down the extra trees to print these pages, matching would-be borrowers with would-be lenders is not a simple process. These ads might not be as titillating as personals, but they would have to go into details such as: "Want to lend $4,500 for three years with quarterly payments at 9.5% annual rate of interest to credit worthy customer – references required." And, "Want to borrow 2 million dollars to finance construction of six, half-million dollar homes on prime suburban land already purchased. Willing to pay 11% over thirty years. Well known developer with over fifty years of successful business activity in the area." But this entails two kinds of "transaction costs." First, the credit worthiness of borrowers is not easy to determine. Particularly small lenders don't want to spend time checking out references of loan applicants. Second, not all mutually beneficial deals are between a single lender and borrower. Many mutually beneficial deals are multiparty swaps. Searching through ads to find all mutually beneficial, multiparty deals takes time – more than most people have – and guaranteeing the commitments and terms of multiparty deals takes time and legal expertise. One way to understand what banks do is to see them as "matchmakers" for borrowers and lenders. But it turns out they are more than efficient matchmakers who reduce transaction costs by informational economies of scale.

Perhaps banks *could* perform their service like the matchmaker in "Fiddler on the Roof" – collecting fees from the parties when they marry. But they don't. Banks don't introduce borrowers and lenders who then contract a "proper" marriage between themselves. Instead, banks engage in legalized bigamy. A bank "marries" its depositors – paying interest for deposits which depositors can redeem on demand. Then the bank "marries" its loan customers – who pay interest on their loans which the bank can only redeem on specified future dates. But notice that if both the bank's "wives" insist on exercising their full legal rights, no bank would be able to fulfill its legal obligations! If depositors exercise their legal right to withdraw all their deposits, and if loan customers refuse to pay back their loans any faster than their loan contract requires, every bank would be insolvent every day of the year. It is only because not all wives with whom banks engage in bigamy choose to simultaneously exercise their full legal rights that banks can get away with bigamy – and make a handsome profit for themselves in the process.

Many depositors assume when they deposit money in their checking account that the bank simply puts their money into a safe, along with all the other deposits, where it sits until they choose to withdraw it. After all, unless it is all kept available there is no way the bank could give all depositors all their money back if they asked for it. But if that is what banks did they could never make any loans, and therefore they could never make any profits! To assume banks hold all the deposits they accept is to think banks offer a kind of collective safety deposit box service for cash. But that is not at all what banks offer when they accept deposits. Banks use those deposits to make loans to customers who pay the bank interest. As long as the bank charges and collects interest on loans that is higher on average than the interest the bank pays depositors, banks can make a profit. But to realize the potential profit from the difference between the loan and deposit rates of interest, banks have to loan the deposits. And if they loan even a small part of the deposits they obviously can't be there in the eventuality that depositors asked to withdraw all their money.

Which leads to a frightening realization: Banks inherently entail the possibility of bankruptcy! There is no way to guarantee that banks will always be able to "honor" their commitments to depositors without making it impossible for banks to make any profits. That is, no matter how safe and conservative bank management, no matter how faithfully borrowers repay bank loans, depositors are inherently at risk. But the logic in banking dynamics is even worse, which is why every government on the planet – no matter how committed to laissez faire, freedom of enterprise, and competitive forces – regulates the banking industry in ways no other industry is subjected to.

How can a bank increase its profits? Profits will be higher if the differential between the rates of interest paid on loans and on deposits is larger. Every bank would like to expand this differential, but how can they? If a bank starts charging higher interest on loans it will risk losing its loan customers to other banks. If it offers to pay less on deposits it risks losing depositors to other banks. In other words, individual banks are limited by competition with other banks from expanding the differential beyond a certain point. Another way of saying the same thing is that the size of the differential is determined by the amount of competition in the banking industry. If there is a lot of competition the differential will be small. If there is less competition the differential will be larger. But for a given level of competition, individual banks are restricted in their ability to increase profits by expanding their own differential. The other deter-minant of bank profits is how many loans they make taking advantage of the differential. If a bank loans out 40% of its deposits and earns $X in profits, it could earn $2X profits by lending out 80% of its deposits. Since there is little an individual bank can do to expand its interest differential, banks concentrate on loaning out as much of their deposits as possible.

Which leads to a second frightening realization: When stockholders press bank officers to increase profits, bank CEOs are driven to loan out more and more of bank deposits. Since insolvency results when depositors ask to withdraw more than the bank has kept as "reserves," the drive for more profits necessarily increases the likelihood of bankruptcy by lowering bank reserves. It is true that stockholders should seek a trade-off between higher profits and insolvency since shareholders lose the value of their investment if the bank they own goes bankrupt. But stockholders are not the only ones who lose when a bank goes bankrupt. While stockholders lose the value of their investment, depositors lose their deposits. So when stockholders weigh the benefit of higher profits against the expected cost of bankruptcy they do not weigh the benefits against the entire cost, but only the fraction of the cost that falls on them. And even with regulations requiring minimum capitalization, it is always the case that the cost of bankruptcy to depositors is a much greater part of the total cost than the cost to shareholders. This means that bank shareholders' interests do not coincide with the public interest in finding the efficient trade-off between higher profitability and lower likelihood of insolvency. Hence the need for government regulation.

This was a lesson that history taught over and over again during the eighteenth and nineteenth centuries as periodic waves of bankruptcy rocked the growing American Republic. Early in the twentieth century Congress charged the Federal Reserve Bank with the task of setting a ***minimum legal reserve requirement*** *that prevents banks from lending out more than a certain fraction of their deposits*. In 1933 Congress also created a federal agency to insure depositors in the eventuality of bankruptcy in its efforts to reassure the public that it was safe to deposit their savings in banks during the Great Depression. Today the Federal Deposit Insurance Corporation (FDIC) will fully redeem deposits up to $100,000 in value if a bank goes bankrupt.

But Federal insurance has created two new problems. First of all, as we discovered in the Savings and Loan Crisis of the mid-1980s, any substantial string of bankruptcies will also bankrupt the insuring agency! When the Savings and Loan Crisis was finally recognized there were roughly 500 insolvent thrift institutions with deposits of

over $200 billion. The Federal Savings and Loan Insurance Corpo-
ration, FSLIC, had less than $2 billion in assets at the time. While
the Federal Reserve Bank was anxious to shut the insolvent Savings
and Loan Associations down to prevent them from accepting new
deposits and creating additional FSLIC liabilities, neither Congress,
led by Speaker Jim Wright from Texas, nor the Reagan White House
wanted to declare the thrifts bankrupt because that would have
required massive additional appropriations for FSLIC. Many of the
insolvent thrifts were in Texas and they convinced Wright to lobby
for delay of bankruptcy procedures. Owners of those insolvent thrifts
had everything to lose from bankruptcy, whereas they could
continue to collect dividends as long as they were permitted to
accept new deposits and make new loans – regardless of whether or
not there was any likelihood they would be able to overcome
insolvency by doing so. The Reagan administration was not anxious
to accept responsibility for the consequences of its financial dereg-
ulatory frenzy in the early 1980s, and didn't want to have to raise
taxes or cut defense spending to come up with the appropriations
necessary to fund FSLIC sufficiently to pay off $200 billion to
depositors – which the Grahm-Ruddman bill limiting deficit
spending would have required at the time. As a result the crisis was
swept under the carpet for three more years, by which time the
deposit liabilities of the insolvent thrifts had doubled. In other
words, the politics of partially funded government insurance cost
the American taxpayer additional hundreds of billions of dollars.
Besides the hundreds of billions spent in the bail-out itself, the
Resolution Trust Corporation established by the Financial Institutions Reform, Recovery and Enforcement Act of 1989 to sell, merge,
or liquidate insolvent thrifts, offered huge tax breaks as inducements
to solvent financial institutions to buy and take over failed institutions, thereby reducing tax revenues for many years to come, and
making it impossible to calculate what the eventual total loss of the
S&L crisis to taxpayers will be.

Federal insurance also aggravates what economists call **moral
hazard** in the banking sector. Bank owners and large depositors
essentially collude in placing and accepting deposits in financial
institutions that pay high interest on deposits which are used to
make risky loans that pay high returns – as long as the borrowers
don't default. But *when there are defaults on risky loans neither
depositors nor shareholders are the major victims of insolvency and
bankruptcy*. Lightly capitalized shareholders lose little in a case of

bankruptcy. And fully insured depositors lose nothing. Meanwhile both have been enjoying high returns while running little or no risk in the process. So government insurance compounds the problem that bank officers cannot be counted on to pursue the public interest in an efficient trade-off between profitability and risk of insolvency by no longer making it necessary for depositors to monitor the lending activities of the financial institutions where they place their deposits. Apparently depositor fear of insolvency was an insufficient restraint on bank lending policy before the advent of public deposit insurance since all governments already had charged their Central Bank with regulating minimum reserve requirements and monitoring the legitimacy of bank loans. Deposit insurance has the unfortunate effect of further weakening depositor incentives to monitor bank behavior.

Finally, notice that banks mean the functioning money supply is considerably larger than the amount of currency circulating in the economy. If we ask how much someone could buy, immediately, in a world without banks the answer would be the amount of currency that person had. But in a world with banks where sellers not only accept currency in exchange for goods and services, but accept checks as well, someone can buy an amount equal to the currency they have *plus* the balance they have in their checking account(s). This means the functioning money supply is equal to the amount of currency circulating in the economy *plus* the sum total balances in household and business checking accounts at banks. Since checking account balances were $616 billion and currency in circulation was only $463 billion in January 1999, currency was less than half the functioning money supply, commonly called M1, at the beginning of 1999.[1]

---

1. More precisely, M1, referred to as the "basic" or "functioning" money supply, includes currency in circulation, "transactions account" balances, and traveler's checks. Beside checking accounts, transaction accounts include NOW accounts, ATS accounts, credit union share drafts, and demand deposits at mutual savings banks. The distinguishing feature of all transaction accounts is they permit direct payment to a third party by check or debit card. M2 and M3 are larger definitions of the money supply which include funds that are less accessible such as savings accounts and money market mutual funds (M2), and repurchase agreements and overnight Eurodollars (M3). By 1999 people held so much money in money market mutual funds and savings accounts that M2 had become more than three times larger than M1.

Which leads to our last frightening realization. Most of the functioning money supply is literally created by private commercial banks when they accept deposits and make loans. But as we have seen, when banks engage in these activities, and thereby "create" most of the functioning money supply, they think only of their own profits and give nary a thought to the sacred public trust of preserving the integrity of "money" in our economy.

MONETARY POLICY: ANOTHER WAY TO SKIN THE CAT

In chapter 6 we studied three fiscal policies: changes in government spending, changes in taxes, and changing both spending and taxes by the same amount in the same direction. While they had different effects on the government budget deficit (or surplus) and on the composition of output, in theory, any one of them was sufficient to eliminate any unemployment or inflation gap. The alternative to fiscal policy is monetary policy which, in theory, can also be used to eliminate unemployment or inflation gaps. If the Federal Reserve Bank changes the money supply it can induce a rise or fall in market interest rates, which in turn can induce a fall or rise in private investment demand, which in turn will induce an even larger change in overall aggregate demand and equilibrium GDP through the "investment expenditure multiplier." Just like fiscal policies, monetary policy can be either expansionary – raising equilibrium GDP to combat unemployment – or deflationary – lowering equilibrium GDP to combat inflation.

While fiscal policy attacks government spending directly, or household consumption demand indirectly by changing personal taxes, monetary policy aims indirectly at the third component of aggregate demand, private investment demand.[2] As we saw in the previous chapter investment demand depends negatively on interest rates. The micro law of supply and demand tells us that changes in the money supply should affect interest rates, which are simply the

2. Our model and language oversimplify. While most federal taxes are personal taxes and therefore affect household disposable income, business taxes potentially affect investment decisions. Moreover, government transfer payments count just as much toward budget deficits as government purchases of military equipment, yet only the latter is part of the aggregate demand for final goods and services. And when the Fed cuts interest rates it makes it cheaper for households as well as businesses to borrow. Beside business investment, monetary policy affects consumer demand for "big ticket items" like appliances, cars, and houses that people buy on credit.

"price" of money. Just as the price of apples drops when the supply of apples increases, interest rates drop when the supply of money increases. The Federal Reserve Bank – called the Central Bank in civilized countries – can change the money supply in any of three ways. It can change the legal minimum reserve requirement. It can conduct "open market operations" by buying or selling treasury bonds in the "open" bond market. Or it can change something called "the discount rate." By changing the money supply the Fed can induce a change in market interest rates to stimulate or retard business investment demand.

When the Fed lowers the legal minimum reserve requirement some of the required reserves held by each bank are no longer required and become excess reserves the banks are "free" to loan. As we saw, when banks make loans this has the effect of increasing the functioning money supply. By increasing the required reserve ratio the Fed can cause a decrease in the functioning money supply. Interestingly, changing the reserve requirement changes the money supply without changing the amount of currency in the economy.

The Fed has its own budget and its own assets, including roughly 8% of the outstanding US treasury bonds in an assortment of sizes and maturity dates. So instead of changing the reserve requirement the Fed could take some of its treasury bonds to the "open" bond market in New York and sell them to the general public who, for simplicity, we assume pays for them with cash. The market for treasury bonds is "open" in the sense that anyone can buy them, and anyone who has some can sell them. While new treasury bonds are sold by the Treasury Department at what are called "Treasury auctions," previously issued treasury bonds are "resold" by their original purchasers who no longer wish to hold them until they mature, to purchasers on the "open bond market." When we talk about the Fed engaging in "open market operations" we are talking about the Fed buying or selling previously issued treasury bonds, that is, we're talking about the bond "resell" market rather than Treasury Department auctions of new bonds. When the Fed sells bonds this isn't a transfer of wealth from the private sector to the Fed or vice versa. It is merely a change in the form in which the Fed

---

Nonetheless, a simple model, which we don't use to make actual predictions in any case, that assumes (1) all of G is demand for public goods, (2) taxes affect only household disposable income, and (3) monetary policy only affects business investment demand is useful for "thinking" purposes and not terribly misleading.

and private sector hold their wealth, or assets. Whereas the Fed used to hold part of its wealth in the form of the bonds it sells, now it holds that wealth in the form of currency. Whereas the private sector used to hold part of its wealth in currency, now it holds that wealth in the form of Treasury bonds. But when the Fed engages in open market operations it does change the amount of currency in the economy – increasing currency in the economy by buying bonds and decreasing currency in the economy by selling bonds.

Finally, the Federal Reserve Bank loans money to private commercial banks that are members of the Federal Reserve Banking System. If these commercial banks borrow more from the Fed and then loan it out, the money supply will increase. If they borrow less from the Fed the money supply will decrease. Just like any other lender, the Fed charges interest on loans – in this case loans it makes to private banks that are members of the Federal Reserve System. And just like any other borrower, these banks will borrow more from the Fed if the interest rate they have to pay is lower, and less if the interest rate they pay is higher. *The name for the interest rate the Fed charges banks who borrow at its "discount window" is the **discount rate**.* So by lowering its discount rate the Fed can induce commercial banks to borrow more currency, thereby increasing the currency circulating in the economy, and by raising the discount rate it can discourage borrowing, thereby decreasing the amount of currency circulating in the economy.

In sum, the logic of monetary policy is as follows: The Fed can increase or decrease the functioning money supply, M1, by changing the minimum reserve requirement, through open market operations, or by changing its discount rate. By changing the money supply the Fed can induce changes in market interest rates, leading to changes in investment demand, leading to even greater changes in aggregate demand and equilibrium GDP. When monetary authorities fear economic recession they increase the money supply, as Chairman Greenspan and the Fed did from mid-1999 through early 2002 when they regularly lowered the discount rate by a quarter and sometimes half percent every month or two. IMF conditionality agreements, on the other hand, routinely insist that monetary authorities reduce their functioning money supply in exchange for emergency IMF bail out loans, for reasons we explore in the next chapter. Since neither increasing nor decreasing the money supply affects government spending or taxes directly, monetary policy has no *direct* effect on the government budget. Of course if expansionary monetary policy lowers unemployment and thereby decreases government spending on unemployment compensation and welfare, it will indirectly lower G. And if expansionary monetary policy increases GDP and therefore GDI and thereby increases tax revenues collected as a percentage of income, it will indirectly raise T. So monetary policy does have an *indirect* effect on the government budget. But unlike fiscal policy, changing the money supply has no direct impact on the government budget. As far as the composition of output is concerned, expansionary monetary policy increases the share of GDP going to private investment, I/Y, and decreases the shares going to public goods, G/Y, and private consumption, C/Y. Deflationary monetary policy has the opposite effect – it chokes off private investment relative to public spending and private consumption. In chapter 9 we explore the effects of *equivalent* monetary and fiscal policies in a simple, short run, closed economy macro model.

THE RELATIONSHIP BETWEEN THE FINANCIAL AND "REAL" ECONOMIES

Increasingly the economic "news" reported in the mainstream media is news about stocks, bonds, and interest rates. During the stock market boom in the 1990s the media acted like cheer leaders for the Dow Jones Average and NASDAQ index. It is was not uncommon for the major US media to report with glee that stock prices rose dramatically after a Labor Department briefing announcing an increase in the number of jobless. In the aftermath of the East Asian financial crisis the media reassured us that stock indices and currency values had largely recovered in Thailand, South Korea, and Indonesia – as if that were what mattered – neglecting to report that employment and production in those economies had *not* rebounded – as if that were unimportant. What should we care about in the economy, and what is the relationship between the financial and "real" sectors of the economy?

In chapter 2 we asked, "What should we demand from our economy?" The answer was an equitable distribution of the burdens and benefits of economic activity, efficient use of our scarce productive resources, economic democracy, solidarity, variety, and environmental sustainability. Nowhere on that wish list did rising stock, bond, or currency prices appear. This does not mean the financial sector has nothing to do with the production and distribution of goods and services. But it does mean the only reason to care about the financial sector is because of its effects on the real sector of the economy. If the financial sector improves economic efficiency and thereby allows us to produce more goods and services, so much the better. But if dynamics in the financial sector cause unemployment and lost production, or increase economic inequality, that is what matters, not the fact that a stock index or currency rose or fell in value. In an era when the hegemony of global finance is unprecedented, it is important not to invert what matters and what is only of derivative interest.

How can money, lending, banks, options, buying on margin, derivatives, or hedge funds increase economic efficiency? Simple: by providing funding for some productive activity in the real economy that otherwise would not have taken place. If monetized exchange allows people to discover a mutually beneficial deal they would have been unlikely to find through barter, money increases the efficiency of the real economy. If I can borrow from you to buy a tool that allows me to work more productively right away, whereas otherwise I would have had to save for a year to buy the tool, a credit market increases my efficiency this year – and the interest rate you and I agree on will distribute the increase in *my* productivity during the year between you, the lender, and me, the borrower. If banks permit more borrowers and lenders to find one another, thereby allowing more people to work more productively sooner than they otherwise would have, the banking system increases efficiency in the real economy. If options, buying on margin, and derivatives mobilize savings that otherwise would have been idle, and extend credit to borrowers who become more productive sooner than had they been forced to wait longer for loans from more traditional sources in the credit system, these financial innovations increase efficiency in the real economy. But while those who profit from the financial system are quick to point out these *positive* potentials, they are loath to point out ways the financial sector can *negatively* impact the real economy. Nor do they dwell on the fact that what the credit system allows them to do is profit from *other people's* increases in productivity.

At its best what the credit system does, in all its different guises, is allow lenders to appropriate increases in the productivity of others. Why do those whose productivity rises agree to pay creditors part of their productivity increase? Because the creditors have the wealth needed to purchase whatever is necessary to increase their productivity while they do not. Moreover, if they wait until they can save sufficient wealth to do without creditors, borrowers lose whatever efficiency gain they could have enjoyed in the meantime. But even when the credit system works well, that is, even when it generates efficiency gains in the real economy, the credit system can increase the degree of inequality in the economy. If the interest rate distributes more than half of the increase in the borrower's efficiency to the lender, and if lenders are generally more wealthy than borrowers in the first place, the credit system will increase wealth inequality.

But beside increasing inequity, the credit system can generate efficiency losses instead of gains in the real economy. In chapter 9 we look at a model that makes clear how rational depositors can cause bank runs. We then look at a model of a real corn economy with banks that shows how banks *can* generate efficiency gains when all goes well, but banks will make the real economy *less* efficient than it would have been with less formal credit markets if there is a bank run. When depositors have reason to fear they will lose their deposits if they fail to withdraw before others do, the model demonstrates how banks will produce efficiency losses, not gains, in the real economy. In a third model we show how international finance can generate efficiency *losses* as well as gains in a "real" global corn economy for similar reasons. The general lesson from these models in chapter 9 is when borrowers and lenders become accustomed to finding each other through bank mediation and banks fail, it is possible for *fewer* borrowers to find lenders than otherwise would have been the case, and therefore for the real economy to become less efficient than it would have been without banks. Similarly, when more highly leveraged international finance makes it more likely that international investors will panic, and capital liberalization makes it easier for them to withdraw tens of billions of dollars of investments from emerging market economies and sell off massive quantities of their currencies overnight when they do panic, tens of millions can lose their jobs and decades of economic progress can go down the drain as banks and businesses in "emerging market economies" go bankrupt. This is how liberalizing the international credit system can make real underdeveloped economies *less* efficient than they were when international finance was more restricted, as it was during the Bretton Woods era. These are among the potential *downsides* of lashing "real" economies more tightly to the back of a credit system when the credit system proves unstable.

Banks, futures, options, margins, derivatives and other "financial innovations" all either expand the list of things speculators can buy and sell, or permit them to increase their leverage – use less of their own wealth and more of someone else's when they invest. In other words these, and whatever new "financial instruments" speculators dream up in the future, simply extend the credit system. If the extension provides funding for some productive activity that would otherwise have not been funded, it can be useful. But all extensions increase dangers in the credit system by (1) increasing the number of places something might go wrong, (2) increasing the probability that if something goes wrong investors will panic and the credit system will crash, or (3) compounding the damage done if the credit system does crash. New "financial products" add new markets where bubbles can form and burst. Increased leverage makes financial structures more fragile and compounds the damage from any bubble that does burst.[3]

There are two rules of behavior in any credit system, and both rules become more critical to follow the more leveraged the system. Rule #1 is the rule all participants want all *other* participants to follow: DON'T PANIC! If everyone follows rule #1 the likelihood of the credit system crashing is lessened. Rule #2 is the rule each participant must be careful to follow herself: PANIC FIRST! If something goes wrong, the first to collect her loan from a debtor in trouble, the first to withdraw her deposits from a troubled bank, the first to sell her option or derivative in a market when a bubble bursts, the first to dump a currency when it is "under pressure," will lose the least. Those who are slow to panic, on the other hand, will take the biggest baths. Once stated, the contradictory nature of the two logical rules for behavior in credit systems make clear the inherent danger in this powerful economic arrangement, and the risk we take when we tie the real economy ever more tightly to a credit system which financial businesses and politicians have recently conspired to make more unstable and fragile.

---

3. For example, derivatives can disguise how many are speculating in a market. Frank Partnoy, a derivative trader turned professor of law and finance at the University of San Diego, described this problem as follows when explaining East Asian currency crises: "It's as if you're in a theater, and say there are 100 people and you have the rush-to-the-exit problem. With derivatives, it's as if without your knowing it, there are another 500 people in the theater, and you can't see them at first. But when the rush to the exit starts, suddenly they drop from the ceiling. This makes the panic all the greater." Quoted by Nicholas Kristof in his article in the *New York Times* on February 17, 1999.

8   International Economics: Mutual Benefit or Imperialism?

Mainstream economics emphasizes the positive possibilities of international trade and investment to such an extent that most economists have difficulty imagining how more free trade, more international lending, or more direct foreign investment could possibly be disadvantageous. They understand why colonial relations might be detrimental to a colony. When Great Britain prevented its North American colonies from trading with Spain, and required them to buy only from England at prices set by England, mainstream economic theory recognizes that Great Britain was benefitted, but her new world colonies were made worse off. But mainstream economists point out that the era of colonialism is behind us. They point out that under free trade any country that is not benefitted by trade with a particular trading partner can look for other trading partners, or not trade at all. They point out that when all are free to lend or borrow in international credit markets any country that is not benefitted by the terms of a particular international loan is free to search for other lenders offering better terms, or not borrow at all. Mainstream theory teaches that as long as international trade and investment is consensual and countries do not mistake what the effects will be, no country can end up worse off, and all countries should end up better off. So now that colonialism is behind us the only reason mainstream economists can see why developing economies would be damaged by international trade or investment is if *they* make a mistake. Only if *they* think a good or service they import will be more beneficial than it turns out to be, only if *they* think an international loan will improve their economic productivity more than it really can, can developing economies be disadvantaged in the eyes of most mainstream economists.

Political economists, on the other hand, argue that international trade and investment are often vehicles through which more advanced economies at the "center" of the global economy exploit less advanced economies in the "periphery" – long after the latter cease to be their colonies. Third world political economists in particular argue that "unequal trade" enriches more advanced economies at the expense of less advanced ones. Many political economists emphasize that direct foreign investment allows multinational companies from advanced economies to take advantage of plentiful raw materials and cheap labor in less developed economies, and to take over lucrative markets from domestic producers. And many political economists point out that international borrowing can ensnare poor countries in debt traps from which it is impossible for them to escape.

Mutual benefit or imperialism? Global village or global pillage? First we explore the logic behind each view – taking pains when reviewing mainstream theory to "render unto Caesar what is Caesar's." Then we see if mainstream and political economists are destined to talk about international economics in different languages with little hope of communication, or if we can sort out the sense of where things lie. We will discover that while international trade and investment *could* improve global efficiency and reduce global inequality, neoliberal, capitalist globalization *will* continue to do just the opposite if it is not stopped.

WHY TRADE CAN INCREASE GLOBAL EFFICIENCY

When we use scarce productive resources to make one good those resources are not available to make another good. That is the sense in which economists say there are **opportunity costs** of making goods. The *opportunity cost of making a unit of good A, for example, can be measured as the number of units of good B we must forego because we used the resources to make the unit of A instead of using them to make good B.* Opportunity costs are important for understanding the logic of international trade because whenever the opportunity costs of producing goods is different in different countries there *can* be positive benefits, or efficiency gains from specialization and trade. And as long as the terms of trade distribute part of the benefit of specialization to both countries, trade *can* be beneficial to both trading partners.

Suppose, for example, by moving productive resources from the shirt industry to the tool industry in the US shirt production falls by 4 shirts for every additional tool produced, while moving resources from the shirt industry to the tool industry in Mexico results in a drop of 8 shirts for every new tool produced. The opportunity cost of a tool in the US is 4 shirts while the opportunity cost of a tool in Mexico is 8 shirts. Conversely, since moving productive resources from the tool to the shirt industry in the US leads to a loss of ¼ tool for every new shirt produced, while moving resources from the tool to the shirt industry in Mexico leads to a loss of ⅛ tool for every new shirt produced, the opportunity cost of a shirt in the US is ¼ tool while the opportunity of a shirt in Mexico is ⅛ tool. Suppose the terms of trade were 6 shirts for 1 tool, or what is the same thing, ⅙ tool for 1 shirt. The US would be better off producing only tools – trading tools for any shirts it wanted to consume – because instead of using the resources necessary to produce 4 shirts, the US could instead produce 1 tool and then trade the tool for 6 shirts. So if the terms of trade are 1 tool for 6 shirts the US is always better off using its resources to produce tools and never shirts – even when it wants to consume shirts. Mexico, on the other hand, would be better off producing only shirts – trading shirts for any tools it wants – because instead of using the resources necessary to produce 1 tool, Mexico could instead produce 8 shirts and trade the 8 shirts for ⅙ tools per shirt times 8 shirts, or 1⅓ tools. So if the terms of trade are 1 tool for 6 shirts Mexico is always better off using its resources to produce shirts and never tools – even when it wants to consume tools. Generalizing we have the central theorem of mainstream trade theory: As long as opportunity costs of producing goods are different in different countries, (1) specialization and trade *can* increase global efficiency, and (2) there are terms of trade that *can* distribute part of the efficiency gain to both trading partners thereby making all countries better off.

Comparative, not absolute advantage drives trade

When David Ricardo first explained the logic of trade he was not concerned with why opportunity costs might be different in different countries. Instead he wanted to dispel the myth that mutually beneficial trade could only take place when one country was better at making one good while the other country was better at producing the other good. Ricardo showed that even if one country was more productive in the production of *both* goods, that is, even if one country had an *absolute advantage* in the production of both goods, the more productive country, not just the less productive country, could gain from specialization and trade. Ricardo demonstrated that the more productive country could benefit by importing the good in which it was relatively, or comparatively less productive, and exporting the good in which it enjoyed a relative, or comparative advantage. In other words, Ricardo showed that *comparative advantage* – not *absolute advantage* – was the crucial factor driving trade.

Suppose in the above example it only takes 1 hour of labor to make either 1 tool or 4 shirts in the US, but it takes 10 hours of labor to make 1 tool or 8 shirts in Mexico. In this case the opportunity costs of tools and shirts in both countries is exactly the same as before, but the US is 10 times more productive than Mexico in tool production and 5 times more productive than Mexico in shirt production. In other words, the US is more productive than Mexico in producing *both* tools and shirts, and enjoys an *absolute advantage* in both industries. Before Ricardo, economists believed a country like the US would have no incentive to trade with a country like Mexico. Certainly the US would not import tools from Mexico because it can produce them 10 times more productively than Mexico can. But why would the US import shirts from Mexico when the US is 5 times more productive than Mexico in shirt production? Notice that the conclusion we derived above – both Mexico *and* the US are better off specializing in the good where they have the lower opportunity cost, or comparative advantage, and trading 6 shirts for 1 tool – still holds. We assumed nothing about how productive either country was when we derived this conclusion. Since the logic was airtight, the conclusion holds even if the US is more productive in the production of both tools and shirts, i.e. has an absolute advantage in both.

Where, you might ask, did the terms of trade, 1 tool for 6 shirts come from? Mainstream theorists hasten to point out that in one sense it does not matter where it came from. If there is even one terms of trade that distributes part of the efficiency gain from specialization and trade to each country, all the conclusions of mainstream trade theory we derived above do follow. But there is more we can say about terms of trade that is very important to political economists concerned with the distributive effects of trade. In our example as long as 1 tool trades for more than 4 shirts but fewer than 8 shirts both countries will benefit from specialization and trade. If 1 tool traded for fewer than 4 shirts the US would have no incentive to trade because instead of producing 1 tool and importing fewer than 4 shirts from Mexico, the US could simply move resources from its own tool industry to its own shirt industry and get 4 shirts for each tool it loses. So the opportunity cost of a tool in the US, 4 shirts, forms a lower bound on the **feasible terms of trade**, i.e. *terms of trade that leave both countries better off*. On the other hand, if 1 tool traded for more than 8 shirts Mexico would have no incentive to trade. By moving resources from its own shirt industry to its own tool industry Mexico only has to give up 8 shirts to get 1 tool. So Mexico has no reason to trade more than 8 shirts to get a tool from the US, and the opportunity cost of a tool in Mexico, 8 shirts, forms an upper bound on the feasible terms of trade. Any terms of trade in the feasible range – 1 tool trades for more than 4 shirts but fewer than 8 shirts – leave both countries better off because it distributes part of the efficiency gain from international specialization to each country. Unless Mexico were a US colony and had no choice, it would presumably refuse to trade more than 8 shirts for 1 tool, and unless the US were a colony of Mexico it would presumably refuse to trade 1 tool for fewer than 4 shirts. We will return to the all-important question of where within the feasible range the actual terms of trade will end up below, when we take up the distributive effects of trade. But note for now that since Mexico is going to be exporting shirts it is better off the *fewer* shirts trade for a tool. That is, Mexico gets a greater share of the efficiency gain the closer the terms of trade are to the opportunity cost of tools *in the US* (4 shirts). Conversely, since the US will export tools, the US is better off the *more* shirts trade for a tool. That is the US gets a greater share of the efficiency gain the closer the terms of trade are to the opportunity cost of tools *in Mexico* (8 shirts).

To review, what Ricardo proved, to the surprise of his nineteenth-century fellow economists, was that differences in opportunity costs is a sufficient condition for mutually beneficial trade, and comparative, rather than absolute advantage was the determining factor in what countries should and should not produce. In our example the opportunity cost of a tool is lower in the US (4 shirts) than it is in Mexico (8 shirts) – which gives the US a comparative advantage in tools. The opportunity cost of a shirt is lower in Mexico (⅛ tool) than it is in the US (¼ tool) – which gives Mexico a comparative advantage in shirts. As we proved above, if the terms of trade are 1 tool for 6 shirts – or more generally 1 tool for more than 4 shirts but fewer than 8 shirts – each country is better off specializing in the production of the good in which it has a comparative advantage and importing the good in which it has a comparative disadvantage. Ricardo also proved that absolute advantage plays no role in determining whether mutually beneficial specialization and trade is possible, nor in determining who should produce what. Instead opportunity costs and comparative advantage are determinant. The intuition in our example is as follows: The US is more productive than Mexico producing tools and shirts, but is *relatively* more productive making tools. That is why the US should produce tools and let Mexico produce shirts. Mexico is less productive than the US producing tools and shirts, but is *relatively* less productive making shirts. That is why Mexico should produce shirts and let the US produce tools – provided terms of trade can be agreed to that distribute part of the efficiency gain to each country.[1]

Trade theory since Ricardo has focused on reasons why opportunity costs differ between countries. Differences in climate or soil are obvious reasons countries might differ in their abilities to produce agricultural goods. Differences in the accessibility of deposits of natural resources are obvious reasons for differences in the opportunity costs of producing oil, coal, gas, and different minerals in different countries. And differences in technological know-how – with significant effects of "learning from doing" – obviously give rise to differences in opportunity costs of producing different manufactured goods. A more subtle source of differences in opportunity costs is different factor endowments. Even if technologies are identical in two countries, and even if the quality of each productive resource is the same, if countries possess productive factors in different proportions the opportunity costs of producing final goods will differ – giving rise to potential benefits from trade.

WHY TRADE CAN DECREASE GLOBAL EFFICIENCY

It is pointless to deny that if opportunity costs of producing goods are different in different countries there are potential efficiency gains from specialization and trade. The theory of comparative advantage (CA) is logically sound when it teaches that global efficiency is increased when countries specialize in making the goods they are relatively better at producing, and import the goods some other

---

1. We have implicitly assumed that we cannot move Mexican workers to the US where they become as productive as US workers. If we could move all Mexican workers to the US and they instantly became as productive as US tool and shirt makers, it would be efficient to do so and make all shirts and shoes in the US. But as long as some workers must remain in Mexico it is more efficient to have them produce something rather than nothing, and more efficient to have them produce shirts rather than tools.

country is relatively better at producing. But this does not mean specialization and trade always improve global efficiency.

Inaccurate prices misidentify comparative advantages

If commercial prices do not accurately reflect the true social opportunity costs of traded goods, free trade can produce a counterproductive pattern of specialization, yielding global efficiency losses rather than gains. If commercial prices inside a country fail to take account of significant external effects they may misidentify where the country's comparative advantage lies. And if international specialization and trade are based on *false* comparative advantages it can lead to international divisions of labor that are less productive than the less specialized patterns of global production they replace.

For example, we know the social costs of modern agricultural production in the US are greater than the private costs because environmentally destructive effects such as soil erosion, pesticide run-off, and depletion of ground water aquifers go uncounted or are undervalued. This translates into commercial prices for corn in the US that underestimate the true social cost of producing corn in the US. On the other hand, when corn is grown in Mexico farmers live in traditional Mexican villages that are relatively disease and crime free and where centuries-old social safety nets exist when family members fall on hard times. Whereas producing shoes, for example, in Mexico requires a Mexican to live in an urban slum or maquiladora zone where disease and crime are higher and social safety nets absent. The positive external effects of rural village life when corn is produced in Mexico are undercounted in the commercial price of Mexican corn. So we know the commercial price of corn divided by the commercial price of shoes is lower than the social cost of corn divided by the social cost of shoes in the US, but higher than the social cost of corn divided by the social cost of shoes in Mexico.

If the external effects are large enough, relative commercial prices in the two countries can *misidentify* which country truly has a comparative advantage in corn, and which country truly has a comparative advantage in shoes. The external effects neglected in US prices make it *look* as though corn production is less costly than it really is. The external effects neglected in Mexican prices make it *look* as though corn production is more costly than it truly is. While the ratio of the commercial price of corn to the commercial price of shoes makes it appear that the US is relatively more productive in corn production and Mexico relatively more productive in shoe production, it may be that the comparative advantage of the US is really in shoe production and Mexico's comparative advantage is actually in corn production. The problem is that even if external effects are significant enough so that taking them into account means it is more efficient to continue producing corn in Mexico and shoes in the US, free trade will lead to counterproductive specialization in which the US expands environmentally damaging corn production, importing more shoes from Mexico, while Mexico moves its population from traditional rural villages to urban slums and maquiladoras to increase shoe production, importing more corn from the US. Efficiency losses like this can happen when treaties like NAFTA increase trade based on differences in relative *commercial prices* rather than on true, relative *social costs* – which can be substantially different.[2]

Unstable international markets create macro inefficiencies

Even if international prices for traditional exports from underdeveloped economies did not decline over the long run compared to the prices they pay for imports, if prices for LDC exports are highly volatile this can damage their economies leading to global efficiency losses as well. In the first half of the twentieth century there were years when the international price of sugar was ten times higher than in other years. In years when Cuba exported sugar at 20 to 30 cents per pound the Cuban economy ran on all cylinders, but in years when sugar prices fell to 2 to 3 cents per pound the Cuban economy sputtered. The international price of tin experienced similar fluctuations during the same time period, periodically wreaking havoc with the Bolivian economy. One problem is that once the export sector reaches full capacity levels of output there is no way to take further advantage of price spikes. But unfortunately, when the bottom falls out of a traditional export market there is no lower limit on how many people can be thrown out of work and how many businesses can go bankrupt. So even if large drops in export prices in bad years were canceled entirely by equally large

---

2. Environmentalists argue that international transportation is a service where commercial prices greatly underestimate true social costs. "Remember the *Exxon Valdez!*" is the environmentalist's equivalent of "Remember the Alamo!" The discrepancy between social and commercial costs of international transportation always makes it appear that specialization and trade are more efficient than they really are.

increases in good years, LDC economies cannot benefit from price spikes as much as they get hurt when prices crash in their traditional export markets. Another problem is that economic development requires a degree of stability. If every decade a crash in the price of sugar or tin means local businesses selling to the growing domestic market go bankrupt as well, it is difficult to develop new sectors of the economy. In short, greater reliance on trade can lead to efficiency losses when international prices prove very unstable.

Adjustment costs are not always insignificant

The adjustment costs of moving people and resources out of one industry and into another can be considerable. If adjustment costs are large they can cancel a significant portion of the efficiency gain from a new pattern of international specialization – irrespective of who pays for them. If people must be retrained, if equipment is scrapped before it wears out, if new industries are located in different regions from old ones so people must move to new locations requiring new schools, parks, libraries, water and sewage systems, etc., leaving perfectly useable social infrastructure idle in "rust belt" regions they vacate, all this duplication and waste should be subtracted from any efficiency gains from further specialization and trade. Since a great deal of the adjustment costs are not paid for by the businesses who make the decisions about whether to specialize and trade, the market fails to sufficiently account for adjustment costs. Consequently, when productivity gains from some new international division of labor are meager and adjustment costs large, we can easily get efficiency losses rather than gains from trade.

Dynamic inefficiency

Finally, the theory of comparative advantage is usually interpreted as implying that a country should specialize even more in its traditional export products, since those would presumably be the industries in which the country enjoys a comparative advantage. But underdeveloped economies are less developed precisely because they have lower levels of productivity than other economies enjoy. If less developed economies further specialize in the sectors they have always specialized in, it may well be *less* likely that they will find ways to increase their productivity. In other words, increasing *static* efficiency by specializing even more in today's comparative advantages may prevent changes that would increase productivity a great deal more, and therefore be at the expense of *dynamic* efficiency.

The hallmark of the Japanese and South Korean economic miracles, and the considerable successes of the other Asian "tigers" who followed their lead, was that they did *not* accept their comparative advantages at any point in time as a *fait accompli*. Instead they aggressively pursued plans to *create* new comparative advantages in industries where it would be easier to achieve larger productivity increases. Japan moved from exporting textiles, toys, and bicycles right after World War II, to exporting steel and automobiles in the 1960s and early 1970s, to exporting electronic equipment and computer products by the late 1970s and early 1980s. This was accomplished through an elaborate system of differential tax rates and terms of credit for businesses in different industries at different times, planned by the Ministry of International Trade and Industry (MITI) and coordinated with the Bank of Japan and the taxing authorities. The whole point of the process was to create new comparative advantages in high productivity industries rather than continue to specialize in industries where productivity growth was slow. Neither Japan, South Korea, nor any of the successful Asian tigers allowed relative commercial prices in the free market to pick their comparative advantages and determine their pattern of industrialization and trade for them. Had they done so it is unlikely that they would have enjoyed their economic miracles.

WHY TRADE USUALLY AGGRAVATES GLOBAL INEQUALITY

While mainstream trade theorists are adamant in their insistence that freer trade always yields efficiency gains, and practically blind to reasons why this may not be the case, they are much quieter about the distributive effects of trade. When forced to address this unpleasant topic the academy admits to the following: (1) How any efficiency gains from trade will be distributed between trading partners depends, or course, on the terms of trade. (2) While any feasible terms of trade make both countries better off, this does not mean all groups within each country are benefitted. There will usually be losers as well as winners from trade. (3) In the short run the internal distributive effects of trade favor the owners and employees of firms in the industries in which a country has a comparative advantage and disfavor the owners and employees of firms producing goods in which a country does not have a comparative advantage. In other words, in the short run owners and workers in exporting industries benefit and owners and workers in importing industries are worse off. (4) In the long run, after resources have moved from industries where imports rise to industries where exports increase, the internal distributive effects of trade favor the owners of relatively abundant factors of production and disfavor the owners of relatively scarce factors of production. But these dispassionate observations about the distributive effects of trade can translate into global economic injustice escalating at an unprecedented pace, as we see below.

Unfair distribution of the benefits of trade between countries

While it is true that trade *could* take place on terms anywhere in the feasible range – which means that trade *could* reduce the inequality between countries if the terms distributed more of the efficiency gains to poorer countries – unfortunately, the international terms of trade *usually* distribute the lion's share of any efficiency gains to countries that were better off in the first place, and thereby aggravate global inequality. The most important reason they do this is that as long as productive capital is scarce globally, that is, as long as having more machines and equipment would allow someone, someplace in the global economy to work more productively, there is good reason to believe the terms of trade will distribute more of the efficiency gains from trade to capital rich countries. Interested readers should see Appendix B in my *Panic Rules! Everything You Need to Know About the Global Economy* (South End Press, 1999) for a simple model that demonstrates this point. There I adapt the simple corn model presented in chapter 3 of this book to include a second good, machines, to provide a good for which corn can be traded, and to play the role of productive capital. The only difference assumed between countries in the model is that "northern" countries begin with more machines than "southern" countries. Consistent with CA theory, the model predicts a global efficiency gain when northern countries specialize in machine production which is relatively capital intensive, export machines, and import corn, while southern countries specialize in corn production which is relatively labor intensive, export corn, and import machines. But the model allows us to go beyond CA theory – which merely establishes the range of feasible terms of trade – to determine where in the feasible range the "free trade" terms of trade between corn and machines will fall. As long as capital is scarce globally, *even when the international markets for corn and machines are both assumed to be competitive*, free market terms of trade give more of the efficiency gain from trade to northern countries than to southern countries, making global inequality greater than it would have been without trade.[3]

The intuition is straightforward: When northern countries specialize in producing machines in which they have a comparative advantage, and southern economies specialize in corn which is their comparative advantage, there should be an efficiency gain. But as long as machines are scarce compared to labor globally, the southern economies compete among themselves for scarce machines, turning the terms of trade against themselves and in favor of the northern countries. In other words, as long as machines are scarce, northern countries who own more machines will be in a position to command a greater share of the efficiency gain from trade than southern countries. The implications are profound: *Even if international markets are competitive, free market terms of trade will aggravate global inequality in the normal course of events.*

Political economists from the Global South have identified additional factors that adversely affect the terms of trade for southern exports compared to southern imports. (1) If capital intensive industries are characterized by a faster pace of innovation than labor intensive industries, the simple corn–machine model discussed above predicts the terms of trade will deteriorate for southern countries. (2) When people's incomes rise the proportion of their income they spend on different goods often changes. Unfortunately many underdeveloped countries export goods people buy

3. In our simple corn model in chapter 3 the interest rate distributed the efficiency gain from the increased productivity of borrowers when their borrowed seed corn allowed them to use the more productive CIT instead of the less productive LIT. In that simple model as long as seed corn was scarce, borrowers competed among themselves and bid interest rates up to the point where the *entire* efficiency gain went to the lenders. In the simple corn–machine model of international trade the terms of trade distribute the efficiency gain when imported machines allow southern countries to produce corn using a more productive technology. In this model as long as machines are scarce, southern countries compete among themselves to import more machines by offering to pay more corn for a machine until the terms of trade become favorable to northern machine exporters, who thereby capture most of the increased efficiency in the southern economies. However, there is one slight difference: Even in simple models, free market terms of trade do not necessarily distribute the *entire* efficiency gain to the northern countries. One interpretation of this difference is that international trade is sometimes a less "efficient" means of international exploitation than international credit markets.

less of when their income rises and import goods people buy more of when their income rises. This erodes the terms of trade for LDCs as world income increases. (3) If trade unions are stronger in more developed economies than less developed economies, wage costs will hold steadier in MDCs than LDCs during global downturns, leading to a deterioration in the terms of trade for LDCs. Finally, (4) if MDCs export products that are more differentiated, or MDC exporters have more market power than LDC exporters, the terms of trade will be even more disadvantageous to LDCs than would be the case if international markets were all equally competitive.

All this leads to the conclusion that if left to market forces the terms of international trade *will* continue to award more developed economies a greater share of any efficiency gains from increased international specialization and trade. But this does not mean that trade must, necessarily, aggravate global inequality. Ironically, the easiest way to reduce global inequality is through trade simply by setting the terms of trade to distribute more of the efficiency gain to poorer countries than richer ones. The existence and size of any efficiency gain from specialization and trade does *not* depend on the terms of trade at all. The terms of trade merely distribute the efficiency gain between the trading partners. The efficiency gain they distribute is the same size no matter where in the feasible range the terms of trade fall. So there are just as many mutually advantageous terms of trade that reduce global inequality as terms that increase global inequality. Moreover, unlike foreign aid where donors do not gain materially, even terms of trade that give poor countries two-thirds of the efficiency gain would still give their more wealthy trading partners one-third of the efficiency gain, and therefore leave wealthier countries better off than they would be without trade. But this will not happen if the terms of trade are left to market forces. This can only happen if international terms of trade are determined through international political negotiation where all parties share a commitment to reducing global inequality as well as increasing global efficiency. The only reason trade cannot be used to reduce global inequality is because the political will to do so is lacking among northern governments.

Unfair distribution of the costs and benefits of trade within countries

When the gap between rich and poor countries increases, global inequality rises. But when the gap between the rich and poor *within* countries increases, global inequality rises as well. Unfortunately inequality of wealth and income inside both MDCs and LDCs has been rising steadily over the past 20 years, and there is good reason to believe the expansion of trade is partly to blame. To understand why trade has aggravated inequalities inside MDCs we need go no farther than mainstream trade theory itself. After David Ricardo's theory of comparative advantage, the most famous theory in international economics is due to two Scandinavian economists, Eli Heckscher and Bertil Ohlin. According to Heckscher-Ohlin theory, countries will have a comparative advantage in goods that use inputs, or factors of production, in which the country is relatively abundant. But this means trade increases the demand for relatively abundant factors of production and decreases the demand for factors that are relatively scarce within countries. In advanced economies where the capital–labor ratio is higher than elsewhere, and therefore capital is "relatively abundant," Heckscher-Ohlin theory predicts that increased trade will increase the demand for capital, increasing its return, and decrease the demand for labor, depressing wages. Of course this is exactly what has occurred in the US, making the AFL-CIO a consistent critic of trade liberalization. In advanced economies where the ratio of skilled to unskilled labor is higher than elsewhere, Heckscher-Ohlin theory also predicts that increased trade will increase the demand for skilled labor and decrease the demand for unskilled labor and thereby increase wage differentials. In a study published by the very mainstream Institute for International Economics in 1997, William Cline estimates that 39% of the increase in wage inequality in the US over the previous 20 years was due solely to increased trade.

However, Heckscher-Ohlin theory cannot explain rising inequality inside the lesser developed economies. As a matter of fact, Heckscher-Ohlin theory predicts just the opposite. Increased trade should increase returns to labor, and unskilled labor in particular, since those are relatively abundant factors in most LDCs, while reducing the returns to capital and skilled labor since those are relatively scarce factors in underdeveloped economies. In other words, Heckscher-Ohlin theory predicts that increased trade should aggravate inequalities within advanced economies, but should decrease inequalities within third world economies.

The problem is not with Heckscher and Ohlin's logic – which like the logic of comparative advantage theory is impeccable. The problem is that all theories implicitly assume no changes in other dynamics the theory does not address. Economic theories are famous for the qualifying phrase *ceteris paribus* – all other things remaining equal. When the real world does not cooperate with the theorist, and allows other dynamics to proceed, we often find the predictions of some particular theory are not borne out. That is not necessarily because the theory was flawed. It can simply be because the predicted effects of the theory are overwhelmed by the effects of some other dynamic the theory never pretended to take into account. In this case I believe the dynamics unaccounted for in Heckscher-Ohlin theory are powerful dynamics affecting third world agriculture.

First, the so-called "Green Revolution" made much of the rural labor force redundant in third world agriculture. Then neoliberal globalization accelerated the replacement of small scale, peasant farming for domestic production by large scale, export-oriented agriculture dominated by large landholders, and increasingly by multinational agribusiness. To be sure third world peasants make a miserable living on the land by first world standards. But they make a better living than their cousins crowded around every major city in the third world from Lima to Sao Paulo to Lagos to Cape Town to Bombay to Bangkok to Manila. While cash incomes are meager in third world agriculture, they are better than joblessness and beggary in third world cities.

Two decades ago large amounts of land in the third world had a sufficiently low value to permit billions of peasant households to live on it, producing mostly for their own consumption, even though their productivity was quite low. The green revolution, globalization, and export oriented agriculture have raised the value of that land. Peasant squatters are no longer tolerated. Peasant renters are thrown off by owners who want to use the land for more valuable export crops. Even peasants who own their family plots fall easy prey to local economic and political elites who now see a far more valuable use for that land and have become more aggressive land-grabbers through a variety of legal and extralegal means. And finally, as third world governments succumb to pressure from the IMF, World Bank, and WTO to relax restrictions on foreign ownership of land, local land sharks are joined by multinational agribusinesses, adding to the human exodus. The combined effect of these forces has driven literally billions of peasants out of rural areas into teeming, third world megacities in a very short period of time. This means there are many more ex-peasants applying for new labor intensive manufacturing jobs produced by trade liberalization and international investment in third world countries than there are new jobs.

Even a casual glance at the scale of the human exodus from traditional agriculture explains why unemployment is increasing, not decreasing, and wage rates are falling, not rising, in underdeveloped economies. Political economists like David Barkin of the Autonomous University of Mexico do not claim that trade liberalization has not created some new jobs in Mexican manufacturing – as Heckscher-Ohlin theory predicts it should have. Instead Barkin[4] and other Mexican political economists point out that disastrous changes in Mexican agriculture, induced in part by terms of the NAFTA agreement, negate any small beneficial Heckscher-Ohlin effects on employment and wages that might have been expected, and explain the large increases in overall *un*employment and the dramatic *fall* in real wages that have occurred since the Mexican government signed the NAFTA treaty.

WHY INTERNATIONAL INVESTMENT CAN INCREASE GLOBAL EFFICIENCY

International investment between the north and south can take the form of multinational companies (MNCs) from more developed countries building subsidiaries in less developed countries.[5] This is called *direct foreign investment*, or DFI. Alternatively, international investment can take the form of multinational banks from MDCs lending to companies or governments in LDCs, or wealthy individuals or mutual funds from MDCs buying stocks of LDC companies, or bonds of LDC companies or governments. This is called *international financial investment*. As was the case with international trade, mainstream economic theory focuses on the potentially beneficial effects of both kinds of international investment and largely ignores the potentially damaging effects.

If machinery and know-how increase productivity more when located in a subsidiary in a southern economy than they do when located in a plant in the home country of the MNC, DFI increases

4. David Barkin, *Wealth, Poverty and Sustainable Development* (Mexico: Editorial JUS, 1998).
5. While most international investment still takes place between northern countries, I focus on north–south investment because that is of greater interest to political economists concerned with global inequality.

global efficiency. If a loan to a foreign borrower increases productivity more abroad than it would have if lent in-country, international financial investment increases global efficiency. Mainstream theory assumes that if profits are higher from DFI than domestic investment this is because the investment raises productivity more abroad than at home. So according to mainstream theory when MNCs invest wherever profits are highest they will serve the interest of global efficiency as well as their own. Similarly, mainstream theory assumes if foreign borrowers are willing to pay higher interest rates than domestic borrowers this is because the loan raises foreign productivity more than it would domestic productivity. So mainstream international finance teaches that when multinational banks lend wherever they can get the highest rate of interest they serve the social interest as well as their own. Of course this is nothing more than Adam Smith's vision of a beneficent invisible hand at work in some new settings. In chapter 9 we study international investment in a simple corn model. Not surprisingly we discover that when we assume northern lenders all find southern borrowers whose productivity is enhanced by the loans they receive, opening an international credit market increases global economic efficiency.

WHY INTERNATIONAL INVESTMENT CAN DECREASE GLOBAL EFFICIENCY

But where mainstream economists see only beneficent invisible hands at work, political economists notice malevolent invisible feet lurking nearby. Political economists focus on why the social interest may not coincide so nicely with the private interests of multinational companies and banks. Just because DFI is more profitable does not mean the plant and machinery are more productive than they would have been at home. DFI might be more profitable because the bargaining power of third world workers is even less than that of their first world counterparts. Or DFI might be more profitable because third world governments are more desperate to woo foreign investors and offer larger tax breaks and lower environmental standards to businesses locating there. Neither of these reasons why profits from DFI might be higher than profits from domestic operations imply that the plant, machinery or know-how raises productivity more abroad than it would have at home. If the reverse were the case, more DFI would decrease global efficiency, not increase it, even if profits from foreign operations are higher than from domestic operations.

It is also not necessarily the case that just because foreign borrowers are willing to pay higher rates of interest, loans are more useful or productive there than at home. When a dictator in Zaire borrowed hundreds of millions at exorbitant interest rates he used the loans to line the pockets of his family and political allies and to buy weapons to intimidate his subjects. There was no increase in economic productivity in Zaire, and consequently little with which to pay back international creditors after Mobutu departed. But a more serious problem with international lending is that when production in developing economies is tied more tightly to the international credit system and the credit system breaks down, real economies and their inhabitants suffer huge losses of production, employment, and capital accumulation. Below I explain why the international credit system aggravates global inequality even when it functions normally and avoids financial crises. But when international investors panic and sell off their currency holdings, stocks, and bonds in an "emerging market economy," there are huge efficiency losses in the emerging market "real" economy, and therefore the "real" global economy as well.

In chapter 9 we explore the downside potential of international finance by appending an international financial sector with unstable potentials to our simple international corn model. This more realistic model illustrates graphically how rational behavior on the part of international investors can lead to international financial crises, and how this can make the real global economy less, rather than more, efficient. The intuition is quite simple: When all goes well in the international financial system it can increase the number of loans that increase economic productivity. But there is a downside as well as an upside potential. What proponents of international financial liberalization don't like to admit is that when we tie real economies more tightly to the international credit system, if a financial crisis occurs, the real global economy suffers efficiency losses, not gains. Moreover, a great deal of the international financial liberalization that has been orchestrated by neoliberals in power at the IMF, World Bank, WTO, OECD, and US Treasury Department has not only lashed emerging market economies more tightly to the international credit system, it as made the international financial system a great deal more unstable and therefore dangerous. In many ways what were called international financial "reforms" in fact created an accident waiting to happen.

WHY INTERNATIONAL INVESTMENT USUALLY AGGRAVATES GLOBAL INEQUALITY

The model of international investment in a simple corn economy in chapter 9 illustrates how international lending *can* increase global efficiency, but also why it *usually* increases global income inequality as well. Global efficiency rises when international loans from northern economies raise productivity more in southern economies than they would have raised productivity domestically. But when capital is scarce globally, as it has always been and will continue to be for the foreseeable future, competition among southern borrowers drives interest rates on international loans up to the point where lenders capture the greater part of the efficiency gain. In the simple international corn model in chapter 9 we assume that the international credit market works perfectly without interruption or crisis, and therefore generates the maximum global efficiency gain. But as long as seed corn is scarce globally, southern borrowers will bid interest rates up to the point where the entire efficiency gain in their productivity is captured by northern lenders. So even when international financial markets work smoothly and efficiently, they *usually* increase income inequality between countries.

As explained above, when we append a more realistic version of international finance to the international corn model in chapter 9, we discover how international financial crises can cause efficiency losses in the "real" economies of developing countries. Moreover, we discover that such crises can result from perfectly rational behavior on the part of international investors. But lost employment and production in Thailand, Malaysia, Indonesia, and South Korea were not the only casualties of the East Asian financial crisis of 1997–98. That crisis, in particular, highlighted how liberalizing international finance can increase global wealth inequality as well as global income inequality. Sandra Sugawara reported from Bangkok in the *Washington Post* on November 28, 1998:

> Hordes of foreign investors are flowing back into Thailand, boosting room rates at top Bangkok hotels despite the recession. Foreign investors have gone on a $6.7 billion shopping spree this year, snapping up bargain-basement steel mills, securities

companies, supermarket chains and other assets. A few pages behind stories about layoffs and bankruptcies are large help-wanted ads run by multinational companies. General Electric Capital Corp., which increased its stake in Thailand this year through three major investments in financing and credit card companies, is seeking hundreds of experts in finance and accounting, according to one ad.

In an article entitled "Asia's Doors Now Wide Open to American Business" Nicholas Kristof expanded on this theme in the *New York Times* on February 1, 1999:

"This is a crisis, but it is also a tremendous opportunity for the US," said Muthiah Alagappa, a Malaysian scholar at the East-West Center in Honolulu. "This strengthens the position of American companies in Asia." A clear indication that the Asian crisis would further the American agenda came in December, when 102 nations agreed to open their financial markets to foreign companies beginning in 1999. It is an important victory for the US, which excels in banking, insurance and securities. Fundamentally that agreement and other changes are coming about because Asian countries, their economies gasping, are now less single-minded in their concern about maintaining control. Desperate for cash, they are less able to pick and choose, less able to withstand American or monetary fund demands that they open up. In Thailand, under pressure from the monetary fund, the government was forced to scrap a regulation that limited foreign corporations to a 25 percent stake in Thai financial companies. In Indonesia, the government has said foreign banks can take a stake in a major new bank that will be formed from several weaker ones. "All our stocks and companies are dirt-cheap," said Jusuf Wanandi, the head of a research institute in Jakarta, Indonesia. "There may be a tendency for foreigners to take over everything."

Kristof concluded:

One of the most far-reaching consequences of the Asian financial crisis will be a greatly expanded American business presence in Asia – particularly in markets like banking that have historically been sensitive and often closed. Market pressures – principally desperation for cash – and some arm-twisting by the US and the IMF mean that Western companies are gaining entry to previously closed Asian markets. Asian countries have been steadily opening their economies in recent years, but they have generally been much more willing to admit McDonalds than Citibank. Governments in the region have sometimes owned banks and almost always controlled them, and leaders frequently regarded pinstriped American bankers as uncontrollable, untrustworthy and unpredictable barbarians at their gates. And now the gates are giving way. And the timing from the US point of view, is perfect: regulations are being eased just as Asian banks, securities, even airlines are coming on the market at bargain prices ... Stock prices and currencies have now plunged so far that it may cost less than one-fifth last summer's prices to buy an Indonesian or Thai company. "This is the best time to buy," said Divyang Shah, an economist in Singapore for IDEA a financial consulting company. "It's like a fire sale."

What I called the "Great Global Asset Swindle" when writing about it in *Z Magazine* in the aftermath of the Asian financial crisis works like this: International investors lose confidence in a third world economy – dumping its currency, bonds and stocks. At the insistence of the IMF, the central bank in the third world country tightens the money supply to boost domestic interest rates to prevent further capital outflows in an unsuccessful attempt to protect the currency. Even healthy domestic companies can no longer obtain or afford loans so they join the ranks of bankrupted domestic businesses available for purchase. As a precondition for receiving the IMF bailout the government abolishes any remaining restrictions on foreign ownership of corporations, banks, and land. With a depreciated local currency, and a long list of bankrupt local businesses, the economy is ready for the acquisition experts from Western multinational corporations and banks who come to the fire sale with a thick wad of almighty dollars in their pockets.

In conclusion, international investment *can* increase global efficiency if it helps allocate productive know-how and resources to uses where they are more valuable. But international investment *can* decrease global efficiency when profitability is *not* coincident with productivity, and particularly when it ties real economies ever more tightly to an unstable credit system that crashes with increasing frequency. International investment *could* reduce global inequality if interest rates on international loans were low enough to distribute more of the efficiency gain to borrowers than to lenders. After all, there is no economic "law" that says international borrowing *must* increase global inequality. Just as there are always fair terms of trade that diminish global inequality, there are obviously interest rates that would permit southern economies to enjoy more of the benefits of improved global efficiency. But those interest rates are seldom free market interest rates. Unfortunately, agencies like the Inter American Development Bank and World Bank have cut back on what they call "subsidized" loans.[6] Worse still, subsidized loans from international agencies are now mainly used as carrots to go along with the stick of international credit boycotts used to cajole and threaten debtor nations reluctant to subject their citizens to the deprivations of IMF austerity programs, and place their most attractive economic assets on the international auction block at bargain basement prices. So, unfortunately, international investment *will* increase inequality when interest rates are determined by market forces in a world where capital is scarce, and where international financial crises create bargain basement sales for third world business assets no longer off limits to foreign bargain hunters. International investment is a two-edged sword. Recently the side of the blade with positive potentials has gone dull, while the side that destroys real developing economies and aggravates global inequality is cutting ever more sharply in the brave, new, neoliberal global economy.

Most mainstream economists believe neoliberal globalization has produced significant efficiency gains, while admittedly increasing global inequality. Evidence of escalating inequality is so overwhelming that nobody dares deny it, and for all who wish to see, it stands out as the most salient characteristic of the global economy during the past quarter-century. But there is *no* evidence whatsoever suggesting efficiency gains. As a matter of fact, there is overwhelming evidence that neoliberal policies have slowed global growth rates significantly. A report prepared by Angus Maddison for the Organization for Economic Cooperation and Development (OECD) titled

6. "Subsidized loans" is the term used to denigrate loans at less than free market interest rates. Since interest rates that promote greater global equality rather than inequality are almost always below free market interest rates, this means the *only* international loans deserving the support of progressives are "subsidized loans," and loans at free market interest rates should be recognized for what they are – vehicles of unjustifiable international exploitation.

Monitoring the World Economy 1820–1992 published in 1995 refuted the popular impression that neoliberal policies had increased world economic growth. Maddison compared growth rates in the seven major regions of the world from 1950 to 1973 – the Bretton Woods era – to growth rates from 1974 to 1992 – the neoliberal era – and found there had been significant *declines* in the annual average rate of growth of GDP per capita in six of the seven regions, and only a slight increase in one region, Asia. Maddison reported that the average annual rate of growth of world GDP per capita during the neoliberal period was only *half* what it had been in the Bretton Woods era. In *Scorecard on Globalization 1980–2000: Twenty Years of Diminished Progress* <www.cepr.net> the Center for Economic Policy Research updated Maddison's work and reconfirmed his conclusion that neoliberal policies continue to be accompanied by a significant *decrease* in the rate of growth of world GDP per capita. If dismantling the Bretton Woods system while promoting capital and trade liberalization had really produced more efficiency gains than losses, it is hard to imagine how world growth rates would have been cut in half!

Ignoring overwhelming evidence of diminished performance, focusing only on the beneficial *potentials* of trade and capital liberalization, and ignoring all adverse effects on the environment and income and wealth inequality are all part of the "free market jubilee" that swept the world's intellectual and policy making elites beginning in the 1980s. One example of uncritical support for global economic liberalization was a series titled "For Richer or Poorer" that ran in the *Washington Post* from December 29, 1996 through January 1, 1997. John Cavanagh, director of the Institute for Policy Studies, and an early critic of corporate sponsored globalization, was limited to a one-column rebuttal published almost two weeks later. Nonetheless, Cavanagh provides an excellent list of adverse consequences of global liberalization in "Failures of Free Trade" which is a fitting conclusion to this part of our chapter: (1) *Rising Inequality*: Cavanagh reports that calculations by IPS researchers "show that at least two-thirds of the world's people are left out, hurt or marginalized by globalization." (2) *Dwindling Jobs and Wages*: Jobs that provide economic security and decent working conditions are disappearing as globalization pits workers in more developed countries against hundreds of millions of desperate men, women and children in underdeveloped economies. (3) *Casino Economies*: "While offering new profit opportunities to the global investing elite," opening up stock and financial markets "is turning Third World economies into casinos vulnerable to the whims of those who manage the world's mutual and other investment funds." (4) *Environmental Plunder*: A large part of the meager economic growth that has occurred in the third world "has been centered on some combination of tearing down forests, over fishing, rapid depletion of minerals and poisoning of land by agri-chemicals." (5) *Community Collapse*: "Many of the rural communities that are bypassed or undermined by globalization were well-functioning social units where hundreds of millions of subsistence farmers and fisher folk have earned a livelihood for decades. While poor in terms of cash income, these communities often score high in terms of nutrition, social peace and even education." (6) *Democracy in Danger*: "In country after country, policies are adapted to serve the needs of global firms ... as corporate contributions become the determining factor in elections the world over."

THE BALANCE OF PAYMENTS ACCOUNTS

Countries engage in international trade and investment activities which economists keep track of in a **balance of payments account** (BOP). When companies sell goods or services produced in the US to buyers from other countries we call this US **exports**. When US businesses or consumers buy goods and services produced in other countries we call this US **imports**. US trading activity is kept track of in what we call the **trade account** of the US balance of payments account. When US businesses buy or build a plant abroad (US direct foreign investment), when foreign companies build subsidiaries in the US (foreign direct foreign investment in the US), when US citizens or corporations buy foreign financial assets (US international financial investment), or foreigners buy US financial assets (foreign financial investment in the US), or when any businesses or citizens repatriate profits or earnings from foreign investments, we call this **international investment** and keep track of all this activity in the **capital account** of the US balance of payments account. The balance of payments are merely an accounting system to keep track of all the international economic activity a country engages in – divided into a trade account and capital account to keep track of trade and investment activity respectively. However, we can use the balance of payment accounts to learn whether the value of a country's currency is likely to rise or fall, and whether a country is "positioned" favorably or unfavorably in the global economy.

When US citizens, corporations, or government agencies engage in any international economic activity, or when foreigners engage in any economic activity with the US, there is always a flow of dollars either into or out of the US. When thinking about the flow of dollars that results from international trade and investment it is easiest to think of an international currency, or foreign exchange market, located somewhere outside the US. When dollars flow out of the US they flow into this international currency market and add to the supply of dollars there, and when dollars flow into the US they come from the international currency market and therefore reduce the supply of dollars in foreign exchange markets. The organizing principle of the balance of payments account is to count any activity that results in an inflow of dollars back into the US (from the international currency market) as a surplus, with a plus sign, and to count any activity that results in an outflow of dollars from the US (into the international currency market) as a deficit, with a minus sign.

The Trade Account: When US businesses or consumers buy imports they take dollars from inside the US out into the international currency market to buy the foreign currency they need to purchase the import. So when US businesses or consumers buy imports, goods flow in – adding to the aggregate supply of goods and services in the US – and dollars flow out of the US to pay for them. When foreigners buy US exports they use their currency to buy dollars in the international currency market to pay the US exporter who brings those dollars back into the US. So when foreigners buy US exports they add to the aggregate demand for US made goods or services, and dollars flow into the US to pay for the goods flowing out.

The Short Run Capital Account: When a US multinational company builds a subsidiary abroad, or when a US pension fund buys foreign bonds, dollars flow out of the US into the international currency market to buy the foreign currency needed to buy the foreign asset.

The Long Run Capital Account: If at some point in the future the US multinational company repatriates profits from its foreign subsidiary, or if the US pension fund repatriates earnings from its foreign bond holdings, they will trade their foreign currency earnings for dollars in the international currency market and bring the dollars back into the US in some future year. Conversely, if foreigners engage in either business or financial investment in the

US, dollars flow into the US during the year in which they make the investment (recorded in the short run capital account), and flow out of the US in some future year if foreigners repatriate profits or earnings (recorded in the long run capital account).

Countries can run a deficit or surplus in any of the three parts of their balance of payments accounts. The trade account can be in surplus if exports exceed imports, or in deficit if imports exceed exports. The short run capital account can be in surplus if new foreign direct and financial investment in the US exceeds new US direct and financial investment abroad during a year, or in deficit if new US international investments exceed new foreign investments in the US. The long run capital account can be in surplus if US corporations and citizens repatriate more profits and earnings back into the US than foreign investors repatriate out of the US to their home countries, or in deficit if foreign repatriations exceed US repatriations during a year. The overall balance of payments deficit or surplus is just the summation of the deficits and surpluses in the trade, short run, and long run capital accounts.

If we simply want to know what is likely to happen to the value of a nation's currency in the near future, we only have to look at the overall balance of payments surplus or deficit. But if we want to know whether a country is doing well or poorly in the international division of labor we have to look at where and why the deficits or surpluses are occurring in the trade, short run, and long run capital accounts.

If the US runs a $100 billion balance of payments deficit in a given year this means there are 100 billion more dollars in the international currency market at the end of the year than there were at the beginning of the year – and we would expect the value of the dollar to fall in foreign exchange markets, *ceteris paribus*. If Japan runs a 10,000 billion yen surplus on its balance of payments account in a given year, this means there are 10,000 billion fewer yen in international currency markets at the end of the year than there were at the beginning of the year – and we would expect the value of the yen to rise, *ceteris paribus*. In this context when we say the value of the dollar has fallen, been *devalued*, or *depreciated* we mean the dollar will buy fewer yen, francs, pesos, etc. in international currency markets, and when we say the value of the yen has risen, been *revalued*, or *appreciated* we mean a yen will buy more dollars, francs, pesos, etc. in foreign exchange markets.

While an overall balance of payments deficit puts downward pressure on a nation's currency, and a balance of payments surplus puts upward pressure on the value of a country's currency, whether or not a country has a BOP deficit or surplus tells us little about how well a country is doing in the global economy. Trade deficits can mean a country is being out-competed by foreign producers, but it could simply mean the country's currency is overvalued making its exports too expensive for foreigners to buy and foreign imports cheap compared to domestically produced goods. A deficit in the short run capital account could mean a country is not attractive to foreign investors, but it could also mean the country's businesses are busy buying and building subsidiaries abroad. Great Britain ran large deficits on its short run capital account during the nineteenth century because it was acquiring an empire on which the sun never set. The US ran large deficits on its short run capital account in the 1950s and 1960s as US businesses expanded rapidly into Europe, Latin America, the Middle East, and Asia in the aftermath of World War II. Clearly those capital account deficits were not signs of economic decline.

OPEN ECONOMY MACRO ECONOMICS AND IMF CONDITION-ALITY AGREEMENTS

In chapters 6 and 7 we learned how aggregate demand explains the causes of some kinds of unemployment and inflation, and studied the logic of fiscal and monetary policies designed to alleviate those problems. But in those chapters we assumed the economy did not participate in, or was "closed" off from, international economic activities. Since fiscal and monetary policy affect a country's exports, imports, international investments, and the value of its currency, we need to extend our thinking when an economy is "open" to international trade and investment. Similarly, while the closed economy macro model in chapter 9 is sufficient for some purposes, we need the open economy macro model in chapter 9 to understand things like the logic of IMF conditionality agreements.

In an open economy, besides domestic production, imports add to the supply of final goods and services available. And besides the demand that comes from the domestic household, business, and government sectors, foreign demand for exports adds to the demand for final goods and services. So when we write the equilibrium condition for an open economy we have:

$Y + M = AS = AD = C + I + G + X$; which is traditionally written:
$Y = C + I + G + X - M$

where M stands for imports and X stands for exports. Imports depend positively on the value of a country's currency, on its rate of inflation, and on the country's income. If the currency appreciates imports become cheaper compared to domestic goods. If the inflation rate is higher than it is in a country's trading partners, imports also become cheaper than domestic goods. Finally, just as consumers will buy more domestically produced goods when their income is higher, they will buy more imported goods as well. Exports depend negatively on the value of a country's currency and on its inflation rate compared to the inflation rates in its trading partners. If a country's currency appreciates its exports become more expensive to foreign buyers. If the inflation rate is higher than it is in a country's trading partners, it also becomes more expensive for foreigners to buy its exports. In the simple open economy macro model in chapter 9 we express imports only as a positive, linear function of domestic income:

$$M = m + MPM(Y); m > 0; 0 < MPM < 1$$

where MPM is the marginal propensity to import out of income, and m is the amount a country will import independent of fluctuations in its national income.

There is an important change in the size of the multipliers when we change from a closed to an open economy model. In a closed economy when production rises to meet new demand and income rises as a result, the new income can go into new taxes, savings, or consumption. To the extent that new income goes into taxes or savings there is no further stimulus to aggregate demand, and no "multiplier effect." To the extent that new income goes into consumption spending it stimulates further production. But in an open economy not all consumption spending stimulates domestic production. If consumers buy domestically produced goods there is still a "multiplier effect" *vis-à-vis* the domestic economy. But to the extent that consumers buy imported goods, their new demand stimulates production abroad, not in their home economy. This implies that income expenditure multipliers in the open economy model must be smaller than in the closed economy model, and that the multipliers for "trading" economies like Japan and Great Britain will be smaller than multipliers for relatively self-contained economies like the US. The marginal propensity to import in Japan and Britain is close to 50% – since those countries export close to half of what they produce and import close to half of what they consume. While the MPM in the US is slightly over 10%, which means the multiplier effect of changes in aggregate demand are greater in the US than in Japan or Britain. The open economy multiplier, [1/(1 – MPC + MPM)], is smaller than its closed economy counterpart, [1/(1 – MPC)]. In other words in an open economy where part of any new income is spent on imports, the overall change in equilibrium GDP, ΔY, is equal to this new, somewhat smaller multiplier times whatever the initial change in aggregate demand many be. If the government changes its spending by ΔG, we multiply this by the new multiplier to find out how much equilibrium GDP will change, ΔY. If the government changes taxes by ΔT we multiply –MPCΔT by the new multiplier. If business investment demand changes by ΔI we multiply this by the new multiplier. Finally, there is a new component of aggregate demand that might change initially: exports. If foreign demand for exports changes by ΔX we multiply this by the new multiplier [1/(1 – MPC + MPM)] to find out how much equilibrium GDP will change as a result.

In the simple, open economy model in chapter 9 we express the net inflow on the capital account of the balance of payments as a positive, linear function of domestic interest rates: KF = 1000r – k where r is expressed as a decimal. This simple relationship is sufficient to capture the most important determinant of changes in short run capital flows. When domestic interest rates fall relative to interest rates in the rest of the world fewer foreigners will invest their financial wealth in a country, and more domestic wealth holders will invest abroad where interest rates are higher. Conversely, a rise in domestic interest rates relative to the rest of the world induces an inflow of foreign financial investment in response to the higher interest payments, and reduces the outflow of domestic financial investment. As regulations on international capital movements have been removed, and as the pool of liquid global wealth has grown, tens of billions of dollars often move in a matter of hours in response to changes in relative interest rates in different countries. This gives us an overall balance of payments equation:

$$BOP = X – M + KF = X – [m + MPC(Y)] + [1000r – k]$$

When we make these amendments to our macro model we can calculate trade and balance of payments deficits or surpluses, as well as unemployment or inflation gaps and government budget deficits or surpluses, for any "state" of the economy. And we can calculate the effects of fiscal and monetary policy on the trade, capital, and balance of payments accounts, as well as their effects on equilibrium GDP, the budget deficit, and the composition of output.

In chapter 9 we use this simple open economy macro model to predict the effects of IMF conditionality agreements and understand why they give rise to such controversy. In exchange for a "bail out loan" that allows the country to pay off international loans coming due that it would otherwise have to default on, IMF "conditionality agreements" typically demand that the recipient government reduce spending and increase taxes, and the central bank reduce the money supply – in addition to demanding removal of restrictions on international trade and investment and foreign ownership. Since the economy is invariably already in recession, fiscal and monetary "austerity" further aggravate the recession. Reducing government spending and increasing taxes both decrease aggregate demand, and therefore decrease employment and production. Reducing the money supply raises interest rates, which reduces investment demand and further decreases aggregate demand, employment, and production. This is why IMF "structural adjustment" and "conditionality" programs elicit strong opposition from citizens of countries whose economies are already producing far below their meager potentials – often resulting in anti-IMF riots.

But it would be wrong to assume that IMF economists are ignorant of standard macro economic theory, or that the IMF is gratuitously sadistic. The IMF policies are designed to increase the probability that the country will be able to repay its international creditors, and makes perfect sense once one realizes this is their goal. If the government is in danger of defaulting on its "sovereign" international debt, forcing it to turn budget deficits into surpluses provides funds for repaying its international creditors. If the private sector is in danger of default, anything that reduces imports and increases exports, or increases the inflow of new international investment will provide foreign exchange needed for debt repayment. Deflationary fiscal and monetary policy reduces aggregate demand and therefore inflation, which tends to increase exports and decrease imports. By reducing aggregate demand deflationary fiscal and monetary policy also reduces output, and therefore income, which further reduces imports. Tight monetary policy raises domestic interest rates which reduces the outflow of domestic financial investment and increases the inflow of new foreign financial investment, providing more foreign exchange to pay off the international creditors whose loans are coming due. Finally, since all in the country who owe foreign creditors receive their income in local currency, anything that keeps the local currency from depreciating will allow debtors to buy more dollars with their local currency, which is what they need to pay their international creditors. IMF austerity programs are well designed to turn stricken economies into more effective debt repayment machines as quickly as possible.

There is little, if any, disagreement among economists about what the short run effects of fiscal and monetary austerity policies will be. Instead, we have a simple conflict of priorities: If the interests of international creditors are given priority, the IMF programs make perfectly good sense. They are only counterproductive if one cares about employment, output, capital accumulation, and prospects for economic development in economies where the poorest 4 billion people in the world live and suffer. This conflict of interest is demonstrated formally in chapter 9 where we apply our simple open economy macro model to a stylized IMF conditionality program for Brazil.

Sometimes the extra complications introduced by the international sector are important to understand why political administrations behave as they do. We close this chapter with an example from the late 1970s. Progressive observers were justifiably disappointed in the economic policies of the Carter Administration from 1976–80. In the 1975 election campaign incumbent President Gerald Ford announced that he considered inflation a more serious problem than unemployment. Democratic challenger Jimmy Carter said he was of exactly the opposite opinion, and promised that, if elected, his administration would work to reduce unemployment first and worry about inflation second. But Carter Administration economic policy from 1976 to 1980 appeared to do just the opposite. It looked to progressive critics as if Carter had reneged on his campaign promise – that while the American electorate had voted for a government that promised to tackle unemployment with conviction, instead they got a government that behaved like the Republican candidate they had not voted for. But the "betrayal" that catapulted Ted Kennedy into the 1980 Democratic primaries to run against an incumbent Democratic president, and the fiscal and monetary policies that maximized the unemployment rate during Carter's first term on election day – a remarkable display of political ineptitude – were not as simple or stupid as they appeared to many outraged liberals at the time.

The US trade account deficit jumped from just over $7 billion to just under $40 billion between 1975 and 1976, and then to almost $65 billion in 1977 putting serious downward pressure on the value of the dollar. What made this particularly worrisome was that Saudi Arabia was Washington's ally inside OPEC and had prevented the OPEC oil price increases from being even greater by increasing its own production and sales. Since the oil price increases were widely believed to be responsible for a substantial part of the stagflation – rising unemployment *and* rising inflation – that rocked the European and US economies in the 1970s, Carter deemed it critical to persuade the Saudis not to abandon their opposition to the majority of their Arab brethren in OPEC who wanted to cut world supplies and boost oil prices even further. But the Saudis were asking why they should continue to trade oil for dollars if the value of the dollar was going to continue to fall – as it surely would if US trade deficits continued to rise. If the dollar was going to fall it was obviously better to leave more oil in the ground where it would only increase in value, rather than pump it out and sell it for dollars that were losing value. As a result, Jimmy Carter's Secretary of the Treasury, Michael Blumenthal, was spending more time in Riyadh, the capital of Saudi Arabia, than in the capital of his own country, Washington DC, in an effort to assure the Saudi government that the Carter Administration was going to shore up the flagging greenback.

If Carter fulfilled his campaign pledge to aggressively combat unemployment this would increase production and income, but also US imports and thereby increase the trade deficit even more. Carter's problem was that the only effective way to hold the line on the trade deficit, at least in the short run, was to cool down, not heat up the American economy. Carter adopted deflationary fiscal policies to slow the economy, and the trade deficit declined in 1979 to $45 billion and disappeared altogether in the election year recession of 1980 just as our simple open economy macro model predicts it should. Our simple model also sheds light on another "inexplicable" Carter Administration "betrayal" – the reappointment and encouragement of Paul Volker as chairman of the Federal Reserve Bank. While the trade account deficit would take two years and a recession to turn around, the Saudis required some more immediate and palpable show of good faith that the Administration was serious about shoring up the dollar. The only way to do that quickly was to raise US interest rates significantly above world levels to induce a massive inflow of finance capital on the short run capital account to counter the trade deficit until it could be reduced. Inflation fighter extraordinaire, Paul Volker was more than willing to do just that. So despite his election promise to prioritize the fight against unemployment over the fight against inflation, Carter reappointed Volker as chairman of the Fed, and Administration officials supported Volker's tight monetary policies despite the fact that unemployment rose from 6% to 8% as election day neared, infuriating many Democrats in Congress who were also up for reelection.

My point is not that Carter chose wisely. With hindsight it is obvious he did not. Carter's overwhelming loss to Ronald Reagan in the 1980 election ushered in the conservative Reagan era that has dominated US politics ever since, and Carter Administration fiscal and monetary policy bears a major responsibility for his election defeat. Instead, my point is that we need an open economy macro model to understand how international complications had more to do with Carter Administration economic policy than did political betrayal or economic stupidity.

9 Macro Economic Models

This chapter contains some simple models that illustrate important themes in banking, macro economics, and international finance. It is the last of three technical chapters that are not necessary to understand the rest of the book. As before, readers who want to be able to analyze economic problems themselves are encouraged to read this chapter.

BANK RUNS

> "That is my money inside that bank, mine!" cried Ramona Ruiz, 67, a retired textile worker who was trying to withdraw funds from an ATM in the city center of Buenos Aires today only to find it empty. "I was being patriotic by not removing my savings earlier. And now I see what a fool I was."[1]

Two people deposit D in a bank.[2] The bank lends these deposits, 2D, to a borrower who, if all goes well, will repay the bank 2R on a future date 2, where R > D. On the other hand, if the bank is forced to sell this loan "asset" to another bank on some date 1 before date 2, it will only receive 2r from the sale of the loan where 2D > 2r > D. Depositors can withdraw their money on either date 1 or date 2. For simplicity we assume depositors have a zero rate of time discount, i.e., if the amount of money is the same the depositors don't care if they get it on date 1 or date 2.

If even one depositor withdraws on date 1 the bank has to liquidate its loan because it has nothing to repay either depositor on date 1 without doing so, receiving 2r from the sale of the loan. If both depositors withdraw on date 1 each gets half of what the bank

---

1. Quoted in "Argentina Restricts Bank Withdrawals," by Anthony Faiola, *Washington Post*, December 2, 2001: A30.
2. This model is adapted from an excellent book by Robert Gibbons, *Game Theory for Applied Economists*, (Princeton University Press, 1992.)

has, r, which is less than each deposited, D. If one withdraws on date 1 but the other does not, the one who withdraws gets D while the other one gets the remainder, 2r − D, which is not only less than D but less than r as well.

If neither depositor withdraws on date 1, the bank does not need to liquidate its loan asset before it reaches maturity and the bank is paid 2R > 2D on date 2 by its loan customer. If both depositors withdraw on date 2 each receives R. Or, if neither withdraws on date 2 the bank pays each depositor R. However, if one depositor withdraws on date 2 while the other does not, the one who does not withdraw is simply paid D and the one who does withdraw is paid the remainder, 2R − D, which is greater than R.

The payoff matrix for the two depositors on date 1 is:

| | Date 1 | |
	Withdraw	Don't Withdraw
Withdraw	(r, r)	(D, 2r − D)
Don't Withdraw	(2r − D, D)	(?, ?)

The payoff matrix for the two depositors on date 2 is:

| | Date 2 | |
	Withdraw	Don't Withdraw
Withdraw	(R, R)	(2R − D, D)
Don't Withdraw	(D, 2R − D)	(R,R)

As in the Price of Power Game (chapter 3), we work backwards beginning with date 2. Both depositors will withdraw on date 2 if the game gets that far. If the other depositor withdraws I get R from withdrawing but only D if I do not. Since R > D I should withdraw if the other depositor withdraws. If the other depositor does not withdraw I get 2R − D by withdrawing but only R by not withdrawing. Since 2R − D > R I should withdraw if the other depositor does not withdraw. So no matter what the other depositor does, I should withdraw on date 2, and so should she. In other words, withdrawal is a "dominant strategy" for both players on date 2.

This allows us to fill in the missing payoffs in the south-east cell of the payoff matrix for date 1. If neither depositor withdraws on date 1 then the game goes to date 2. But now we know that if the game does go to date 2 both depositors will withdraw and each will receive R. So we can fill in R as the payoff to each depositor if both don't withdraw on date 1, replacing (?, ?) with (R, R).

On date 1 if the other depositor withdraws I get r from withdrawing and 2r – D if I do not. Since r > 2r – D I should withdraw if the other depositor withdraws. If the other depositor does not withdraw I get D by withdrawing but (eventually) R by not withdrawing. Since R > D, on date 1 I should not withdraw if the other depositor does not withdraw. There is no dominant strategy equilibrium on date 1. Each depositor's best move depends on what the other does. If I think the other depositor is going to withdraw, I should withdraw. Moreover, if that's what happens – we both withdraw – neither one of us would have any regrets over our own choice, and therefore if we had it to do again we would both presumably withdraw again. On the other hand, if I thought the other depositor was not going to withdraw on date 1, I should not withdraw either. Moreover, if we both don't withdraw, neither will have any regrets and wish to change our choice.[3] So *either* mutual withdrawal *or* mutual non-withdrawal are possible stable outcomes. But only one of these stable outcomes is efficient. Since (R, R) is better than (r, r) for both depositors, it is unambiguously more efficient. What we have discovered, unfortunately, is that this is only one of two equilibria. The other equilibrium outcome, mutual withdrawal on date 1, where each depositor withdraws for fear the other may withdraw, is inefficient and illustrates the logic of bank runs.

Notice that the model does not *predict* bank runs, any more than it predicts that depositors will always leave their deposits in banks until bank loans mature and all depositors get back more than they deposited in the first place. Instead, the model helps us see why *both*

---

3. What I have just explained means that both (withdraw, withdraw) and (don't, don't) are *Nash equilibria* (after the mathematician John Nash) for the date 1 game. They are both outcomes where neither party would regret their choice after the fact, so presumably if either outcome occurred, it would keep occurring – hence the word "equilibrium." Neither of the other two possible outcomes is a Nash equilibrium: If I withdrew on date 1 and you did not, you would regret your choice and withdraw next time if you assumed I was going to continue to withdraw on date 1. On the other hand, I might regret my choice and not withdraw next time if I could be sure you weren't going to change to withdraw because I'd just burned you. Similarly, if I don't withdraw but you do we would each want to change our choice if we felt the other was not going to change theirs.

outcomes are possible – the outcome where the bank promotes economic efficiency by helping both depositors do better than had they hidden their $D < R$ under their mattresses, and the socially counterproductive outcome where bank failure leaves both depositors worse off than had they hidden their $D > r$ under their mattresses. The model also makes clear the importance of depositor expectations about the behavior of other depositors in a banking system. If depositors trust other depositors not to make early withdrawals, all benefit ($R > D$, $R > D$). Whereas if depositors are suspicious that others may make early withdrawals, all lose ($r < D$, $r < D$). One way to think about deposit insurance and the minimum legal reserve requirement, is as a way to improve the likelihood that depositors will not panic, and therefore that the banking system will generate efficiency gains rather than losses.

INTERNATIONAL FINANCIAL CRISES

The same model can also be applied to international finance and help explain international financial crises and "contagion." I chose the title *Panic Rules!* for a book[4] about the global economy written right after the Asian Financial Crisis of 1997–98 because the "panic rules" described in chapter 7 were a useful way to begin to think about what had happened in those unfortunate Asian economies. You remember from chapter 7, there are two rules of behavior in any credit system: Rule #1 is the rule all participants want all *other* participants to follow: DON'T PANIC! Rule #2 is the rule all participants must be careful to follow themselves: PANIC FIRST! These "panic rules" succinctly summarize both the promise and the dangers of any credit system. If you substitute "international investors" for the word "depositors," and "emerging market economy" for the word "bank" in the bank run model above, the model helps explain both the promise and danger inherent in today's liberalized international financial system. Or, if you substitute "currency speculator" for "depositor," and "emerging market currency" for "bank" you can learn much from the model about the potential benefits *and* dangers associated with making a currency "convertible" and eliminating all "controls" on who can buy and sell how much. As I explained in chapters 7 and 8, before even asking if a credit system distributes

4. *Panic Rules! Everything You Need to Know About the Global Economy* (South End Press, 1999).

efficiency gains equitably between borrowers and lenders, we need to ask if the credit system, or innovation in an existing credit system, will actually yield efficiency gains rather than losses. The above model makes clear, there is *always* a possibility in *any* credit system that we could suffer efficiency losses (r < D, r < D), rather than enjoy efficiency gains (R > D, R > D), if participants obey Panic Rule #2 rather than #1. Those who speak of the benefits of financial deregulation, and new financial "instruments" invariably assume the positive alternative for their "product" and seldom warn us of the downside possibilities. It is true that *if* R is sufficiently greater than D, *if* r is not much less than D, and most importantly, *if* the probability of participants obeying rule #1 rather than #2 is sufficiently high, the expected value of the effects of the credit system will be positive. But the last "*if*" in particular cannot merely be *assumed*. It needs to be considered carefully. Insurance programs, reserve requirements, a lender of last resort, rules of disclosure, and a host of other factors all affect the probability that participants will obey one rule rather than the other – which our model makes clear is the all-important issue. When these safeguards are absent or weak, as they are in today's international credit system, and when "new financial product innovations" like derivatives magnify the downside risks, rational investors are more prone to obey Panic Rule #2 and the chances of efficiency losses are correspondingly greater.

INTERNATIONAL INVESTMENT IN A SIMPLE CORN MODEL

This model is a simple adaptation of the corn model from chapter 3. Instead of people we have countries. Instead of borrowing and lending between people we have an "international credit market" where countries lend to, and borrow from, one another. Instead of a labor market where people play the role of employer and the role of employee, direct foreign investment (DFI) allows northern countries to hire labor in southern countries to work using capital intensive technologies in northern-owned, multinational businesses located in southern economies.

There are 100 countries in the global economy, each with the same number of citizens. There is one produced good, corn, which all like to consume. Corn is produced from inputs of labor and seed corn. All countries are equally skilled and productive, and all have knowledge of the technologies that exist for producing corn. Each country needs to consume 1 unit of corn per year, after which they wish to maximize their leisure and only accumulate corn if they can do so without loss of leisure. There are two ways of producing corn, the "labor intensive technique" and the "capital intensive technique."

Labor intensive technique, LIT:
6 units of labor + 0 units of seed corn yield 1 unit of corn

Capital intensive technique, CIT:
1 unit of labor + 1 unit of seed corn yield 2 units of corn

In either case it takes a year for the corn to be produced and seed corn is tied up for the entire year, disappearing by year's end. *Our measure of global inequality is the difference between the number of units of labor worked by the country that works the most, and number of units of labor worked by the country that works the least. Our measure of global efficiency is the average units of labor worked per unit of net corn produced in the world.* There are 50 units of seed corn in the world; 10 northern countries each have 5 units of seed corn, and 90 southern countries have no seed corn at all.

I assume readers are familiar with how to analyze outcomes in the simple corn model from chapter 3 and compare outcomes under three international economic "regimes": (1) Under autarky there is no international investment of any kind permitted. In other words, there is neither international financial investment nor direct foreign investment. (2) An international credit market allows countries to lend and borrow seed corn as they please. We generously assume that when we open an international credit market all mutually beneficial deals between lending and borrowing countries are discovered and signed, i.e. that the credit market functions perfectly without crises and efficiency losses of any kind.[5] (3) Direct foreign investment (DFI) permits countries to hire labor from other countries to work in factories owned by the "foreign" country located inside the "host" country. By assuming the labor market inside host countries equilibrates we implicitly assume foreign and domestic

---

5. We drop this assumption below in the model that follows which substitutes a more realistic version of international finance for the "naïve" international credit market assumed here. The more realistic model allows for efficiency losses as well as efficiency gains from extending the international credit system.

employers pay the same wage rate. If foreign multinationals paid higher wages than domestic employers our results would be slightly less unequal.

Under **autarky** each southern country will work 6 units of labor in the LIT while each northern country will work 1 unit of labor in the CIT. The degree of global inequality will be 6 – 1 or 5. The average number of days worked per unit of net corn produced, or efficiency of the global economy will be [90(6) + 10(1)]/[100] = 5.500

If we legalize an **international credit market** the interest rate, r, on international loans will be ⅚ unit of seed corn per year. Each southern country will work 6 units of labor either in the LIT or with borrowed seed corn in the CIT. Each northern country will lend 5C, collect (⅚)5 or 4.167C in interest, consume 1C and accumulate 3.167C without having to work at all. The degree of global inequality would increase from 5 to 6, although the degree of inequality would really be greater than 6 if we took into account corn accumulated by the northern countries. The efficiency of the global economy would increase since the average number of days worked per unit of net corn produced in the world would fall from 5.500 to [90(6) + 10(0)]/[100 + 10(3.167)] or 4.101. The intuition behind these results is that under autarky northern countries do not have any incentive to put all their seed corn to productive use. Each northern country uses only 1 of its 5 units of seed corn – the other 4 units are an idle productive resource. The international credit market gives northern countries an incentive to lend their seed corn to southern countries where the borrowed seed corn increases the productivity of southern labor. Because seed corn is scarce globally, the northern countries are able to capture the entire efficiency gain from the increased productivity in the southern countries.

If some technical change improved the efficiency of the LIT so it only required 4 units of labor to produce a unit of corn, the international rate of interest, r, would fall from ⅚ to ¾ units of corn per year. Global efficiency would increase since the average number of days needed to produce a unit of net corn in the world would fall to [90(4) + 10(0)]/[100 + 10(2.75)] = 2.824 which is less than 4.101. The international rate of interest, r, decreases because the difference between the productivity of the CIT and LIT technologies is now less so southern countries are not willing to pay as much for the seed corn they need to use the CIT. Global efficiency increases because all production in the LIT is more productive, or efficient. Inequality decreases because lenders get less of the efficiency gain and borrowers more when r is lower. *Notice that improving the productivity of more labor intensive technologies not only increases global efficiency, it ameliorates global inequality.*

On the other hand, if some technical change improved the efficiency of the CIT so that it only required half a unit of labor together with 1 unit of seed corn to produce 2 units of corn, gross (or 1 unit of net corn), the international interest rate would rise from $5/6$ to $9/10$ unit of corn per year. Global efficiency would increase since the average number of days needed to produce a unit of net corn in the world would fall to $[90(6) + 10(0)]/[100 + 10(3.5)] = 4.0$ which is less than 4.101. The international rate of interest, r, increases because the difference between the productivity of the CIT and LIT technologies is now greater so southern countries are willing to pay more to get access to the seed corn they need to use the CIT. Global efficiency increases because all production in the CIT is more productive, or efficient. Inequality increases because lenders get less of the efficiency gain and borrowers more when r is higher. *Notice that improving the productivity of more capital intensive technologies increases global efficiency but aggravates global inequality.*

If instead of an international credit market, we legalize **direct foreign investment**, the wage rate in southern economies will be $w = 1/6$. Each southern country will have to work 6 units of labor, whether in the LIT in domestic owned businesses or in the CIT in northern owned businesses located in the southern, or "host" country or some combination of the two. Each northern country will hire 5 units of southern labor to work in the northern country's businesses located in southern countries, producing 10C gross, 5C net, paying $(1/6)(5) = 0.833C$ in wages, and receiving 4.167C profits. So each northern country will consume 1C and accumulate 3.167C without working at all. The degree of global inequality would increase from 5 to 6, although inequality would now really be greater than 6 if we took into account corn accumulated by the northern countries. The efficiency of the global economy would increase since the average number of days worked per unit of net corn produced in the world would fall from 5.500 to $[90(6) + 10(0)]/[100 + 10(3.167)]$ $= 4.101$. Again, the intuition behind these results is that direct foreign investment gives northern countries an incentive to use seed corn that was idle under autarky to employ southern labor that was previously working in the LIT under autarky, in northern businesses located in the south using the CIT – thereby raising the productivity of some southern labor. Because seed corn is scarce globally, the northern countries are able to capture the entire efficiency gain from the increased productivity in the southern countries.

BANKS IN A SIMPLE CORN MODEL

By combining the insights from the bank run model with the simple corn model from chapter 3 we can illustrate how banks can increase economic efficiency, but also how they might lead to efficiency losses. As before the economy consists of 1000 members. There is one produced good, corn, which all must consume. Corn is produced from inputs of labor and seed corn. All are equally skilled and productive, and all know how to use the two technologies that exist for producing corn. We assume each person needs to consume exactly 1 unit of corn per week, after which she wants to maximize her leisure. We assume people only accumulate corn if they can do so without loss of leisure. As before there are two ways to make corn: a labor intensive technique (LIT) and a capital intensive technique (CIT):

Labor Intensive Technique:
6 days of labor + 0 units of seed corn yields 1 unit of corn

Capital Intensive Technique:
1 day of labor + 1 unit of seed corn yields 2 units of corn

As always we measure the degree of inequality in the economy (imperfectly) as the difference between the maximum and minimum number of days anyone works, and efficiency as the number of days it takes on average to produce a unit of net corn. We examine a situation where 100 of the 1000 people have 5 units of seed corn each, while the other 900 people have no seed corn at all.

Under autarky each seedless person will work 6 days in the LIT and each seedy person will work 1 day in the CIT. The degree of inequality will be $6 - 1 = 5$. The efficiency of the economy will be: $[900(6) + 100(1)]/1000 = 5.500$ days of work needed on average to produce a unit of net corn.

Imperfect lending without banks

Before we implicitly assumed that if borrowing and lending were made legal all mutually beneficial loans would be made. Financial economists explain this is a naïve and unwarranted assumption. It ignores the fact that there are considerable "transaction costs"

associated with lenders and borrowers finding one another and successfully negotiating deals. Enthusiasts point out how banks reduce
transaction costs for borrowers and lenders by allowing lenders to
simply deposit funds at a single location where the rate of interest on
bank deposits is taken as a given, and by allowing borrowers to apply
at a single location where the rate of interest on bank loans is taken
as a given. Easy to find, nothing to negotiate. So we overcome our
naïvity and get "real" by assuming that without the assistance of
banks only half the mutually beneficial loans would be made. We
assume that only 50 of the 100 seedy would find borrowers, and the
other 50 would fail to do so without the mediation of banks.

The rate of interest would still be $\frac{5}{6}$ since any borrower would be
willing to pay that much but no more. Consequently the seedless
would work 6 days, as before, whether or not they borrowed and
worked in the CIT, or did not borrow and worked in the LIT. The 50
seedless who lend out their corn would each collect $(5)(\frac{5}{6}) = 4.167C$
interest, consume 1C, accumulate 3.167C and not work at all. The
seedy who did not find borrowers would work 1 day in the CIT,
consume 1C, and accumulate no corn.

The efficiency of the economy would be $[900(6) + 50(1) +
50(0)]/[1000 + 50(3.167)] = 4.705$ days on average to produce a unit
of net corn. This is an improvement from autarky where the average
number of days worked to produce a unit of net corn was 5.500. The
degree of inequality would be 6 as compared to 5 under autarky –
even without accounting for the 3.167C the 50 seedy who lend out
their corn and do not work at all accumulate.

Lending with banks when all goes well

We open a bank and assume this permits all 100 seedy people to find
borrowers simply by depositing their seed corn in the bank. The bank
will be able to charge an interest rate of $\frac{5}{6}$ on loans of seed corn to
the seedy, but to make a profit suppose it only pays $\frac{4}{6}$ on deposits.
If there is no legal reserve requirement, the bank could loan out all
500 units of seed corn deposited by the seedy, and the bank would
get $(\frac{1}{6})(500) = 83.33C$ in profits. Each of the 100 seedy depositors
gets $(\frac{4}{6})(5) = 3.33C$ interest, consumes 1C, and accumulates 2.33C
without working at all. Each of the seedless works 6 days whether
they borrow from the bank or do not, consume 1C and accumulate
none. The efficiency of the economy with a bank where all seedy
deposit their corn, where none panic and make early withdrawals,
where all corn deposits are loaned out to the seedless who use them

productively to work in the CIT, and where all seedless repay their loans, plus interest at the end of the week is: $[900(6) + 100(0)]/[1000 + 83.33 + 100(2.33)] = 4.101$ if we assume for convenience that there are no days worked at the bank. Of course this is the same degree of efficiency we calculated back in chapter 3 when we assumed "naïvely" that all mutually beneficial deals between borrowers and lenders took place without a bank. The degree of inequality remains 6 (although none of the seedy accumulate 3.167C now, they all accumulate 2.33C, and the bank has profits of 83.33 for zero work.)

Lending with banks when all does not go well

Suppose the seedy must deposit their seed corn in the bank before 12 p.m. on Saturday of the previous week in order to get their $\frac{1}{6}$ weekly rate of interest, and suppose the bank lends seed corn to the seedless borrowers beginning Monday morning at 9 a.m. Over the weekend a rumor spreads among the seedy depositors that the weather bureau is predicting no rain for the week, in which case harvests from corn grown in the CIT will be depleted to the point where borrowers will not only be unable to pay interest owed the bank, they will not even be able to pay back all the principle they borrowed: $(r \ll D)$. Our bank run model makes clear why rational depositors would switch from "don't withdraw" before the week begins but only at week's end, to "withdraw" immediately if they believe bad weather will prevent the seedless from being able to pay the bank back the principle, much less interest on their loans the following Sunday. So this Sunday all the seedy run (rationally) to find an ATM machine and withdraw their 5 units of corn from the bank. However, to everyone's surprise a soaking rain begins at 2 a.m. Monday morning, and by the time the work day begins on Monday morning it is clear that productivity in the CIT during the week will be as high as ever.

In the extreme the bank would have no corn to lend on Monday morning, and if the seedy had lost the habit of searching for borrowers themselves so none of them found borrowers before the week's work began, the economy would sink back into autarky. But this means the economy would be even less efficient than before the bank was opened! In the extreme no seed corn would be lent in the aftermath of a bank panic – through either the bank or private arrangements – and the average days worked per unit of net corn produced would rise from 4.101 when the bank-credit system worked perfectly all the way back up to 5.500 under autarky. But

5.500 days on average to produce a unit of net corn is *worse* than 4.705 days on average to produce a unit of net corn – which is what the imperfect credit market achieved before we opened a bank. This means the economy is less efficient when the bank fails than when there was no bank at all and some, but not all lenders found borrowers on their own. In other words, it is possible that an imperfect, informal credit market where lending takes place without bank mediation can be more efficient than a bank-credit system when there is a bank crisis. To the extent that not all the seedy make withdrawals, and those who do find borrowers themselves, the efficiency loss would be less. But it is certainly possible that if bank panics are deep enough and occur often enough the economy could end up less efficient with a banking system than it would have been without one. What this simple model illustrates is how instability in the financial sector might obstruct more productivity enhancing loans than it facilitates, and thereby make the "real" economy less, rather than more efficient.

INTERNATIONAL FINANCE IN AN INTERNATIONAL CORN MODEL

We can reinterpret the above model to illustrate the relationship between the financial and real sectors of the global economy as well. Instead of appending the bank run model to the simple corn model of the "real" domestic economy as we just did, interpret the financial model as a model of the international financial system and append it to the international corn model of the "real" global economy analyzed above. The financial model illustrates why the international financial system has both "upside" *and* "downside" possibilities. The international financial system can increase global efficiency by expanding the number of mutually beneficial international deals that get struck when international investors obey Panic Rule #1 and (don't withdraw, don't withdraw) leads to the more efficient Nash equilibrium (R, R). But a fragile, highly leveraged, international financial system can also decrease global efficiency if international investors obey Panic Rule #2 and (withdraw, withdraw) leads to the less efficient Nash equilibrium (r, r).

Compare four possible outcomes: (1) International autarky, (2) international lending without finance, (3) international finance where investors do not panic, and (4) international finance where investors do panic. If we assume some, but not all mutually beneficial international loans get made without international financial mediation there is a partial, but not complete efficiency gain from lending without finance compared to autarky. If we assume the remaining mutually beneficial international loans would get made through financial mediation *provided investors do not panic,* and therefore the financial system settles on its efficient Nash equilibrium (R, R), we get a further efficiency gain from international financial mediation. But *if instead, investors do panic,* so the international financial system settles on the inefficient Nash equilibrium (r, r), and if the ensuing international financial crisis causes lending to drop by more than the amount that would have occurred without financial intermediation, the international financial system causes efficiency losses rather than gains. In 1997–98 a half dozen East Asian economies discovered this little advertised fact about capital liberalization the hard way. Argentina is providing a reminder in 2001–02 for all who failed to heed the lesson the first time.

FISCAL AND MONETARY POLICY IN A CLOSED ECONOMY MACRO MODEL

We can use a simple *closed* economy, short run macro model to compare the effects of equivalent fiscal and monetary policies. All figures are in billions of dollars.

$Y = C + I + G$ is the equilibrium condition saying that aggregate supply, the Y on the left side of the equation, equals aggregate demand, the sum total of household consumption demand, C, business investment demand, I, and government spending, G.

$C = 90 + \frac{3}{4}(Y-T)$ is the consumption function, indicating that the US household sector will consume $90 billion independent of income, and three-quarters of every dollar of after tax, or disposable, income they have.

$I = 200 - 1000r$ is the investment function where r is the rate of interest expressed as a decimal. It says investment depends negatively on the rate of interest. Whenever interest rates change by 1% investment demand will change by $10 billion.

$G^* = 40$ and $T^* = 40$. Government spending and taxes are both initially $40 billion. Finally, potential GDP, or Y(f) is $900.

(1) Calculate Y(e) if r is equal to 10%, i.e. r* = 0.10

Y(e) = 90 + ¾(Y(e) – 40) + 200 – 1000(0.10) + 40
Y(e) – ¾Y(e) = 90 – 30 + 100 + 40
¼Y(e) = 200
Y(e) = 800

(2) In what state is the economy? Is there unemployment? Is there inflation? What is the size of the unemployment or inflation gap in the economy?

Y(f) – Y(e) = 100: There is an unemployment gap of 100. So there will be cyclical unemployment, but there should not be demand pull inflation. Of course there could be cost push inflation, but the simple Keyensian model would not allow us to see that.

(3) Is there a government budget deficit or surplus? How much?

Since T(1) – G(1) = 40 – 40 = 0 the government budget is balanced initially.

(4) What is the composition of output initially?

G(1)/Y(1) = 40/800 = 5%; I(1)/Y(1) = 100/800 = 12.5%; C(1)/Y(1) = 660/800 = 82.5%

(5) How much would the government have to change its spending in order to eliminate the unemployment gap?

We need the new equilibrium Y to be 100 billion bigger than the initial equilibrium Y, that is, $Y_2 - Y_1 = \Delta Y = 100$. Using the government spending multiplier formula:

$\Delta Y = [1/(1 - ¾)] \Delta G$
$100 = [4] \Delta G$
$\Delta G = 25$

(6) What would be the deficit (or surplus) in the government budget in this case?

T(2) – G(2) = 40 – [40 – 25] = –25 billion *deficit.*

(7) What would the composition of output now be?

$G(2)/Y(2) = 65/900 = 7.22\%$; $I(2)/Y(2) = 100/900 = 11.11\%$;
$C(2)/Y(2) = 735/900 = 81.67\%$

(8) Suppose there was a Republican or "New Democrat" administration, and instead of eliminating the unemployment gap by increasing government spending the administration wanted to eliminate the gap with an *equivalent* tax policy. By how much would the government have to reduce taxes to eliminate the unemployment gap?

Using the tax multiplier formula:

$\Delta Y = [-\frac{3}{4}/(1 - \frac{3}{4})] \Delta T$
$100 = [-3] \Delta T$
$\Delta T = -33.33$

(9) What would be the deficit (or surplus) in the government budget in this case?

$T(3) - G(3) = [40 - 33.33] = 6.66 - 40 = -33.33$ billion *deficit.*

(10) What would the composition of output be in this case?

$G(3)/Y(3) = 40/900 = 4.44\%$; $I(3)/Y(3) = 100/900 = 11.11\%$;
$C(3)/Y(3) = 760/900 = 84.44\%$

(11) What could the government do to eliminate the gap *without creating a budget deficit?*

Using the Balanced Budget multiplier formula:

$\Delta Y = [1]\Delta BB$
$100 = \Delta BB = \Delta G = \Delta T$

So if the government increased G *and* T by 100 billion aggregate demand and equilibrium GDP would both rise by 100 increasing GDP from 800 to 900 billion, and the budget would remain balanced with $G(4) = T(4) = 40 + 100 = 140$.

(12) What would the composition of output be in this case?

$G(4)/Y(4) = 140/900 = 15.55\%$; $I(4)/Y(4) = 100/900 = 11.11\%$;
$C(4)/Y(4) = 660/900 = 73.33\%$

Obviously different fiscal policies that are *equivalent* in the sense of eliminating the same size unemployment gap have different effects on the government budget. We can see by the answers to questions 3, 6, 9 and 11 that while increasing spending and taxes by the same amount does not change the balance in the government budget, increasing G alone increases the deficit, but decreasing T alone increases the government budget deficit even more.

We can observe the effects different fiscal policies have on the composition of output by comparing the answers to questions 4, 7, 10, and 12. Increasing G to eliminate the unemployment gap raises the share of public goods and reduces the shares of private investment and consumption. Cutting taxes increases the share of private consumption and decreases the share of public goods and private investment. Raising both G and T increases the share of public goods dramatically, and decreases the share of private consumption dramatically, and the share of private investment slightly.

In sum, while any of the three fiscal policies can be used to eliminate an unemployment (or inflation) gap, *equivalent fiscal policies* do *not* have the same effect on either government budget deficits, nor on the composition of output.

What if the White House and Congress cannot agree on a fiscal stimulus package, as was the case after September 11, 2001 when the Bush Administration insisted on more tax cuts for the wealthy and Democrats in Congress pressed for increases in unemployment benefits? When there is gridlock over fiscal policy sometimes the Fed has to step in and provide stimulus with monetary policy. Suppose the Fed wanted to provide a stimulus *equivalent* to the three fiscal policies just studied. That is, what if the Fed wanted to increase the money supply by enough to increase aggregate demand by 100 billion from 800 to 900 billion.

(13) The investment multiplier is the same as the government spending multiplier because in the short run the macro economy doesn't know or care whether the initial increase in spending came from the federal government buying more aircraft carriers or from private business buying more capital equipment. Therefore:

$\Delta Y = [1/(1 - \tfrac{3}{4})] \, \Delta I$
$100 = [4] \, \Delta I$
$\Delta I = 25$

(14) But how much must interest rates fall to produce a 25 billion increase in private investment? We initially used the investment equation, I = 200 − 1000r, to solve for I(1) when r(1) was 10% or 0.10

$$I(1) = 200 − 1000r(1) = 200 − 1000(0.10) = 200 − 100 = 100$$

We now use the same equation to see what r(2) must be to give us an I(2) = I(1) + ΔI:

$$I(2) = 100 + 25 = 125 = 200 − 1000r(2); 125 − 200 = −75 = −1000r(2);$$
$$−75/−1000 = 0.075 = r(2)$$

So r(2) − r(1) = 0.075 − 0.100 = − 0.025 = Δr. We need interest rates to drop by 2.5%

(15) Suppose interest rates in the economy drop by 1% whenever the functioning money supply, M1 increases by 10 billion dollars. Since the Fed wants interest rates to fall by 2.5% they would have to get M1 to increase by 25 billion. The Fed could do this through an appropriate purchase of bonds in the open market, decrease in the discount rate, or reduction in the minimum legal reserve requirement.

(16) When the Fed buys bonds, decreases the discount rate, or reduces the reserve requirement there is no direct effect on the government budget at all. It doesn't change G and it doesn't change T.[6] Therefore the government budget would remain balanced at G(5) = T(5) = 40.

(17) What would be the composition of output in the case of an expansionary monetary policy that is *equivalent* to any of the three expansionary fiscal policies we studied?

$$G(5)/Y(5) = 40/900 = 4.44\%; \quad I(5)/Y(5) = 125/900 = 13.89\%;$$
$$C(5)/Y(5) = 735/900 = 81.67\%$$

6. If expansionary monetary policy works it will increase production and income. Since a rise in national income will increase federal tax collections, this will reduce the government budget deficit. But this is an *indirect* effect on the budget deficit. Monetary policy, unlike fiscal policy, has no *direct* effect on the budget deficit. Moreover in our simple model taxes are not a function of income so monetary policy has no indirect effect in our model either.

Expansionary monetary policy increases the share of private investment and decreases the shares of both public and private consumption.

IMF CONDITIONALITY AGREEMENTS IN AN OPEN ECONOMY MACRO MODEL

We can use a simple *open* economy, short run macro model to demonstrate the effects of IMF agreements which require countries to implement deflationary fiscal and monetary policies as a "condition" for obtaining an IMF "bailout" loan to prevent default. The model shows us how deflationary fiscal and monetary policy can turn balance of payments deficits into surpluses and increase the value of a country's currency – thereby increasing the ability of these countries to repay their international debts. But it also shows us why these policies will reduce employment, production, income, and domestic investment in these countries – and thereby sheds light on why the Washington Consensus is often unpopular with many citizens of debtor countries.

Assume the following information characterized the Brazilian economy in the fall of 1998: All figures are in billions of reales.

$Y + M = C + I + G + X$ is the equilibrium condition for the economy. Y is domestic production, (and therefore also income) and M is imports. So $Y + M$ represents the aggregate supply of final goods and services. C is household consumption demand, I is domestic investment demand, G is government spending, and X is foreign demand for Brazilian exports. So $C+I+G+X$ represents the aggregate demand for final goods and services. The equilibrium condition says the aggregate supply of final goods and services is equal to the aggregate demand for final goods and services when the goods market is in equilibrium. It is traditionally written as: $Y = C+I+G+X-M$

$C = 60 + (\frac{4}{5})(Y-T)$ is the Brazilian consumption function.

$I = 150 - 1000r$ expresses domestic Brazilian investment as a linear negative function of the real rate of interest in Brazil (expressed as a decimal).

$BOP = X - M + KF$ is the balance of payments accounting identity. If $BOP < 0$ there is a net outflow of reales into international currency markets, increasing their supply by BOP. If BOP > 0 there is a net inflow of reales from international currency markets decreasing their supply in foreign exchange markets by BOP. The BOP includes both the trade account, X – M, and the capital account, KF (see below).

G = 120 is what the government spends initially: T = 100 is initial tax collections.

M = 50 + ($\frac{1}{10}$)Y is the import equation where Y stands for national income in this expression. Brazilian people and businesses import more when national income is higher. Their marginal propensity to import out of income, or MPM, is $\frac{1}{10}$.

X = 120 is foreign demand for Brazilian exports.

KF = 1000r – 60 expresses the net inflow of short run financial capital as a function of domestic interest rates. When interest rates are higher in Brazil more foreign financial capital is likely to flow into Brazil, attracted by the high interest rate paid, and less Brazilian wealth is likely to flow out. When the real interest rate is 6%, or 0.06 the inflow exactly matches the outflow. For real interest rates higher than 6% there is a net inflow, for interest rates below 6% there is a net outflow.

Y(f) = 1000 is Brazil's potential GDP.

We assume the international value of the real increases (decreases) by 1% whenever the supply of reales in international currency markets decreases (increases) by 10 billion reales.

We assume interest rates inside Brazil increase (decrease) by 1% whenever the functioning money supply, M1, decreases (increases) by 20 billion reales.

The government spending and investment income–expenditure multipliers are both equal to [1\(1–MPC+MPM)] in this simple open economy macro model reflecting the extra "leakage" in the income expenditure multiplier chain caused by imports.

(1) Calculate the initial equilibrium GDP, Y(1), if the interest rate in Brazil is 5% (r = 0.05).

$Y(1) = 60 + (\frac{4}{5})[Y(1)–100] + 150 – 1000(0.05) + 120 + 120 – [50 + (\frac{1}{10})Y(1)]$

$Y(1) – (\frac{4}{5})Y(1) + (\frac{1}{10})Y(1) = (\frac{3}{10})Y(1) = 60 – 80 + 150 + 120 + 120 – 50 = 270$

$Y(1) = (\frac{10}{3})(270) = 900$

(2) What size is the unemployment gap in the Brazilian economy initially?

$Y(f) – Y(1) = 1000 – 900 = 100$ unemployment gap.

(3) What is the deficit in the Brazilian government budget initially?

$T(1) – G(1) = 100 – 120 = –20$; a 20 billion real budget deficit.

(4) What is Brazil's trade deficit initially?

$X(1) – M(1) = 120 – [50 + (\frac{1}{10})Y(1)] = 120 – 50 – (\frac{1}{10})900 = –20$; a 20 billion real trade deficit.

(5) What is the deficit on Brazil's capital account initially?

$KF(1) = 1000(0.05) – 60 = –10$, a 10 billion real capital account deficit.

(6) What is Brazil's Balance of Payments deficit initially?

$BOP(1) = X(1) – M(1) + KF(1) = –20 –10 = –30$ billion real BOP deficit.

(7) As things stand, by how much and in what direction would the value of the real change?

$BOP(1)/10 = –30/10 = –3\%$; the value of the real would drop by 3% by year's end.

(8) If the Central Bank of Brazil takes no action regarding the money supply, by how much and in what direction would the money supply inside Brazil, M1, change by year's end?

Absent any intervention by the Brazilian central bank, the BOP deficit of 30 would decrease the domestic money supply by 30 billion reales. Assuming the monetary authorities did not want this to happen, they would have to take some "countervailing monetary policy" to keep the domestic money supply where it was at the beginning of the year.

(9) What percentage of GDP in Brazil is devoted to investment initially?

$I(1)/Y(1) = 100/900 = 0.111$ or 11.1%

When Brazilians look at their economy they see an economy with too much unemployment, producing too far below its capacity, and perhaps devoting too little of its output to increasing its capital stock so as to increase potential GDP in the future. When the IMF looks at the same economy they see a government budget deficit – meaning the government might not be able to pay off foreigners holding Brazilian government bonds when they come due. They see a trade and balance of payments deficit, rather than surplus – which is what is needed for Brazil to be able to pay off its international creditors. And they see a depreciating real – which means all Brazilians, whether the government or private banks and companies, will have a harder time buying the dollars they need with the reales they have to pay off international loans due in dollars. Where Brazilians and the IMF see eye to eye is that Brazil is not going to be able to meet its outstanding international obligations without an emergency loan from the IMF, and that the consequences of default would be disastrous for both Brazil and international investors.

Suppose in the fall of 1998 the IMF insists that in exchange for an IMF bailout loan the Brazilian government has to *decrease* its spending by 30 billion reales.

(10) How large will the unemployment gap in Brazil now become?

The government spending multiplier is $[1/(1 – \frac{4}{5} + \frac{1}{10})] = \frac{10}{3}$. So we multiply $\Delta G = -30$ by $(\frac{10}{3})$ to get $\Delta Y = -100$, the drop in equilibrium GDP. So equilibrium GDP drops by 100 from 900 to 800 billion reales and the unemployment gap increases from 100 to 200 billion reales.

(11) What will the deficit or surplus in the Brazilian government budget now be?

$T(2) = T(1) = 100 – G(2) = 100 – (120 – 30) = + 10$ billion real surplus. This provides the Brazilian government with something to pay foreign bond holders when those bonds come due. Even if the bonds are denominated in dollars, the Brazilian government can sell its 10 billion real surplus for dollars to make payments in dollars.

(12) What will happen to Brazil's trade deficit?

$X(2) = X(1) = 120 - M(2) = 120 - [50 + (\frac{1}{10})800] = -10$; down from 20 billion, but still a 10 billion real trade deficit.

(13) What will happen to Brazil's capital account?

Since $r(2) = r(1) = 0.05$ there is no change in KF, and $KF(2) = KF(1) = -10$

(14) What will Brazil's Balance of Payments deficit or surplus now be?

$BOP(2) = X(2) - M(2) + KF(2) = -10 - 10 = -20$; down from 30 billion, but still a 20 billion real BOP deficit.

(15) What will happen to the value of the real?

$BOP(2)/10 = -20/10 = -2\%$ drop in the value of the real; down from a 3% devaluation, but still falling.

The trade and balance of payments deficits continue to threaten Brazil's overall ability to repay foreign creditors. And while the downward pressure on the real has eased slightly, if the real continues to drop, even the government surplus may be insufficient to allow for repayment of the "sovereign" debt if it is largely denominated in dollars that become more expensive for the government to buy. Despite complaints by Brazil about rising unemployment and falling income, the IMF decides it cannot "stand pat."

When Brazil needs a further loan in the spring of 1999 another opportunity to insist on additional conditions arises. In exchange for an additional IMF bailout loan in March, 1999 the IMF requires the Central Bank of Brazil to tighten up on the money supply. Suppose the IMF insists that the Central Bank of Brazil sell enough reales on the Brazilian bond market to reduce the Brazilian money supply, M1, by 60 billion reales as an additional conditionality.

(16) How much will the rate of interest in Brazil rise?

Since every time the functioning money supply, M1, decreases by 20 billion reales interest rates in Brazil rise by 1%, a 60 billion decrease in the money supply leads to a 60/20 = 3% rise in real interest rates in Brazil, so: $r(3) = r(1) + \Delta r = 5\% + 3\% = 8\%$

(17) How much will business investment fall in Brazil?

$I(3) = 150 - 1000r(3) = 150 - 1000(0.08) = 70$, a drop of 30 billion reales from 100.

(18) What will the unemployment gap in Brazil become now?

The investment expenditure multiplier is the same size as the government spending multiplier we calculated was [$10/3$]. So we have to multiply $\Delta I = -30$ by ($10/3$) which gives $\Delta Y = -100$, a further drop in Y(e). Since Y(e) had already fallen to 800 billion reales, it now falls another 100 billion reales and the new Y(e), Y(3), is $800 - 100 = 700$ billion reales. This increases the unemployment gap to $1000 - 700 = 300$ billion reales.

(19) What will happen to Brazil's government budget surplus?

Monetary policy does not directly affect the government budget deficit, so it will remain the same as it was after the decrease in government spending, a 10 billion real surplus.

(20) What will happen to Brazil's trade account?

$X(3) - M(3) = 120 - [50 + (1/10)700] = 120 - 50 - 70 = 0$; and Brazil's trade account is finally balanced.

(21) What will happen to Brazil's capital account?

$KF(3) = 1000r(3) - 60 = 1000(0.08) - 60 = + 20$; a 20 billion real surplus on the capital account.

(22) What will happen to Brazil's overall Balance of Payments?

$BOP(3) = X(3) - M(3) + KF(3) = 0 + 20 = +20$; so finally there is a BOP surplus to use to pay off international creditors.

(23) How much and in what direction will the value of the real now change?

$BOP(3)/10 = +20/10 = + 2\%$ rise in the value of the real; finally the downward pressure on the value of the real has been reversed. If the value of the real does rise it will be easier for all Brazilian creditors to pay off dollar denominated loans.

(24) What percentage of Brazilian GDP will now be devoted to investment?

$I(3)/Y(3) = [150 - 1000(0.08)]/700 = 70/700 = 10\% < 11.1\% = 100/900 = I(1)/Y(1)$. This means that Brazil is not only investing 30 billion reales less than it was before, it is devoting an even lower *percentage* of its output to increasing its capital stock, and thereby its potential GDP, than before.

Presto! By mid-1999 Brazil has been successfully turned into a "debt repayment machine" while the Brazilian economy sinks further and further into recession, and long run economic development becomes an even more distant dream.

WAGE-LED GROWTH IN A LONG RUN, POLITICAL ECONOMY MACRO MODEL

The general framework

There is only one good produced which we call a shmoo. It is an all-purpose good that both workers and capitalists eat, wear, and live in. Moreover, shmoos are also used to produce shmoos. In other words shmoos are also an investment good, and the capital stock, K, with which labor works to produce shmoos, consists of shmoos. Let X be the number of shmoos produced per year and C be the number of shmoos consumed per year. We assume any shmoos not consumed are added to the capital stock, i.e. invested, I, and for convenience we assume the rate of depreciation of the capital stock is zero. L is the number of person-years employed during the year, and c is the number of shmoos consumed per person-year of employment *by both workers and capitalists*.[7] This means that total annual consumption of shmoos, C, is equal to cL. If we let g be the rate of growth of the capital stock, then total annual investment of shmoos, I, is equal to gK since we have assumed no depreciation.

---

7. In other words, c is not the amount workers consume per year of employment, it is the amount workers and capitalists *together* consume per year of employment.

Our first identity says that all shmoos produced are either consumed or added to the capital stock, i.e. invested:

(1) $X = C + I = cL + gK$

Next we assume a very simple "fixed coefficient" production function. To make a shmoo it takes a certain number of person-years of labor, $a(0)$ – the labor input coefficient – and it takes a certain number of shmoos of capital stock, $a(1)$ – the capital input coefficient. With fixed coefficient production functions there is no way to substitute more labor to make shmoos with less capital, or more capital to make shmoos with less labor. To make X shmoos it takes $a(0)X$ person-years of labor and $a(1)X$ shmoos of capital stock. If we only have $a(1)X$ shmoos in the capital stock it will do no good to hire more than $a(0)X$ person-years of labor because only X shmoos can be produced in any case, and if only $a(0)X$ person-years of labor are hired only $a(1)X$ shmoos from the capital stock will be used, the rest will be effectively idle.

So L will always be equal to $a(0)X$. If output, X, is low and the labor force, N, is large this may mean that $a(0)X = L < N$ and we have unemployed labor. Similarly, if output, X, is low and the capital stock, K, is large it may be the case that $a(1)X < K$ and we will have unutilized capital stock. The difference is that whereas employers do not have to hire N if they only want $L < N$, they are stuck with the capital stock they have, K. If this proves to be more capital than they need to utilize to produce the amount they want to produce, $a(1)X$, then some of their capital stock will be idle at their expense, so to speak. Therefore, L/X always equals $a(0)$, but K/X equals $a(1)$ only at full capacity levels of output. When not all the capital stock is being utilized $K/X > a(1)$. It is useful to define an index of capacity utilization, $u = X/K$, which ranges from a minimum value of 0 when output is zero to a maximum value of $1/a(1)$ when X is full capacity output, and therefore $K/X = a(1)$ and $X/K = 1/a(1)$. How changes in exogenous variables affect our capacity utilization index, $0 \leq u \leq 1/a(1)$, will prove crucial in the performance of the economy in our model.

We now divide equation (1) by X and simplify to get equation (2):

$X/X = c(L/X) + g(K/X)$

(2) $1 = ca(0) + g/u$; which can also be written: $ca(0) = [1 - g/u]$

Just as shmoos produced go either to consumption or investment, income goes either to workers or capitalists. *Our second identity says that total income is equal to the sum of the income of workers and capitalists.*

(3) $PX = WL + rPK$

Where P is the dollar price of a shmoo, W is the dollar wage rate per person-year of employment, and r is the rate of profit capitalists receive. PX gives the dollar value of production, or GDP, which, according to the pie principle, must be equal to the dollar value of income, or GDI in the economy. WL gives the dollar value of all wages paid. And since PK is the dollar value of the capital stock, multiplying the dollar value of the capital stock by the rate of profit capitalists "earn" per dollar "invested" in capital stock gives us the dollar value of capitalists' income. Again we divide equation (3) by X and simplify to get equation (4):

$PX/X = W(L/X) + rP(K/X)$; $P = Wa(0) + rP/u$; dividing this equation by P yields:

(4) $1 = wa(0) + r/u$, where $w = W/P$, the real wage, which can be written: $wa(0) = [1 - r/u]$

Next we assume that while workers consume all their income, capitalists save part of their income, and let s represent the fraction of their income capitalists save.[8] And we write *our third and last identity: The value of total consumption must equal the value of workers' consumption plus the value of capitalists' consumption.* Total consumption is cL so the dollar value of total consumption is PcL. Total employment is L so the dollar value of total labor income is WL, which is also the dollar value of workers' consumption since they consume all their income. The dollar value of total income to capital is rPK, but capitalists only consume (1–s)rPK. Therefore:

(5) $PcL = WL + (1-s)rPK$

---

8. Assuming a zero rate of saving for workers is convenient. None of our results would change if workers did save part of their income, as long as their saving rate was lower than the saving rate of capitalists.

Dividing equation (5) by PX gives:

PcL/PX = WL/PX = (1–s)rPK/PX; c(L/X) = w(L/X) + (1–s)r(K/X);
ca(0) = [wa(0) + (1–s)r/u]

Substituting this expression for ca(0) into equation (2) gives:

1 = [wa(0) + (1–s)r/u] + g/u; but from equation (4) wa(0) = [1 – r/u]
which gives:
1 = 1 – r/u + (1–s)r/u + g/u; or 0 = – r/u + r/u – sr/u + g/u;
or sr/u = g/u which leaves:
(6)   g = sr

We call equations (2), (4), and (6) our *General Framework*. It contains the logical implications of the basic framework of our long run macro model. In our framework we assume shmoos not consumed are invested. We assume a zero rate of depreciation on the capital stock. We assume there are two classes, workers whose income consists entirely of wages, and capitalists whose income consists entirely of profits. And we assume capitalists save out of their income but workers do not. In this framework of assumptions we can write three tautologies which reduce to equations (2), (4), and (6):

(2)   1 = ca(0) + g/u
(4)   1 = wa(0) + r/u
(6)   g = sr

We also have u ≤ 1/a(1) as an inequality constraint in the basic framework.

There are five "endogenous" variables we want to solve for: c, g, w, r, and u. There are three "exogenous" variables, or "parameters," a(0), a(1) and s, which we take as givens when solving for the endogenous variables. But we will be very interested in how changes in these parameters (and others) affect the values of the endogenous variables. For instance, we will ask how an increase in capitalists saving rate, s, affects c, g, w, r and u. And we will ask how labor saving technical change – a reduction in a(0) – and how capital saving technical change – a reduction in a(1) – affect the endogenous variables. But at this point we cannot solve for the values of five endogenous variables with only three equations and one inequality constraint. We need more equations. Fortunately we have yet to make any assumptions about what motivates capitalists to invest more or less, or how the goods and labor markets function. By adding a political economy theory of business investment, and a political economy theory about the struggle between employers and employees over real wages, we can "close" the basic model with two more equations that allow us to solve our long run political economy macro economic model for the values of the five endogenous variables.

A Keynesian theory of investment

Keynes provided key insights into business investment behavior. First, he argued that investment would depend in part on what he called capitalists' "animal spirits," i.e. psychological and speculative factors that were impossible to capture in formal models. In our model we represent these "animal spirits" by $\alpha > 0$. When capitalists become more optimistic α increases, and when they get more pessimistic α decreases. Second, Keynes reasoned that capitalists would want to invest more if the rate of profit on invested capital was higher. In our model we represent this relationship by βr with $\beta > 0$. Finally, Keynes observed that since the purpose of investment is to increase the capital stock, capitalists would be *less* likely to invest when the utilization rate of the existing capital stock was low. Why add more to the capital stock when you are not using what is already available? We represent this relationship by τu with $\tau > 0$, signifying that capitalists' desire to increase their capital stock is positively related to the current level of capacity utilization. These behavioral assumptions about the rate at which capitalist entrepreneurs would like to expand the capital stock, g, are incorporated into equation (7):

(7) $g = \alpha + \beta r + \tau u$ with α, β, τ all > 0

A Marxian theory of wage determination

Marx provided key insights into how the real wage is determined. He argued that beside labor's productivity, the real wage in capitalist economies will depend on the bargaining strengths of labor and capital. If employees become more powerful the real wage will increase, whereas if employers become more powerful the real wage will decrease. We will model the effect of bargaining power on the real wage by multiplying labor's productivity by a parameter whose value increases when workers' bargaining power increases and decreases when capitalists' power increases. The real wage is W/P or w. Labor productivity is $[1/a(0)]$. Our bargaining power parameter is $[1/(1+m)]$ where $m > -1$ giving us:

(8) $w = [1/a(0)][1/(1+m)]$; with $m > -1$

When $m = 0$, $[1/(1+m)] = 1$ and the real wage is exactly equal to labor's productivity. For $m > 0$ $[1/(1+m)] < 1$, and therefore workers receive less than their productivity. For $-1 < m < 0$ $[1/(1+m)] > 1$, and therefore workers receive more than their productivity. When m increases workers' real wage declines, and when m decreases their real wage rises.[9]

Solving the model

When added to our basic framework of equations (2), (4), and (6) and the inequality $u \leq 1/a(1)$, equations (7) and (8) give us five equations in five unknowns: c, g, w, r, and u. We proceed to solve the five equations for the values of the five unknowns in terms of the model's parameters: a(0), a(1), s, m, α, β, and τ. Then we will be able to explore the implications of the model by seeing the effect of changes in key parameters on the values of endogenous variables.

Equation (8) already expresses the equilibrium value of the real wage, w^*, in terms of the parameters a(0) and m:

(a) $w^* = 1/a(0)(1+m)$

Unfortunately, solving for r^* is more difficult: We begin with equations (6) and (7). Equation (6) tells us that when deciding how to divide their income between consumption and savings, capitalists'

---

9. Notice that m can be interpreted as the "mark up" above the variable cost of production capitalists charge for a shmoo. $W/P = w = [1/a(0)][1/(1+m)]$; $P/W = a(0)[1+m]$; and $P = Wa(0)[1+m]$ – which says that the price of a shmoo is the labor, or variable cost of making a shmoo times one *plus* the "mark up," m. In the initial formulation of a model similar to the one developed here the political economist Michael Kalecki argued that in "monopoly capitalism" capitalists would be able to mark up prices above their costs depending on their "degree of monopoly power." He wrote equation (8) as $P = Wa(0)[1+m]$ and argued that the size of m depended on the degree of monopoly power capitalists had in product markets. The capitalist/worker and capitalist/consumer bargaining power interpretations are formally equivalent.

savings *will* add shmoos to the capital stock so as to yield a growth rate of K, g, equal to sr. On the other hand, equation (7) tells us that in their role as entrepreneurs and investors, capitalists *want* to add shmoos to the capital stock so as to yield a growth rate of K, g, equal to $\alpha + \beta r + \tau u$. In equilibrium capitalists' behavior as managers of their wealth must be reconciled with their behavior as entrepreneurs and investors, i.e. we can set our two expressions for g in equations (6) and (7) equal to one another: $sr^* = g = \alpha + \beta r^* + \tau u^*$; or $sr^* = \alpha + \beta r^* + \tau u^*$. Now we use equation (4) to solve for u^* in terms of r^* in order to get an expression for r^* entirely in terms of parameters:

$1 = w^*a(0) + r^*/u^*$; substituting for w^* from (a) we get:
$1 = [1/a(0)(1+m)]a(0) + r^*/u^*$ which gives: $1 = 1/(1+m) + r^*/u^*$;
or $u^* = u^*/(1+m) + r^*$; or $(1+m)u^* = u^* + (1+m)r^*$;
or $u^* + mu^* - u^* = (1+m)r^*$; or $mu^* = (1+m)r^*$; or $u^* = (1+m)r^*/m$.
Substituting this expression for u^* into $sr^* = \alpha + \beta r^* + \tau u^*$ gives:
$sr^* = \alpha + \beta r^* + \tau(1+m)r^*/m$.
Collecting all terms in r^* on the left side gives:
$sr^* - \beta r^* - \tau(1+m)r^*/m = \alpha$; or $r^*[s - \beta - \tau(1+m)/m] = \alpha$; and finally:

(b) $r^* = \alpha / [s - \beta - \tau(1+m)/m]$

Substituting this expression for r^* into equation (6) now yields g^* immediately:

(c) $g^* = s\alpha / [s - \beta - \tau(1+m)/m]$

And substituting the solution for r^* from (b) into our equation for $u^* = (1+m)r^*/m$ gives:

$u^* = \alpha / [s - \beta - \tau(1+m)/m]/[(1+m)/m]$;
or $u^* = \alpha(1+m)/m[s - \beta - \tau(1+m)/m]$;
or $u^* = \alpha(1+m) / [sm - \beta m - \tau(1+m)]$; and finally:

(d) $u^* = \alpha(1+m) / [m(s - \beta - \tau) - \tau]$

To solve for c^* we use equation (2): $1 = c^*a(0) + g^*/u^*$; or $c^* = [1 - g^*/u^*]/a(0)$, and substitute for g^* from (c) and for u^* from the more convenient formulation for u^* in italics before our final simplification in (d): $c^* = (1 - \{s\alpha / [s - \beta - \tau(1+m)/m]\}/ \{\alpha(1+m)/m[s - \beta - \tau(1+m)/m]\})/a(0)$. Since the two long expressions in brackets, [ ] cancel each other, this simplifies nicely to:

(e) $c^* = [1 - sm/(1+m)]/a(0)$

Equations (a), (b), (c), (d), and (e) are the "reduced form" of the model and give the equilibrium value of each endogenous variable in terms only of the values of parameters. We can use these equations to see how changes in the value of any parameter affect the equilibrium values of the endogenous variables. Of particular interest is how changes in the savings behavior of capitalists as wealth holders, changes in the investment behavior of capitalists as entrepreneurs, and changes in the bargaining power of workers versus capitalists affect consumption and growth and the values of our two distributive variables, the rate of profit and the real wage.

An increase in capitalists' propensity to save

Looking at equation (a) reveals that if capitalists decide to save more of their income and consume less, there is no effect on the real wage because s does not appear in the expression for w^*. Inspecting equation (b) reveals that an increase in s will decrease r^* because s appears as a positive term in the denominator, so an increase in s increases the size of the denominator which decreases the overall fraction and therefore r^*. The relationship between s and g^* is a little more complicated. We just discovered that when s increases r^* decreases. But $g^* = sr^*$ so the question is if r^* decreases by a greater percentage than s increases. If r^* were equal to α/s then the percentage decrease in r^* when s increases would be the same as the percentage increase in s because g^* would equal $s[\alpha/s] = \alpha$ and not change when s increases. But instead r^* is equal to α divided by s minus some constant, call it k. Since $(s - k)$ necessarily grows by a greater percentage than s does when s increases, $\alpha/(s - k)$ must decrease by a greater percentage than α/s does when s increases, and therefore by a greater percentage than s increases, which means that g^* must decrease when s increases. Inspecting (d) reveals that u^* must decrease when s increases because s appears in a positive term of the denominator in the expression for u^*. Finally, inspecting (e) reveals that c^* must decrease when s increases since s appears in a negative term in the numerator of the expression for c^*. In sum, when s increases u^*, r^*, g^*, and c^* all decrease, while w^* remains constant.

What is the intuition behind these results? Equations (2) and (4) can help us see what is happening. According to equation (2) as long as u is held constant, if g falls c must rise and vice versa. This is because if u does not change the number of shmoos we produce, X, does not change. So if g falls, meaning fewer shmoos are invested, there must be more shmoos for consumption, and c must rise. According to equation (4) as long as u is held constant, if w falls r must rise and vice versa. This is because if u does not change the number or shmoos we produce does not change and therefore total income does not change. So if w falls and therefore labor income falls, capitalist income must rise, and r must rise. However in our political economy model u does not stay constant when s increases. Instead u decreases when s increases because when capitalists increase their savings rate they decrease their consumption demand, leading producers to lower production, which lowers u. Since there are now fewer shmoos produced it is possible for fewer shmoos to be consumed *and* fewer shmoos to be invested than before. Similarly, less production means less income, which is how capital's income can fall *even though* labor's income remains constant. Equations (2) and (4) confirm this relationship: When u falls either g, c, or both must fall if the right side of equation (2) is to remain equal to 1. Similarly when u falls either r, w, or both must fall if the right side of equation (4) is to remain equal to 1. When s rises u* falls and r* must fall according to equation (4) since w* remains constant. Apparently when capitalists decrease their demand to consume shmoos by raising their savings rate they decrease capacity utilization and shmoo production sufficiently that not only does the number of shmoos consumed fall, so does the number of shmoos invested, which equation (2) reveals to be possible.

In sum, when production and therefore income are constant we have a "zero sum game" between consumption and growth, and between workers and capitalists. If we think of the distribution of output between present consumption and investment as a conflict of interest between the present and future generation we can say that as long as production, i.e. capacity utilization, is constant there is an unavoidable conflict between the interests of the present generation, higher c, and the interests of the future generation, higher g. Just as there is an unavoidable conflict of interests between capitalists, higher r, and workers, higher w as long as income is constant – which it will be if capacity utilization remains the same. However, if something changes capacity utilization, i.e. production and income, the economy changes from a zero sum game to either a negative sum game or a positive sum game. Anything that lowers capacity utilization, u*, as an increase in s does, creates a negative sum game, as we discovered: g* and c* both fell, and r* fell even though w* remained constant. Obviously we will be on the lookout for changes in parameters that raise long run capacity utilization since that should allow some group to benefit without some other group losing.

An increase in capitalists' propensity to invest

If capitalists become more optimistic and decide they wanted to invest more, i.e. if α increases, equation (d) tells us u^* will increase allowing for a positive sum change. Equation (b) tells us r^* will increase while equation (a) tells us w^* will not decrease but stay constant. Equation (c) tells us g^* will increase while equation (e) tells us c^* will not decrease but stay constant. In sum, an increase in α raises u^*, r^*, and g^* while w^* and c^* remain constant. So by keeping the economy closer to full capacity utilization over the long run an increase in capitalists' animal spirits in their role of entrepreneurs and investors allows the rate of profit to rise without the wage rate falling, and allows the growth rate to increase without consumption falling. An increase in α benefits capitalists, but not at the expense of workers, and benefits future generations, but not at the expense of the present generation.

An increase in workers' bargaining power

What if workers increase their bargaining power and increase their real wage while labor productivity remains constant? In our model w^* can only increase while $[1/a(0)]$ stays constant when m decreases. Unless u^* increases r^* must decrease if w^* increases. But rewriting equation (d) slightly reveals that if m falls u^* must rise. Rewrite (d): $u^* = [(1+m)/m][\alpha/(s - \beta - \tau - \tau/m)]$ and note that $[(1+m)/m]$ must increase when m decreases, and $[\alpha/(s - \beta - \tau - \tau/m)]$ also increases when m decreases since τ/m rises when m falls, subtracting a larger term from s, making the denominator smaller, and therefore the fraction larger. With both terms in brackets increasing when m falls, u^* must increase when m falls yielding positive sum results. Inspection of equation (b) reveals that r^* indeed does increase when m falls: As before $(1+m)/m$ rises when m falls, making $\tau(1+m)/m$ larger, making the denominator smaller, and the fraction, and therefore r^* larger. Surprisingly capitalists benefit from a higher rate of profit when workers' bargaining power and real wages increase. Since $g^* = sr^*$ and r^* is greater when m is smaller the rate of growth also rises when workers' bargaining power increases. But inspection of (e) reveals that the increase in g^* is not at the expense of c^*: As noted, $(1+m)/m$ increases when m decreases, which means $m/(1+m)$

decreases when m decreases. So $s(m/(1+m))$ decreases when m decreases making the numerator larger and therefore c^* larger. In sum, a fall in m increases the real wage rate, w^*, without an increase in labor productivity, but also increases u^*, r^*, g^*, and c^*. The intuition behind this result is that an increase in workers' bargaining power, which raises real wages, increases the demand for shmoos since workers consume a higher percentage of their income than capitalists. This raises long run capacity utilization and makes capitalists *as well as* workers better off, and allows *both* future generations *and* the present generation to be better off as well.[10]

Our political economy model explains why "wage-led growth" is possible – even in the long run – if redistributing income from capital to labor keeps capacity utilization higher over the long run. But it also explains how capitalists can "foul their own nest," so to speak, when their bargaining power increases over workers. The 1980s and 1990s were marked by a dramatic increase in capitalist bargaining power in the developed economies for a number of reasons. We also witnessed a failure of real wages to keep pace with labor productivity increases, and lower economic growth rates than during the "golden era of capitalism" from 1950 through the mid-1970s. Obviously stagnant real wages and low economic growth rates are bad for workers and future generations. But our model points out that the "neoliberal economy" of the 1980s and 1990s was not even necessarily best for capitalists. Our model predicts that low levels of capacity utilization, which have also been characteristic of the neoliberal period, tend to lower profit rates for capitalists as well. As capitalists became ever more powerful and pushed real wages farther and farther below labor productivity, stagnant demand and idle capacity may well have created a negative sum game in which capitalists' profits were lower than they might otherwise have been.

10. Labor saving technical change is represented in our model by a fall in $a(0)$. Inspection of equations (a), (b), (c), (d), and (e) reveal that labor saving technical change increases w^* and c^* while leaving r^* and g^* unchanged. That is, labor saving technical change benefits workers and the present generation, but not at the expense of capitalists or future generations. Capital saving technical change does not change any of our endogenous variables because as long as there is any idle capacity economizing on the capital stock generates no efficiency gain.

10 What Is To Be Undone? The Economics of Competition and Greed

In *Capitalism and Freedom* (University of Chicago Press, 1964) Nobel Laureate and Dean of conservative economists, Milton Friedman, argued that only capitalism can provide economic freedom, allocate resources efficiently, and motivate people successfully. He also argued that capitalism is no less equitable than other kinds of economies, and a necessary condition for political freedom. Almost 40 years later neoliberal capitalism stands triumphant over the demise of both of its twentieth-century challengers – communism and social democracy – and its supporters are more confident than ever that laissez faire capitalism is the best economy of all. Since the "fall of the wall" and eclipse of social democracy have tied the tongues of many former critics of capitalism, I respond to Friedman's claims one by one, and present the case that free market capitalism is inherently inequitable, anti-democratic, and inefficient.

FREE ENTERPRISE EQUALS ECONOMIC FREEDOM – NOT

Friedman says the most important virtue of free enterprise is that it provides economic freedom, by which he means the freedom to do whatever one wishes with one's person and property – including the right to contract with others over their use of your person or property. He says economic freedom is important in and of itself, but also important because it unleashes people's economic creativity and promotes political freedom.

Political economists believe that people should control their economic lives, and only when they do so is it possible to tap their full economic potential. We also believe economic democracy promotes political democracy. But we find Friedman's concept of economic freedom inadequate, his argument that free enterprise allows people to control their economic lives highly misleading, his claim that free enterprise is efficient, rather than merely energetic, unpersuasive, and his conclusion that free enterprise promotes political democracy preposterous.

In chapter 2 I argued that it is important for people to control their economic lives irrespective of the quality of decisions they make. In other words, beside efficient and equitable outcomes we want workers and consumers to have input into economic decisions in proportion to the degree they are affected by those decisions – we want economic *self-management*. Friedman plays on the obvious truth that it is good when people are free to do what they want to substitute the concept of "economic freedom" for a more meaningful definition of economic democracy. Since this distortion is at the core of capitalist mythology it is important to treat it seriously.

The first problem with Friedman's concept of economic freedom is that in capitalism there are important situations where the economic freedom of one person conflicts with the economic freedom of another person. If polluters are free to pollute, then victims of pollution are not free to live in pollution free environments. If employers are free to use their productive property as they see fit, then their employees are not free to use their laboring capacities as they see fit. If the wealthy are free to leave their children large bequests, then new generations will not be free to enjoy equal economic opportunities. If those who own banks are free from a government imposed minimum reserve requirement, ordinary depositors are not free to save safely. So it is not enough simply to shout "let economic freedom ring" – as appealing as that may sound.

In capitalism whose economic freedom takes priority over whose is settled by the property rights system. Once we realize that economic freedom as defined by Friedman is meaningless without a specification of property rights – that it is the property rights system in capitalism that dictates who gets to decide what – the focus of attention shifts to where it should have been in the first place: How does the property rights system distribute decision making authority? Does the property rights system give people decision making authority in proportion to how much they are affected by an economic decision? Or, by giving priority to property rights over human rights, and by distributing property ownership unequally, does a property rights system leave most people little control over their economic destinies and award a few control over the economic fates of the many?

So the first problem with Milton Friedman's way of conceptualizing the notion that people should control their own economic lives is that it merely begs the question and defers all problems to an unspecified property rights system. The second problem is that while Friedman and other champions of capitalism wax poetic on the subject of economic freedom, they have remarkably little to say about what is a better or worse property rights system. Most of what little they do say reduces to two observations: (1) Whatever the distribution of property rights, it is crucial that property rights be clear cut and complete, since otherwise there will be inefficiency due to "property right ambiguity." (2) Since in their opinion it is difficult to argue that any distribution of property rights is preferable to any other on moral or theoretical grounds, there is no reason in their opinion to change the distribution of property rights history bequeathed us. In sum, Friedman defends the property rights status quo and considers only clarification of ambiguities a legitimate area for public policy. What is entirely lacking is any attempt to develop criteria for better and worse distributions of property rights, not to speak of discussion of how property rights might be distributed to best approximate economic self-management.

However, conservatives' silence on the issue of what besides clarity and respecting the status quo constitutes a desirable system of property rights does not extend to the issue of employer versus employee rights. According to Friedman there is no conflict between employees' and employers' economic freedoms as long as employment contracts are agreed to by both parties under competitive conditions. As long as the employment relation is voluntary, and as long as labor markets are competitive so nobody is compelled to work for a particular employer, or compelled to hire a particular employee, the economic freedoms of all are preserved according to Friedman and his conservative followers. In their eyes, when an employee agrees to work for an employer she is merely exercising her economic freedom to do with her laboring capacities as she sees fit. She could use her "human capital" herself if she wished. But she should be free to relinquish her right to use her laboring capacities to another for an agreed wage payment if she decides that is a better deal. What's more, if she were prohibited from making this choice her economic freedom would be violated, just as the economic freedom of the employer to use his productive property as he sees fit would be violated if he were barred from hiring employees to work with it under his direction. Accordingly, Friedman concludes that "union shops" are violations of employee as well as employer economic freedom under capitalism, and socialism's ban on private enterprise is the ultimate violation of people's economic freedom to hire and be hired by one another should they so choose.

The first problem with this defense of private enterprise as the cornerstone of economic freedom is that not all people have, or could ever have, an equal opportunity to become employers rather than employees. In real capitalist economies a few will become employers, the vast majority will work for someone else, and some will be self-employed. Moreover, *who* will be employers, employees, or self-employed is determined for the most part *neither* randomly *nor* by peoples' relative preferences for self-managed versus other-directed work. In the corn model in chapter 3 we discovered that *only* under egalitarian distributions of seed corn would relative preferences for self-managed work determine who became employers and who became employees. Under inegalitarian distributions those with more seed corn became employers and those with less became employees *irrespective* of people's relative preferences for self-management or aversions to being bossed around. One of the most profound insights provided by the simple corn model is that while it is true, in a sense, that employees "choose" alienated labor, they do not necessarily do so because they have a weaker desire for self-management than those they go to work for. The distribution of wealth "tilts" the private enterprise playing field so that some will benefit more by becoming employers and others will benefit more by becoming employees *independent* of people's work preferences. In different terms, the poor have to "pay a price" to manage their own laboring capacities while the rich are rewarded for bossing others.

Defenders of capitalism's answer to this criticism is that anyone who wants to work badly enough for herself can borrow whatever is necessary to become an employer in the credit market. They go on to point out that *assuming perfect credit markets*, anyone who can run an efficient business can borrow enough to do so, and thereby avoid having to play the role of employee herself. But this line of reasoning (1) assumes more than any real capitalism can offer – credit on equal terms for all – and (2) ignores that even competitive credit markets can impose a steep price on the poor for self-management which the wealthy are not required to pay. In a world with uncertainty and imperfect information – not to speak of patents and technological and financial economies of scale – those with more collateral and credentials will receive credit on preferential terms while the rest of us will be subject to credit rationing in one form or another. To expect any different is to expect lenders to be fools. So being referred to the credit market is not going to even the playing field for the poor. And even if all did receive credit on equal terms, our simple corn model in chapter 3 demonstrates that the poor who avoid the status of employer by borrowing in credit markets – where we generously assumed anyone could borrow as much as she wanted at the market rate of interest – effectively pay their wealthy creditors for the right to manage their own laboring capacities – a right that should be as "inalienable" as the right to vote on political issues. There is a bottom line and the buck must stop somewhere: Those without wealth to begin with have an uphill road to avoid employee status in capitalist economies, with or without credit markets, no matter how close to perfect those credit markets might be.

But even if the capitalist playing field were level, and the probability of becoming an employer rather than an employee was exactly the same for everyone, this would not mean the employer–employee relationship was a desirable one. Of course random assignment would be a far sight better than having relative wealth determine who will boss and who will be bossed. But is it better than having neither bosses nor bossed? In other words, is it better than an economy where *all* enjoy self-management?

Here is a useful analogy: A slave system where slaves apply to be slaves for slave masters of their choice is better than one where slave owners trade slaves among themselves. A slave system where people are assigned randomly to be slaves or slave masters is better than one where only blacks are slaves and only whites can be slave owners. But abolition of slavery is better than even the least objectionable kind of slavery. The same holds for wage slavery. A labor market where employees are free to apply to work for employers of their choice is better than one where employers trade employees among themselves. A system where who become employers and who become employees is truly a random walk is better than one where the wealthy predictably become the employers and the poor predictably become employees. But abolition of wage slavery – replacing the roles of employer and employee with self-management for all – is better than even the least objectionable system of private enterprise.

Friedman goes on to argue that beside being good in itself, economic freedom promotes political freedom. His first argument is that in a free enterprise economy people have a choice of non-government employers. This means people are not reliant on the government for their economic livelihood and therefore will be free to speak their minds, and in particular, free to oppose government policies. Friedman's second argument is that if wealth were distributed equally none would have sufficient discretionary wealth to fund political causes. Since wealth is distributed very unequally in capitalist economies, Friedman concludes that there are always multiple funding sources available for any and all political causes.

Economic democracy *is* political democracy's best friend, and authoritarian economies *are* political democracy's worst enemy. But that does not mean that private enterprise promotes political freedom and democracy. One problem with Friedman's first argument is that private employers can intimidate employees who are afraid to lose their jobs if they support political causes their employers disagree with – just as a government employer can. In other words, Friedman is blind to the dictatorship of the propertied, and sees government as the only conceivable perpetrator of coercion. A second fallacy with his first argument is that a monolithic state employer is not the only alternative to a wealthy capitalist employer. State monopoly on employment opportunities in Soviet-style economies *was* a serious obstacle to freedom of political expression in those societies. But in the next chapter we will see that nobody has reason to fear for her job because of her political views in a participatory economy or in an employee managed, market socialist economy since the State exerts no influence over who gets hired or fired in enterprises in either of these economies. Comparing capitalism only to communism, and implicitly assuming there are no other alternatives is the oldest play in the capitalist team play book.

The obvious problem with Friedman's second argument – that unequal wealth provides alternative sources of funding for political causes – is that by his own admission, those with vastly greater wealth will control access to the means of political expression. This effectively disenfranchises the poor who have no recourse but to appeal to the wealthy to finance their political causes. Jerry Brown was right when he argued in the 1992 Democratic Presidential primaries that politicians in both major parties in the US are essentially bought and paid for by wealthy financial interests who pre-select which candidates can mount viable primary campaigns. Ralph Nader was right when he argued during the 2000 general election that both the Republican *and* Democratic parties had been effectively bought by corporations, and should be seen for what they are, two wings of a single party of business, the Republicrats. Every viable politician has to ask how his stand on an issue will affect both his voter appeal *and* his funding appeal – with the effect on donations from wealthy contributors becoming ever more crucial to electability in the US where expensive television ads are increasingly critical. While we needn't feel sorry for them, more and more US senators are choosing retirement in face of the daunting task of raising literally tens of thousands of dollars per day starting the day after they're elected in order to be viable candidates for re-election six years later.

The fact that Ross Perot and Steve Forbes Jr. could gain serious public consideration for their mostly hare-brained political ideas by financing presidential bids out of their own deep pockets, whereas 99% of the population cannot pay for a single ad in the *New York Times*, much less finance a credible presidential campaign, is hardly evidence that capitalism makes it possible for all political opinions to get a hearing, much less evidence of equal political opportunities under capitalism. Moreover, why does Milton Friedman think the economically powerful and wealthy will finance political causes aimed at reducing their wealth and power? At best, Friedman's view of the wealthy as "patrons of the political arts" would predictably provide more adequate funding for some schools of "political art" than others. Simply put, Friedman's attempt to make a political virtue out of the large disparities of economic power capitalism creates is ludicrous. Unequal economic power breeds unequal political power – not political democracy – as any school child knows.

FREE ENTERPRISE IS EFFICIENT – NOT

Friedman and mainstream economists argue that free enterprise promotes technological efficiency. They point out that any capitalist who discovers a way to reduce the amount of an input necessary to make an output will be able to lower her production costs below those of her competitors, and thereby earn higher than average profits. Moreover, other producers will be driven to adopt the new, more productive technique for fear of being driven out of business by more innovative competitors. In this way they argue that competition for profit promotes the search for and adoption of more efficient technologies. While competition sometimes drives entrepreneurs to seek and implement technological improvements, Friedman fails to point out that there are compelling reasons to believe competition for profits also drives firms to make technological choices contrary to the social interest.

Monopoly and oligopolistic markets not only yield static inefficiencies by restricting supply to drive up market price, they promote dynamic inefficiencies as well. Examples of large companies conspiring to suppress technological innovations because it would depreciate their fixed capital, or reduce opportunities for repeated sales because a product lasted longer, are legion. While this cause of technological inefficiency in real capitalist economies riddled with non-competitive market structures is important, I concentrate below on a more difficult theoretical point, namely that even in competitive environments, capitalists will often make socially counterproductive choices of technology.

Biased price signals

In chapter 4 we discovered that externalities lead to market prices that do not accurately reflect true social costs and benefits. Since capitalists understandably use market prices, not true social costs, when deciding if a new technology is cost reducing, inaccuracies due to external effects can lead to socially counterproductive decisions regarding technologies. Furthermore, the Sraffian model of price and income determination in chapter 5 reveals that the higher the rate of profit in the economy, and the lower the wage rate, the more likely it is that capitalists will implement new capital-saving, labor-using technologies that are profitable but socially inefficient, and reject new capital-using, labor-saving technologies that are socially efficient but unprofitable. In other words, the Sraffa model reveals another reason why prices in capitalism are biased in a way that leads profit maximizing capitalists to make inefficient choices of technology: The greater the bargaining power of capital over labor, the more likely the price system will provide false signals leading to socially counterproductive choices of technologies.

Conflict theory of the firm

The *conflict theory of the firm* spells out why profit maximization requires capitalists to choose less efficient technologies if more efficient technologies lower their bargaining power over their employees sufficiently. The logic I review informally here is illustrated formally in the application of the "price of power game" to the conflict theory of the firm in chapter 5. There is an inherent conflict of interest between employers and employees over how high or low the wage will be, and how much effort employees will have to exert for that wage. If we define the real wage in terms of dollars of compensation per unit of effort expended this reduces to a struggle over the real wage. For the most part employers are free to choose among alternative technologies available and free to establish whatever internal personnel policies they wish. Or at least, employers have considerable discretion in these areas. Political economists from the conflict school point out that it would be irrational for employers to consider the impact of technological choices and personnel policies on productivity *only* when these choices *also* affect employers' bargaining power *vis-à-vis* their employees. Since profits depend not only on the size of net output, but on how the net output is divided between wages and profits, rational employers will consider how their choices affect *both* the size *and* distribution of the firm's net output.

Suppose technology A is slightly less productive than technology B, but technology A substantially reduces employees' bargaining power while technology B increases the employer's bargaining power significantly. A profit maximizing employer would have no choice but to opt for the less productive technology A. For example, consider automobile manufacturers' choice between assembly line versus work team technologies. Suppose when quality and reliability are taken into account, making automobiles in work teams is slightly more productive than making cars on an assembly line. But suppose team production is more skill enhancing and builds employee solidarity, while assembly line production reduces the knowledge component of work for most employees and reduces employee solidarity by isolating employees from one another. If the "bargaining power effect" outweighs the "productivity effect," competition for profits will drive auto makers to opt for assembly line production even though it is less efficient.

The disagreement between political economists from the conflict school and our mainstream colleagues is *not* whether or not employers and employees *have* a conflict of interest over wages and effort levels – since everyone recognizes that – but whether or not this conflict leads to economic inefficiencies. Beside leading to inefficient technologies, this permanent conflict of interest between employers and employees over how to distribute the net product, or value added, also wastes valuable resources and personnel on supervisory efforts, creates incentives for employees to resist innovation and technical change, and most importantly wastes the creative economic potential of the vast majority of the populace. For the most part employees' conceptual capabilities go under-used and repressed by their employers who cannot trust them, because while employers and their employees may share an interest in greater efficiency, they have conflicting interests over the effects of firm policies on bargaining power.

FREE ENTERPRISE REDUCES ECONOMIC DISCRIMINATION – NOT

Mainstream economists insist that competition for profits among employers will reduce discrimination. They point out that if an employer has "a taste" for discrimination and insists on paying white employees more than equivalent black employees, or male employees more than equivalent female employees, the discriminating employer will have a higher wage bill than an employer who does not discriminate and pays equivalent employees equally. Mainstream theorists conclude that eventually employers who do not discriminate should compete those who do out of business. Similarly, they point out that the business of any employer who fails to hire or promote the most qualified people due to overt or unconscious discrimination will be less productive than businesses which hire and promote purely on merit. So according to mainstream economists a firm that engages in discriminatory hiring or promotion practices should also be competed out of business by firms that do not. While mainstream theory is quick to see the profit reducing aspects of economic discrimination on the part of employers, it is blind to the profit increasing effects of discrimination. By recognizing the importance of bargaining power in the ongoing struggle between employers and their employees over the distribution of value added, the conflict theory of the firm helps us see why profit maximization does not preclude, but in fact *requires* economic discrimination even when employers operate in competitive labor and goods markets.

Discrimination in hiring, assignment, promotion, and payment have all been used to aggravate suspicions and antagonisms that already exist between women and men, and between people of different races and ethnic backgrounds. Historical settings where ample reasons for suspicion and mistrust already exist provide ready-made pressure points which employers can manipulate to "divide and conquer" their employees. When employees are mutually suspicious they can be more easily induced to inform on one another regarding lackadaisical efforts – making it easier for the employer to extract more "labor done" from the "labor hired." When employees are unsupportive of one another they will be easier for their employer to bargain with over wages when their contract comes up. What the conflict theory reveals is that since discriminatory practices by an individual employer have these positive effects on profits, profit maximization requires engaging in discriminatory practices up to the point where the negative effects of discrimination on profits – which are the exclusive focus of mainstream theory – outweigh the profit enhancing effects – which only political economists identify. In other words, competition for profits will drive employers to engage in discriminatory practices up to the point where the redistributive effect of discrimination – increasing the employer's share of value added by decreasing employees' bargaining power – equals the negative impact of discrimination on productivity or the wage bill.

The implications of discovering that economic discrimination is part and parcel of profit maximization are important. First, since mainstream theorists are correct that discrimination often reduces economic efficiency, it provides yet another reason to believe that capitalism will not be efficient. But more importantly this means that it is not the employers who discriminate who will eventually be driven out of business by those who do not, but just the reverse. Employers who steadfastly refuse to discriminate will be driven out of business by those who pay attention only to the bottom line – and therefore engage in profit enhancing discriminatory behavior. The implication for public policy is huge. If mainstream economists were correct, competitive labor and capital markets would tend to eliminate discriminatory employment practices, at least in the long run. In which case, if minorities and women were willing to continue to pay the price for society's patience, we could expect discrimination to diminish without government involvement. But the conflict theory demonstrates that even assuming no collusion among employers, it is profitable for individual employers to aggravate racial antagonisms among their employees up to the point where the costs of doing so outweigh the additional profits that come from negotiating with a less powerful group of employees. Therefore it is foolish to wait for capitalism to eliminate discrimination if unaided. Instead laws outlawing discrimination and affirmative action programs are absolutely necessary if discrimination is to be reduced in capitalist economies. Moreover, the struggle against discrimination through active intervention must constantly "swim upstream" in capitalism because employers who do discriminate are rewarded with higher profits, and employers who refuse to discriminate are punished by shareholders who care only about their bottom line.[1]

The increasingly popular view in the US that government protection and affirmative action have done their job and are no longer necessary could not be farther from the truth.[2] As the government's anti-discriminatory efforts weakened, the discrepancy between the wages of equivalent black and white workers increased by 50% from 10.9% in 1979 to 16.4% in 1989.[3] A study by the Government Accounting Office released in January 2002 revealed that the female wage gap was no longer shrinking, but had widened significantly between 1995 and 2000. Shannon Henry reported in an article titled "Male–Female Salary Gap Growing, Study Says" published in the *Washington Post* on January 24, 2002: "Female managers are not only making less money than men in many industries, but the wage gap widened during the economic boom years of 1995 to 2000, according to a congressional study to be released today. The study found that a full-time female communications manager earned 86 cents for every dollar a male made in her industry in 1995. In 2000, she made only 73 cents of the man's dollar." The conflict theory merely explains what is readily apparent to anyone who wishes to see.

FREE ENTERPRISE IS FAIR – NOT

Imagine a capitalist economy where discrimination was successfully outlawed. Even under these best of circumstances private enterprise market economies would distribute the burdens and benefits of

---

1. See Michael Reich, *Racial Inequality* (Princeton University Press, 1981): 204–15 for a simple, yet powerful model proving that wage discrimination is a necessary condition for profit maximization for individual capitalist employers operating in competitive markets.
2. See Barbara Bergman, *In Defense of Affirmative Action* (Basic Books, 1996) for persuasive evidence that affirmative action programs *do* help groups that are discriminated against, and that discrimination quickly reappears in their absence.
3. Lawrence Mishel and Jared Bernstein, *The State of Working America: 1994–95* (ME Sharpe, 1994): 187. "Equivalent" means comparing black and white workers with the same level of education, work experience, etc.

economic activity according to the conservative maxim 1: to each according to the market value of the contribution of his or her labor and productive property. But we have already seen why capitalist distribution is inequitable. Distribution according to this maxim means that the grandson of a Rockefeller who never works a day in his life will consume a thousand times more than a hard working doctor, simply because the former inherited ownership of large amounts of productive property. In a world where recent estimates indicate the combined wealth of the world's 447 billionaires is greater than the income of the poorest half of the world's people, capitalist inequity can hardly be dismissed as a minor liability, as Friedman does. As long as there are feasible economies that distribute the burdens and benefits of economic activity more equitably than capitalism – and in the next chapter we will see that there are – those who offer rationalizations for inequities in capitalism are nothing more than accomplices in the crime of economic injustice.

MARKETS EQUAL ECONOMIC FREEDOM – NOT

Milton Friedman argues that the principle virtue of markets is that they promote economic freedom:

> The basic problem of social organization is how to coordinate the economic activities of large numbers of people ... The challenge to the believer in liberty is to reconcile this widespread interdependence with individual freedom. Fundamentally there are only two ways of coordinating the economic activities of millions. One is central direction involving the use of coercion – the technique of the army and of the modern totalitarian state. The other is voluntary cooperation of individuals – the technique of the market place. The possibility of coordination through voluntary cooperation rests on the elementary, yet frequently denied, proposition that both parties to an economic transaction benefit from it, *provided the transaction is bilaterally voluntary and informed*. So long as effective freedom of exchange is maintained, the central feature of the market organization of economic activity is that it prevents one person from interfering with another in respect of most of his activities. The consumer is protected from coercion by the seller because of the presence of other sellers with whom he can deal. The seller is protected from coercion by the consumer because of other consumers to whom he can sell. The employee is

protected from coercion by the employer because of other employers for whom he can work, and so on. And the market does this impersonally and without centralized authority.[4]

The first problem is that it is not one person one vote, but one dollar one vote in the market place. Some claim this as a virtue: If I have a particularly strong preference for a good I can cast more dollar ballots to reflect the intensity of my desire. But this is conflating two issues. There is nothing wrong with a system of social choice that permits people to express the intensity of their desires. In fact, this is necessary if we are to achieve self-managed decision making. But, *there is something wrong when people have vastly different numbers of dollar ballots to cast in market elections.* Few would hold up as a paragon of freedom a political election in which some were permitted to vote thousands of times and others were permitted to vote only once, or not at all. But this is exactly the kind of freedom the market provides. Those with more income have a greater impact on what suppliers in markets will be signaled to provide than those with less income, which explains why "market freedom" often leads to outcomes we know do not reflect what most people need or want. Why are there so many plastic surgeons when many communities suffer for lack of basic family practitioners? How can the demand for cosmetic plastic surgery be so high and the demand for basic family health care so low? There are many more who vote in the health care market for basic health care than for plastic surgery. Moreover, the intensity of people's desires for basic health care is higher than the intensity of desires for plastic surgery. But those voting for plastic surgery in healthcare markets have many more votes to cast for even their less pressing desires than most voting for basic health care have even for life and death needs. Hence the provision of medical services of marginal benefit, like plastic surgery, and the failure to provide essential medical services for the poor, when health care decisions are left to the market place.

Second, in the simple corn model in chapter 3 we saw how exchanges in labor and credit markets that are bilaterally voluntary and informed can still lead to growing inequalities – even when employees and borrowers are supposedly "protected from coercion" by a multiplicity of employers and lenders to choose from. The lie behind Friedman's portrayal of market exchanges as non-coercive is

4. Milton Friedman, *Capitalism and Freedom*: 12–13.

that he ignores the importance of what those who confront each other in the market place arrive with. As we saw in the corn model, when some arrive at the labor market with seed corn and others have none, it is entirely predictable that the seedy will end up being the employers and the seedless their employees. Moreover, as long as seed corn is scarce it is predictable that the seedy employers will capture the lion's share of the efficiency gain from the labor exchange as profits, even though the employers don't work at all. Similarly, those who arrive at the credit market with more seed corn will lend to those with less, and as long as seed corn is scarce the lenders will capture the lion's share of the resulting increase in the borrowers' productivity as interest, even though the lenders don't work at all. Friedman can call these outcomes non-coercive if he wants, on grounds that the seedless volunteered to exchange their laboring capacities for a wage, and borrowers agreed to pay interest knowing full well what the consequences would be. But this merely displaces the source of coercion. It is their seedlessness that "coerces" employees and borrowers to "volunteer" to be fleeced. Are we to believe they would have "volunteered" to be the ones who showed up at the labor or credit market place seedless in the first place?

Friedman opens the door when he acknowledges that exchange under non-competitive conditions is coercive even though exchanges under non-competitive conditions are also bilaterally voluntary, informed and mutually beneficial. In a one-company town since I am free to remain unemployed, I am presumably better off working than not working if you find me employed. In a one-bank town since I am free not to borrow at all, I am presumably better off if I borrow than I would have been had I not. But not even Milton Friedman has the *chutzpah* to call these non-competitive market outcomes non-coercive – even though the agreement is voluntary and may be mutually beneficial in both cases. Once we recognize that voluntary exchanges under non-competitive conditions are coercive since only one party to the exchange has the opportunity to choose among *different* partners, it is easy to see how exchanges under competitive conditions can be coercive as well. *When initial conditions are unequal, voluntary, informed and mutually beneficial exchanges will be coercive and lead to inequitable outcomes even if exchanges take place under competitive conditions.*

The third problem with Friedman's assertion that market decisions are free from coercion is that buyers and sellers often come to agreements with adverse consequences for third parties who have no say in the matter whatsoever. Friedman acknowledges that victims of what he calls "neighborhood effects" are coerced, but presumes these are minor inconveniences that seldom occur. As we saw in chapter 4, many political economists believe that external effects are the rule rather than the exception in market exchanges, thereby leaving many disenfranchised and "coerced" when buyers and sellers make decisions that affect them without giving a thought to consulting their interests.

The fourth problem is that Friedman assumes away the best solution for coordinating economic activities. He simply asserts: "there are only two ways of coordinating the economic activities of millions – central direction involving the use of coercion – and voluntary cooperation – the technique of the market place." In the next chapter we will explore the alternative of democratic planning. We will see how participatory economies permit all to partake in economic decision making in proportion to the degree they are affected by outcomes. Since a participatory economy uses participatory planning instead of markets to coordinate economic activities, Friedman would have us believe that participatory planning must fall into the category of "central direction involving the use of coercion." But as you will see, this is most certainly not the case, invalidating Friedman's assertion that there are only two ways of coordinating economic activities – a crucial assumption Friedman offers no argument for whatsoever.

In sum, few economic decisions are such that only those who own a property right that allows them to make the decision unilaterally are affected by the outcome. So to believe that when those whose ownership of property gives them the legal right to make decisions in the market place, others are not subjected to coercion, is to swallow a myth. It is best to have all those affected by a decision take part in making it. And it is more honest to recognize that not everyone usually gets exactly what they want when choices affect many people, rather than pretend that everyone always gets what they want in market decisions, while people are only forced to accept outcomes they don't like from political decisions.

MARKETS ARE FAIR – NOT

Is capitalism unfair only because people get unjustifiable income from ownership of productive property? Or, are labor markets also unfair? Even if wages and salaries were determined in competitive labor markets free from discrimination, a surgeon who is on the golf course by 2 p.m. would consume ten times more than a garbage collector working 50 hours per week because the surgeon was genetically gifted and benefitted from vast quantities of socially costly education. Free labor and capital markets mean that most who are wealthy are so *not* because they worked harder or sacrificed more than others, but because they inherited wealth, talent, or simply got lucky. In chapter 2 we concluded that distribution according to maxim 2 – to each according to the value of her labor's contribution – is inequitable because income from human capital is unfair for the same reasons income from physical capital is unfair: Differences in the values of people's contributions for reasons *other than* differences in effort or sacrifice are beyond people's abilities to control, and carry no moral weight in any case.

But wages in real world capitalism are considerably more inequitable than marginal revenue product wages would be. Minorities and women are generally not paid the market value of their labor's contribution. Because of economic discrimination in hiring, promotion, and pay, because of occupational ghettos, and because of unequal educational opportunities, inequities in real world capitalism are far worse than they would be in ideal models.

MARKETS ARE EFFICIENT – NOT

In chapter 4 we explored a number of reasons for believing markets are guided by a malevolent, invisible foot as often as by a beneficent invisible hand when they allocate our scarce productive resources. We discovered that Milton Friedman and received wisdom not withstanding, there are good reasons to believe markets allocate resources very inefficiently and concluded: "Convenient deals with mutual benefits for buyer and seller should not be confused with economic efficiency. When some kinds of preferences are consistently underrepresented because of transaction cost and free rider problems, when consumers adjust their preferences to biases in the market price system and thereby aggravate those biases, and when profits can be increased as often by externalizing costs onto parties external to market exchanges as from productive behavior, theory predicts that free market exchange will often result in a *mis*allocation of scarce productive resources. Moreover, when markets are less than perfectly competitive – which they almost always are – and fail to equilibrate instantaneously – which they always do – the results are that much worse."

When pressed, all economists concede that externalities, non-competitive market structures, and market disequilibria lead to allocative inefficiencies. Since mainstream economists take capitalism for granted, the debate among them is whether "market failure" or "government failure" is worse. That is, mainstream economists argue among themselves over whether government policies aimed at reducing inefficiencies due to externalities, non-competitive market structures, and disequilibria create even greater inefficiencies than those they eliminate. Conservative mainstream economists emphasize the dangers of "government failure" when politicians and bureaucrats sacrifice efficiency to their personal agendas. Liberal mainstream economists emphasize how much inefficiency due to market failures can be reduced by responsible government policies if only opposition from business special interests could be overcome.

Not surprisingly, political economists generally side with liberals in the mainstream in our attempts to ameliorate the inefficiencies and inequities of capitalism. But until recently most political economists also emphasized that as much as we try to reduce the ill effects of market failures, even the best efforts will always fall short of what a truly desirable economy could yield for a host of theoretical and practical reasons. While anti-trust policy can be used to make industries more competitive, they frequently sacrifice economies of scale and dynamic efficiency in service of allocative efficiency when they break up large firms. Moreover, even when the public interest is obviously served, anti-trust cases are hard to win when opposed by corporate power as the Microsoft anti-trust case attests. Using fiscal and monetary policies to "fine tune" real economies honeycombed with uncertainties and speculative dynamics impossible to capture in even the most elaborate macro economic forecasting models, is far more difficult than theoretical models lead one to suspect. Political economists also used to emphasize that an increasingly integrated global economy and powerful domestic business interests often obstruct effective fiscal and monetary policy.

Sectoral imbalances pose a different kind of disequilibria and inefficiency. When an industry expands less rapidly than industries it buys from and sells to, it can become a "bottleneck" retarding overall growth and under-utilizing productive capacities in related industries. "Indicative planning" or "industrial policy" attempts to reduce this kind of market inefficiency by anticipating sectoral imbalances and reducing them through differential tax and credit policies. Industries identified as bottlenecks are favored with lower business taxes and preferential credit to stimulate their growth, while "surplus industries" expanding more rapidly than related industries are discouraged by higher taxes and credit rationing in some form or another. Whether the government can guess better than the market, whether differential tax and credit policies are an open invitation to corruption, and whether indicative planning inevitably reduces economic democracy as economic elites dominate the planning process are all questions posed by mainstream and political economists alike.

It is ironic that from the 1930s through the 1970s when significant progress was made in the theory and practice of regulation, fiscal and monetary policies, and indicative planning, most political economists held firmly to the conviction that market failures were a serious, if not fatal flaw in capitalism. But since 1989 as environmental externalities become ever more apparent, and government after government abandons regulatory policies, full-employment stabilization policies, and industrial policies, many political economists have inexplicably altered their assessment. Now, problems due to market failures of one kind or another that were once deemed damning are considered by some political economists to be tolerable – despite *declining* economic performances from *more* free market economies. Of course, I am not suggesting there are no reasons for the about face in opinion. The dramatic increase in the political and ideological hegemony of pro-market forces is obvious to all, as is the demise of what was widely assumed to be the only alternative to market allocations – central planning. As a result, economists who criticize market inefficiencies are even more marginalized within the profession than before – an obvious incentive for muting criticism once voiced more freely. However, the change in political climate has no *logical* bearing on the degree to which market allocations are, in fact, inefficient due to market failures. Market failures and their pernicious effects continue unabated no matter how impolitic it is to mention them.

In sum, private enterprise and markets *both* cause unacceptable inequities. Private enterprise and markets *both* cause significant inefficiencies. Private enterprise and markets *both* disenfranchise the vast majority from participating in economic decision making in proportion to the degree they are affected, and stand as a growing danger to, rather than bulwark of, political freedom. The only difference between twenty-first-century and twentieth-century capitalism will be that "born again" capitalism may well kill us all since it begins with "initial conditions" – 5 billion people, modern industrial technology, and an already damaged ecosystem – that can do in mother earth in fairly short order. God has given capitalism the rainbow sign. No more water, the fire next time.

WHAT WENT WRONG?

One hundred years ago economic radicals expected the twentieth century to be capitalism's last. Progressives expected democracy and economic justice to advance in tandem and replace a wasteful system based on competition and greed with a more efficient, equitable economy in which workers and consumers planned how to cooperate through democratic procedures. But the heirs apparent to nineteenth-century anti-capitalism – twentieth-century communism and social democracy – each failed to advance the causes of economic justice and democracy. So instead of hearing its last hurrah, capitalism beat back all challengers, leaving us with economies that are no more democratic or equitable than economies a century ago.

Communist economies were public enterprise systems governed by central planning. After spreading its influence over large parts of the globe from 1917 to 1989, these economies vanished in only a few years at the end of the century.[5] The Communist economic system did not suffer from the same deficiencies as capitalism. Centrally planned economies in the Soviet Bloc were terribly flawed in different ways. While the fatal flaw in capitalism is its antisocial bias, the fatal flaw in central planning was its anti-democratic bias. It is clear that centrally planned economies run by totalitarian political parties, largely immune from popular pressure, and increasingly free to feather the nests of their leaders and members, were not likely to produce the best outcomes. For this reason some progressive anti-capitalists continue to favor central planning on grounds that many of the problems that appeared could, conceivably, be blamed

5. See Michael Albert and Robin Hahnel, "Revolutions in the East" *Z Magazine*, April 1990, for an interpretation of the "demise of Communism" written before the collapse of the Soviet Union.

on the negative effect of undemocratic political systems on the economy. But these apologists for central planning grossly underestimate the fatal flaw in even "best case" central planning: Central planning is terribly biased against popular participation in economic decision making. It was precisely this flaw that made central planning such a convenient accomplice for totalitarian political elites. The marriage of the single vanguard party state and economic central planning was truly a marriage made in the hell of two totalitarian dynamics, and predictably political and economic democracy were the first victims.

Combined with a more democratic political system, and redone to closer approximate a best case version, centrally planned economies no doubt would have performed better. But they could never have delivered economic self-management, they would always have been slow to innovate as apathy and frustration took their inevitable toll, and they would always have been susceptible to growing inequities and inefficiencies as the effects of differential economic power grew. Under central planning neither planners, managers, nor workers had incentives to promote the social economic interest. Nor did appending markets for final goods to the planning system enfranchise consumers in meaningful ways. But central planning would have been incompatible with economic democracy even if it had overcome its information and incentive liabilities. And the truth is that it survived as long as it did only because it was propped up by unprecedented totalitarian political power. In the end Communist parties sacrificed economic democracy along with political democracy in the name of economic justice and efficiency they never delivered.[6]

Social democratic parties avoided the totalitarian errors of communism only to abandon their commitment to pursuing the economics of equitable cooperation. While social democratic reforms within national economies gained ground for 30 years after World War II, these reforms proved ever harder to defend as capital became more mobile internationally, and as ideological and political opposition to capitalism crumbled with the "fall of the wall" in 1989. To rephrase an old adage: It proved harder and harder to build social

6. For a thorough critique of centrally planned economies written a decade before the "fall of the wall" see Michael Albert and Robin Hahnel, *Marxism and Socialist Theory,* and *Socialism Today and Tomorrow* both published by South End Press in 1981.

democracy in one country. But social democracy also abandoned its base among the disadvantaged by accepting, rather than challenging, the ideological underpinnings of labor markets, and made peace with capitalism by accepting the inevitability of an economic system based on competition and greed. After more than a half-century of alternating in and out of power, European social democratic parties lost sight of the difference between "reformer of" and "apologist for" capitalism.

In the end, both would-be heirs to nineteenth-century economic radicalism delivered neither economic justice nor economic democracy. And, largely as a result, both communism and social democracy had one foot, if not both, firmly in the dustbin of history as the door closed on the century each presumed would bear its name.

Misconceptions about economic justice and democracy also undermined efforts to replace the economics of competition and greed with the economics of equitable cooperation in the twentieth century. For example, few union leaders today could tell you if they thought the workers they represent are exploited because they are *not* paid their marginal revenue product, or exploited precisely because they *are* paid their marginal revenue product. No wonder the most powerful progressive movement of the twentieth century, the union movement, became confused and hypocritical on the subject most central to its own mission. As passionate as union leaders are about economic justice, they have a remarkably difficult time saying clearly what it is. Instead, most union leaders find themselves in the position the late US Supreme Court Justice Potter Stewart found himself when required to make a ruling on pornography. In his immortal words: "I shall not today attempt further to define pornography, but I know it when I see it." It seems few union leaders can define economic justice, but almost all believe they know economic *in*justice when they see it.

In a similar way "economic democracy" became an ever more vague "buzz" word as the twentieth century progressed, instead of standing forthrightly for decision making power in proportion to the degree one is affected. In this context it is easy to confuse total quality management (TQM), employee stock-ownership plans (ESOPs), and employee ownership accompanied by traditional management hierarchies with *real* economic democracy. TQM and ESOPs are concessions to the fact that people not only want a say and stake in what they are doing, but they perform better when they feel that they have a say. Since the essence of the capitalist labor exchange deprives employees of control over their labor, employers sometimes find it useful to resort to appearances and partial concessions.

While progressives have every reason to validate people's desires for economic justice and real participation, and work to expand partial concessions, we should never fool ourselves – or others – that appearances are reality, or that real economic justice and democracy can be achieved until traditional ownership, management, and allocation institutions are replaced by new institutional forms. Progressives increasingly fell victim to this trap as the twentieth century unfolded.

Finally, some great opportunities to advance the causes of economic justice and democracy in the twentieth century were lost. To name a few examples: (1) While underdevelopment and international opposition were contributing factors, the primary blame for the failure of the Russian Revolution lies with anti-democratic choices made by the Revolutionary leadership in the first few years after overthrowing Czarist tyranny. (2) A living example of economic justice and democracy at work in the Spanish Republic did not die primarily because of internal flaws, but instead because it was crushed by fascist military might in the Spanish Civil War when progressives in the "democratic countries" failed to pressure their governments to effectively counter intervention by Mussolini and Hitler. (3) The liberatory potentials of national liberation movements in Africa, Latin America, Asia, and the Middle East after World War II were squandered by undemocratic political and economic models as much as they were casualties of the Cold War. And (4) the decline of the New Left in Europe and North America after the 1960s was due more to poor theory, analysis, and strategy than to political repression, much less improvements in the performance of capitalism. There was nothing inevitable about these and other failures. And there was no lack of opportunities to advance the cause of economic justice and democracy in the twentieth century, where a better performance on the part of progressives could have changed outcomes. The lesson we need to learn is that unless progressives respond better to the opportunities that present themselves to replace the economics of competition and greed with the economics of equitable cooperation in the twenty-first century than we did in the century that just ended, the outcome will be no better.

11 What Is To Be Done? The Economics of Equitable Cooperation

What should we do if we have the opportunity to start over again? We could hold a lottery – or perhaps have a brawl – to decide who owns what productive resources. The unfortunate losers would have to hire themselves out to work for the more fortunate winners, and the goods the losers produced could then be "freely" exchanged by their owners – the people who didn't produce them. Of course this is the capitalist "solution" to the economic problem which has been spreading its sway for roughly three centuries and now stands triumphant.

Alternatively, we could make the best educated – or perhaps most ruthless among us – responsible for planning how to use society's scarce productive resources and for telling the rest of us what to do. But that was tried with unsatisfactory results. After a troubled three-quarters of a century communism and "command planning" are where they should be, in the dustbins of history. So whether centrally planned economies caused more or less alienation, apathy, inefficiency, inequity and environmental destruction than their capitalist rivals is, practically speaking, a moot point.

The important conclusion from all our recent experiments in managing our economic affairs is that neither the economics of competition and greed, nor the economics of command, is the answer to our economic problems. In this last chapter we explore ideas of political economists who remain convinced that the economics of equitable cooperation is not beyond humanity's grasp.

NOT ALL CAPITALISMS ARE CREATED EQUAL

Not all versions of capitalism are equally horrific. Moreover, since the capitalist ruling class shows no signs of relinquishing power as quickly and easily as Communist rulers did in Eastern Europe and the Soviet Union, creating the economics of equitable cooperation will have to go on inside capitalist economies for the foreseeable future. How can capitalism be humanized?

Taming finance

What's good for the wealthy and the financial companies who serve their interests is *not* necessarily good for the rest of us. If we listen to advice from the financial industry we will never restrict any of their activities – to our detriment. Paul Volker, who served as Chairman of the Board of Governors of the Federal Reserve System from 1979 through 1987, had this to say about financial regulation in a luncheon address to the Overseas Development Council Conference on "Making Globalization Work" on March 18, 1999:

> I've been involved in financial supervision and regulation for about 40 of my 70 years, mostly on the regulatory and supervisory side but also on the side of those being regulated. I have to tell you from long experience, bank regulators and supervisors are placed on a pedestal only in the *aftermath* of crises. In benign periods – in periods of boom and exuberance – banking supervision and banking regulations have very little political support and strong industry opposition.

Even when there are no crises, an unbridled financial sector will almost always distribute the lion's share of efficiency gains from extending the credit system to those who were better off in the first place, and thereby widen wealth and income inequalities. But free market finance is particularly dangerous and prone to crisis, as people as different as Keynes and Volker warn us. Simply put, an unregulated, or badly regulated financial sector is an accident waiting to happen. Therefore it must be regulated in the public interest to diminish the likelihood of financial crises of one kind or another, and to distribute the costs of financial crises more equitably when they do occur.

The Financial Markets Center (www.fmcenter.org/front.asp) in Philomont Virginia is a small progressive institute devoted to research and organizing about financial reforms in the United States. Its director of programs, Jane D'Arista, and executive director, Tom Schlesinger, have developed a cornucopia of financial reform proposals over the decades ranging from modest reforms that diminish outright corruption and thievery, to substantial reforms to protect the real economy from "financial shocks," to ambitious reforms that would redistribute the benefits of financial activities from the wealthy to the poor and democratize monetary policy. Community development corporations and development banks can be useful parts of reform efforts to revitalize ghettos and combat urban unemployment. In the international arena a "Tobin tax" on international currency transactions is a minimal first step toward taming international finance. Robert Blecker provides an excellent evaluation of this and other suggestions for international financial reform in *Taming Global Finance* (M.E. Sharpe, 1999). Beside judging if a particular reform is "winnable," those who work on financial reforms must judge how the reform will affect efficiency and stability in the real economy, if it will decrease or further increase income and wealth inequality, whether it will give ordinary people more or less control over their economic destinies, and most importantly, if winning the reform will strengthen the broad movement struggling to replace the economics of competition and greed with the economics of equitable cooperation.

Full employment macro policies

There is no reason aggregate demand cannot be managed through fiscal and monetary policies to keep actual production close to potential GDP and cyclical unemployment to a minimum. That is, there is no technical, or intellectual reason. Of course there are political reasons that prevent governments from making capitalism as efficient as it can be. Because the wealthy fear inflation more than unemployment, they exert political pressure on governments to prioritize the fight against inflation, even when inflation is not a danger, to the detriment of combating unemployment. Because employee bargaining power increases when labor markets are tight over long time periods, employers pressure governments to permit periodic recessions in the name of fighting inflation.

In an increasingly integrated global economy where demand for exports is an important component of aggregate demand in most countries, and where differential interest rates produce large movements of wealth holdings from one country to another, fiscal and monetary policies must be better coordinated internationally. Obviously, when the world's hegemonic super power persists in behaving unilaterally, international macro economic policy coordination is obstructed. However, these are merely the political obstacles to stabilization policies that not only could make the economy more efficient, but strengthens the broad movement struggling for equitable cooperation in other ways.

Wage increases and improvements in working conditions are easier to win in a full employment economy. Affirmative action programs designed to rectify racial and gender discrimination are easier to win when the economic pie is growing rather than stagnant or shrinking. Union organizing drives are more likely to be successful when labor markets are tight than when unemployment rates are high. The reason privileged sectors in capitalism obstruct efforts to pursue full employment macro policies – it diminishes their bargaining power – is precisely the reason those fighting for equitable cooperation should work for it.

Industrial policy

The French practiced what they called "indicative planning" with such success in the 1950s that the British government tried to copy the policy (unsuccessfully) in the early 1960s.[1] The German model of capitalism, then the Japanese model, and finally what became known as "the Asian development model" all used industrial policy to great advantage. In brief, the policy consists of identifying key sectors in the economy that are important to prioritize in order to increase overall economic growth rates. In the 1950s the French *Commusariat du Plan* identified "bottleneck sectors" whose sluggish growth was holding back the rest of the economy and arranged with the Finance Ministry and a State-owned development bank for lower business tax rates and interest rates for firms investing in those sectors. During the heyday of the post-World War II Japanese economic miracle, the Ministry of International Trade and Industry, MITI, identified "industries of the future" expected to be crucial to Japanese international economic strategy, and arranged with the Finance Ministry and Bank of Japan for firms in those industries to be taxed and receive credit on preferential terms. In effect MITI treated comparative advantage as something to be created rather than meekly accepted as "national fate." As a result Japan became a world powerhouse first in low cost, light manufactured goods, then in high quality steel and automobiles, and eventually in electronics

---

1. Andrew Shonfield provides an excellent evaluation of both the French policy and the failed British attempt to copy it in *Modern Capitalism* (Oxford University Press, 1974).

and computers.[2] Among the Asian Tigers, South Korea and Taiwan copied Japan's successful industrial policies most closely, with great success.[3]

There are three important things for progressive reformers to bear in mind about industrial policy: (1) Real capitalist economies are often plagued by temporary disequilibria among sectors that cause inefficiencies, and many capitalist economies are trapped playing a role in the international division of labor that dooms them to produce goods where opportunities to increase wages and profits are minimal. Industrial policies can be used to eliminate short run imbalances between sectors, or to guide an economy out of a "vicious cycle" of specialization onto a more "virtuous" long run development strategy. Since free marketeers like those in power at the IMF, World Bank, and US Department of the Treasury since the 1980s are oblivious to the static and dynamic inefficiencies of markets, they see no purpose to such policies, label them "crony capitalism," and pressure governments to abandon them no matter how successful they may have been. (2) Industrial policies to help create new comparative advantages are crucial if less developed economies are ever to break out of their vicious cycle of poverty, and therefore are an important part of forging a path toward more productive economies in the third world, and a more egalitarian global economy. Industrial policy is also crucial to redirect investment in advanced economies away from priorities overvalued by the market, like private luxuries for the affluent, toward priorities the market neglects, like housing for the poor, education, and environmental protection. (3) However, it is important to realize that industrial policy is highly susceptible to being hijacked by the largest corporations and high ranking government bureaucrats. If this occurs industrial policy can further reduce the power of workers, consumers, farmers, and small businesses if they are excluded from the industrial planning "power

2. President Nixon created a commission to study *The United States in the Global Economy* in the early 1970s. Peter Gary Peterson who headed the commission was so impressed with the advantages of Japanese industrial policy that he added a special appendix to the GAO report titled "The Japanese Economic Miracle," in which he urged the US government to imitate Japanese industrial policy.
3. See Alice Amsden, *Asia's Next Giant: South Korea and Late Industrialization* (Oxford University Press, 1989), and more recently *The Rise of 'the Rest': Challenges to the West from Late-Industrialization Economies* (Oxford University Press, 2001).

game." In fact, it can be argued that successful industrial policies in France, Japan, South Korea, and Taiwan made their economies *less* democratic. Industrial policy is a kind of capitalist planning, not to be confused with the kind of democratic, or participatory planning discussed below. On the other hand it was used effectively without reducing economic democracy in Norway, and if progressive reformers win disadvantaged sectors seats at the planning table it can improve investment priorities and increase rather than diminish economic democracy in capitalist economies.

Wage-led growth

In capitalism the low road growth strategy is to suppress wages to increase profits and hope the wealthy plow those profits back into productive investments that expand the capital stock and increase potential GDP. Beside being inequitable, this strategy runs the risk that the wealthy will not invest their profits to expand the domestic capital stock but consume them or save them abroad. In the latter case not only will the profits not be used to add machines to the capital stock, aggregate demand may falter and reduce actual production farther below a stagnant potential GDP.

The high road to growth in capitalism is to raise wages to keep aggregate demand high, trusting that if there are profitable sales opportunities capitalists will find ways to expand capacity to take advantage of them. Besides being more equitable, this strategy minimizes lost output due to lack of aggregate demand and reduces unemployment in economies where chronic underemployment is a major social problem. The only risk in this strategy is that there will be too little savings to lend to businesses trying to expand their productive capacity.

Progressives in developing economies and their allies in the advanced economies need to reject neoliberal, low road growth programs peddled by the US Treasury, IMF, World Bank, and WTO and point out that there *is* an alternative – wage-led growth and production oriented toward domestic basic needs. Every developing economy needs some dynamic export industries if for no other reason than to import cutting edge technologies. But subordinating the entire economy to export-led, low road growth is a recipe for disaster.

Progressive not regressive taxes

Taxes can redistribute income and wealth. If a tax on income requires those with higher income to pay a higher *percentage* of their income in taxes than those with lower income, the tax reduces income inequality and we call it *progressive*. Similarly, if a tax on wealth requires those with more wealth to pay a higher *percentage* of their wealth in taxes than those with less wealth, the tax reduces wealth inequality and is *progressive*. On the other hand if those with higher income or wealth pay a lower percentage of their income or wealth on a tax than those with less income or wealth, then we call the tax *regressive*. It is important to note that if those with more income can shield a greater part of their income from a tax by claiming more deductions than those with less income, even if the rate on taxable income rises with income, the tax will be less progressive than it appears, and it may actually be regressive. In 1998 those with less than $7,000 of taxable income in the US did not have to pay any income taxes. Those with incomes between $7,000 and $30,000 had to pay 15% of each additional dollar of income. Those with incomes between $30,000 and $65,000 had to pay 28% of each additional dollar of income, and the marginal tax rate rose to 39.6% for people with taxable incomes in excess of $300,000. However, studies indicate that the federal individual income tax is much less progressive than it appears to be once exclusions of income, deductions, and credits are taken into account. These exceptions to the complete taxation of income, also known as loopholes or preferences, tend to be distributed disproportionately to higher income persons. The reason is that the greatest loopholes pertain to savings, home ownership, and capital income of various types, and higher income persons have greater capacity to save, greater housing wealth, and larger shares of capital income.

Moreover, many federal taxes such as Social Security and Medicare, or FICA taxes, are highly regressive, and state sales taxes and local property taxes are highly regressive as well. It is generally believed that despite progressive income tax rates, federal taxes as a whole are barely progressive, and the overall tax system including state and local taxes is regressive. In other words, in the US the current tax system actually redistributes income from the poor to the rich. Obviously equitable cooperation requires exactly the reverse. There are a number of organizations with tax reform proposals that would replace regressive taxes with more progressive ones and make progressive taxes even more progressive – Citizens for Tax Justice (www.ctj.org) and United for a Fair Economy (www.ufenet.org) to name two. Unfortunately we have been "progressing" rapidly in reverse in the United States over the past 25 years as the wealthy have used their growing political influence with politicians they fund to shift the tax burden off themselves, where it belongs, onto the less fortunate, where it does not.

Tax bads not goods

What makes more sense than taxing socially destructive behavior rather than behavior that is socially desirable? Economists since Alfred Pigou have known that efficiency requires taxing pollutants an amount equal to the damage suffered by the pollution's victims. Moreover, if governments did this they would raise a great deal of revenue. But even if the tax is collected from the firms who pollute, the cost of the tax will be distributed between the firms who pollute and the consumers of the products they produce. To the extent that firms pass the pollution tax on in the form of higher prices, consumers pay part of pollution taxes along with producers. There is nothing wrong with this from the perspective of efficient incentives. Part of the reason pollution taxes improve efficiency in a market economy is that they discourage consumption of goods whose production requires pollution precisely by making those products more expensive for consumers.

But studies of *tax incidence – who ultimately bears what part of a tax –* have concluded that lower income people would bear a great deal of the burden of many pollution taxes. In other words, many pollution taxes would be highly regressive and therefore aggravate economic injustice. On the other hand, as we have seen, the federal, state, and local governments in the US already collect taxes that are even more regressive than pollution taxes. In 1998 social security taxes were the second greatest source of US federal tax revenues: 35% of all federal revenues came from social security taxes where employees contributed 7.65% of their wages and employers contributed an equal amount. If every dollar collected in pollution taxes were paired with a dollar reduction in social security taxes paid by employees we would substitute taxes on "bads" – pollution – for taxes on "goods" – productive work – and make the federal tax system more progressive as well. Redefining Progress (www.rprogress.org) is one organization calling for sensible proposals for environmental tax reforms as part of an overall program to achieve "accurate prices" that reflect environmental costs.

A mixed economy

The truth is that sectors like education, healthcare, and housing for the poor, sectors like telecommunications and energy where technology makes monopoly difficult to avoid, and sectors like the banking industry that have a major impact on investment patterns often do *not* perform well in private hands. In Europe and many developing economies during the golden era of capitalism governments established public enterprises through a variety of means to operate in these sectors producing a *mixed economy*, i.e. an economy with a mixture of private and publicly owned firms.

Privatization of public enterprises was a major thrust of Thatcher governments in Great Britain during the 1980s, and has been a constant theme of neoliberals and the IMF over the past 20 years in developing economies. Fighting to protect public enterprises from privatizations that are often fire sales for political rulers' wealthy backers and/or foreign multinationals is often called for. Sometimes it is necessary to preserve public services at equitable prices. The sale of the Bolivian water utility to Bechtel Corporation in 1998 led to such dramatic price hikes that it spurred a popular movement that forced the Bolivian government to rescind the deal. In Washington DC a coalition of progressive forces has been battling the Financial Control Board imposed by the US Congress to oversee city finances to prevent privatization of the city's last public hospital that is required by law to accept any patient in need, DC General. Sometimes opposing privatization is necessary to keep public enterprises which are key allies for governments in their industrial or economic development strategies. Publicly owned banks have played important roles in guiding economies in settings as varied as France in the 1950s and a number of Latin American and African countries in the 1960s and 1970s. While technically private, many banks in Japan and South Korea were so reliant on support from those countries' Central Banks that they could be counted on to cooperate with government industrial policies that brought about the Japanese and Korean economic miracles. Over the past ten years the US government, with a large assist from the IMF in the case of South Korea, has seized on every opportunity to force Korea and Japan to rescind laws barring foreign ownership of their banking sector. Not only does this allow foreign banks to gobble up lucrative assets when crises hit, it eliminates government influence over banking policies that was once an important part of successful industrial policy.

Subordinating finance to the service of the real economy rather than the reverse, pursuing full employment fiscal and monetary policies and intelligent industrial policies, embracing a wage-led rather than profit-led growth strategy, reforming the tax system to be more efficient and more equitable, and accepting public ownership where practical is nothing more than a "full Keynesian program." It may seem radical in an era of free market triumphalism, but it once fell well within the mainstream. But this full Keynesian program falls far short of redressing the fundamental inequities and power imbalances of capitalism, much less establishing an institutional framework conducive to equitable cooperation. Nevertheless, the only "golden age" capitalism has ever known was the era when this program was ascendant, and the only capitalist economies where substantial segments of the workforce ever rose to middle class status were economies guided by these policies – whether they were called Keynesian or not. But there are ways to make capitalism even more just and democratic, and political economists believe that fighting for reforms that go beyond Keynesian measures is a crucial part of building the economics of equitable cooperation.

Living wages

Establishing a minimum wage, and raising it faster than the inflation rate, is both equitable *and* "good economics." Similarly, living wage campaigns in a number of American cities have been among the strongest initiatives to make US capitalism more equitable over the past ten years. Minimum and living wages are important programs to steer capitalism toward the high road to growth.

Opponents invariably argue that minimum wage laws and increases in the minimum wage hurt the people they are supposed to help by increasing unemployment. Unless the demand for labor is infinitely inelastic raising wages does decrease employment to some extent as simple supply and demand analysis reveals. What opponents do not want to admit is: (1) Demand for labor is often wage-inelastic in the short run. (2) Even in the short run raising the wage rate, unlike raising other prices, can be expected to shift the demand curve for labor to the right as well as move us up the demand curve for labor. Because workers spend a higher percentage of their income than employers, wage increases increase the aggregate demand for goods and services in the short run which will make employers *more* likely to hire workers because they will have less trouble selling the goods those workers make. While wage increases move us up a given labor demand curve and reduce employment, shifting the labor demand curve out – as wage increases also do – increases employment. That is also simple supply and demand analysis, but just not the kind opponents of minimum wages want to consider. (3) The wage rate is a distributive variable, and as our Sraffian model of wage, profit, and price determination in chapter 5 demonstrates, there are an infinite number of combinations of long run equilibrium wage rates and profit rates that are possible in any capitalist economy. The only difference between combinations where the wage rate is high and profit rate low, and combinations where the profit rate is high and the wage rate low, is that the former are more equitable and the latter less so! So in the long run increasing the minimum wage just moves us to a more equitable distribution of benefits in capitalist economies. As long as appropriate macro economic policies are used to preserve full employment of the labor force there need be no loss of employment in the long run at all. Thomas Palley provides an excellent defense of "the new economics of the minimum wage" in "Building Prosperity from the Bottom Up," in the September/October 1998 issue of *Challenge* magazine.

Opponents' criticism that living wage campaigns in a single city will cost jobs in that city as employers move to other locations is more compelling on theoretical grounds. It is nothing more than an example of the "race to the bottom effect" which critics of corporate sponsored globalization are right to worry about. For that matter, it is no different from making local environmental regulations stronger, or local business taxes higher. Anything that raises costs to businesses in one locale makes it more likely that they will move their business and jobs to another locale. But the lessons those working on living wage campaigns need to draw from this is not to give up, but to expand the living wage into adjoining jurisdictions, and to press for restrictions on the right of businesses to pick up and move. Just as a national minimum wage is better than minimum wages in some states but not others, the more jurisdictions covered by a living wage, the less likely there will be job losses because businesses would have to move farther. And while it is common today to think "freedom of enterprise" means businesses are free to do whatever they want – including murderous releases of toxic pollutants and life-threatening working conditions – the fact is that corporations are licensed by governments and can be held accountable to community needs. In the 1980s the Ohio Public Interest Campaign, OPIC, collected enough signatures to get an initiative on the ballot that would have placed serious restrictions on how quickly, and for what reasons, corporations in Ohio could shut down and move out of state. Unfortunately the initiative was defeated when businesses outspent supporters by more than ten to one.

Theory aside, there is strong empirical evidence that local living wages have *not* led to significant job losses where they have been enacted. Partly this is because living wage ordinances often only cover city employees and employees of private employers who do business with the city. Robert Pollin and Stephanie Luce present evidence regarding job loss along with an excellent analysis of a number of living wage campaigns in *The Living Wage: Building a Fair Economy* (The New Press, 1998). As of February 2002 70 cities and counties in the US had adopted some form of living wage. Successful living wage campaigns also provide opportunities to press private employers not covered by a city ordinance to pay their employees a living wage. The living wage ordinance in the city of Cambridge helped workers, local unions, students, and progressive faculty at Harvard University win substantial wage concessions from a recalcitrant institution and its neoliberal president, Laurence Summers, in the winter of 2001 – after a long campaign that included student occupations of university offices. A much less publicized campaign at American University in Washington DC where I work issued a report in February 2002 titled "A Living Wage for Workers at American University: A Question of Fairness and Social Responsibility" recommending an hourly wage of $14.95 in 2001 dollars for a 35-hour workweek based on standards for the DC metropolitan region developed by the Economic Policy Institute and Wider Opportunities for Women. Oakland passed one of the nation's first living wage ordinances in 1998, but due to the City Charter this law did not apply to the Port of Oakland. A local coalition is trying to win passage of "Measure I" that would force the port authority to pay 1500 low wage workers at the airport and seaport wages consistent with the living wage established by the city ordinance.

A safe safety net

The Scandinavian economies in the 1960s and early 1970s were the only capitalist economies to ever provide a safety net worthy of the name. In the US the so-called "War on Poverty" in the 1960s established a Welfare system that was noteworthy for how bureaucratic, inefficient, and demeaning it was, and how pitiful it was compared to Scandinavian and German welfare programs. But even that was more than those who were fortunate enough not to need a safety net in the US could stand. The centerpiece of the Republican Party "Contract for America" in 1994 was to reform Welfare by abolishing it. Newt Gingrich found in New Democrat Bill Clinton a president willing to collaborate with the same House Republicans who voted to impeach him four years later to "end Welfare as we know it" in the President's infamous words. Only because the prolonged economic boom prevented the full consequences of eliminating all economic support for single mothers and their children from becoming visible, were Americans saved from seeing what we had done to our most unfortunate fellow citizens – until recently. The recession of 2001 – the first recession since Welfare programs were savaged by the Republican *and* Democratic parties – started to reveal what we, as a society, have done. Max Sawicky and his co-authors provide an excellent analysis in *The End of Welfare? Consequences of the Federal Devolution for the Nation* (EPI Books, 2000). Building a safety net for the victims of capitalism that is worthy of the name is the most pressing domestic task facing those of us who would make US capitalism more equitable and humane.

Worker and consumer empowerment

The essence of capitalism, of course, is that those who own the means of production decide what their employees will produce and how they will go about their work. Capitalism denies workers and consumers *direct* decision making power over how they work and what they consume, and gives them in exchange something called "producer and consumer sovereignty." Producer sovereignty operates through labor markets where the ability of employees to vote with their feet supposedly provides incentives for their employers to take their wishes into account when deciding what they order them to do. Consumer sovereignty operates through goods markets where the ability of consumers to vote with their pocket books supposedly provides incentives for capitalists to take their wishes into account when deciding what they order their employees to produce. If labor and goods markets are competitive, the story goes, workers and consumers will exert *indirect* influence over issues that concern them.

This indirect influence operates far from perfectly even when markets are more competitive, much less when markets are less competitive. The "point" of capitalism is that economic power is concentrated in the hands of employers who own the means of production, or in modern capitalism, in the hands of corporations. Modern capitalism means corporate power.

But since humans want control over their lives, and work better when they have more control over the economic decisions that affect them, the essence of capitalism is problematic and gives rise to the following dynamic: Employees sometimes try to win some of the direct power capitalism denies them. Employers sometimes pretend to give their employees some direct power because their employees work better if they think they have power. Employee stock options, total quality programs, joint worker–management committees, and a host of programs that go under the all-embracing title "autogestion" in Europe, are the outgrowth of this dynamic. The secret to evaluating different forms of worker and consumer empowerment in capitalism is to try to distinguish between appearance and reality. Anything that *really* enhances employee or consumer power moves us toward the economics of equitable cooperation. But programs that increase employers' ability to get more of what they want out of their employees by deceiving them into thinking they have some power when, in fact, they do not, promote the economics of competition and greed, not the economics of equitable cooperation. Unfortunately it is not always easy to know which is which, or when a concession has been won by employees rather than bestowed by employers like the Trojan horse.

BEYOND CAPITALISM

Even the most efficient and equitable capitalist economies cannot restore the environment, provide people with economic self-management, distribute the burdens and benefits of economic activity equitably, and promote solidarity and variety while avoiding wastefulness. That is one reason we must go beyond capitalism to build the economics of equitable cooperation. Another reason is that reforms to humanize capitalism are always at risk of being reversed. If we leave private enterprise and markets in place the economics of competition and greed will threaten reforms and lead to renewed attempts to weaken restraints they place on capitalists.

In the United States, the Humphrey–Hawkins full employment act was signed in 1978 after decades of lobbying by organized labor and civil rights groups, only to become a dead letter under a Democratic president, Jimmy Carter, and a Democratic Congress as soon as the ink was dry. Financial regulatory reforms prompted by the Crash of 1929 and the Great Depression were scuttled by the Reagan Administration in the early 1980s which invited the financial industry to rewrite rules that had long irked them but protected the rest of us. Welfare reforms dating from the "War on Poverty" in the 1960s were rolled back when a Democratic president, Bill Clinton, collaborated with a Republican Congress in the mid-1990s. Privatization of Social Security was first raised by the Clinton White House, and will be pursued relentlessly by the Bush Administration as soon as they believe the public has once again forgotten that a stock market that goes up can also go down. In Great Britain in the 1980s Margaret Thatcher's Tory governments reversed reforms that had made British capitalism more stable and equitable. More recently Tony Blair's "New Labour" governments have continued the process of dismantling reforms "Old Labour" and its progressive allies once worked decades to win. But the most successful attempts to humanize capitalism were in the Scandinavian economies during the 1960s and early 1970s. Norway and Sweden had a full Keynesian program, the most generous welfare system to date, and the Meidinger Commission in Sweden had begun to press for significant worker participation in firm governance. But starting in the mid-1970s all these reforms came under attack in Scandinavia, and all have been rolled back to a greater or lesser extent. Like the triumph of free market over Keynesian capitalism in the United States and Great Britain, the backward trajectory of social democracy in Scandinavia also stands as a reminder of why we must go beyond capitalism if we expect to sustain progress toward the economics of equitable cooperation.

Replace private ownership with workers' self-management

In capitalism people are rewarded according to the value of the contribution of the productive capital they own as well as the value of the contribution of their labor. At least that is how people would be rewarded in an ideal model of capitalism. In real capitalism discrimination, market power, asymmetrical information, and luck distribute income and wealth even more unfairly. But even under ideal circumstances, in capitalism a Rockefeller heir who never works a day in his life can enjoy an income hundreds of times greater than that of a skilled brain surgeon. For this reason many political economists believe private ownership is incompatible with economic justice and must be abolished. Similarly, political economists who believe that people have a right to manage their own labor call for the abolition of private enterprise because giving absentee owners the legal right to decide what their employees will produce and how they will produce it violates a more fundamental human right of their employees. Some support a mixture of public and private enterprise merely for pragmatic reasons. Other progressives support mixed economies as a road to the abolition of private enterprise altogether, and creation of a public enterprise economy where property income no longer exists and workers, rather than absentee owners, choose their managers or manage themselves. All political economists who espouse public enterprise market models[4] or democratic planning models do so because we believe private enterprise is incompatible with economic justice and democracy, and therefore must eventually be replaced.

Replace markets with democratic planning

Others of us think markets must also eventually be replaced by appropriate systems of democratic planning if we are to sustain a system of equitable cooperation. Of course that does not mean that all who would replace markets with democratic planning agree on how best to go about it. The Spring 2002 issue of *Science & Society* (Vol. 66, No. 1) was devoted entirely to different models of democratic planning. Nine political economists presented their ideas about how democratic planning can best be organized, and commented on one another's proposals. In his introduction the special editor for the issue, Pat Devine,[5] explained:

4. Yugoslavia was a living example of a workers' self-managed, market economy from 1952 until the collapse of Yugoslavia in the late 1980s. Few know that the Yugoslav economy had the highest rate of economic growth in the world over much of that time period – even higher than Japan during the heyday of the "Japanese economic miracle." Benjamin Ward, Branko Horvat, and Jaroslav Vanek provided excellent theoretical analyses of Yugoslav-type economies in the 1960s and 1970s. Alec Nove (*The Economics of Feasible Socialism*, Allen and Unwin, 1983), David Schweickart (*Against Capitalism*, Westview Press, 1996) and Michael Howard (*Self-Management and the Crisis of Socialism*, Rowan and Littlefield Press, 2000) are among the most recent to present and defend theoretical models of employee managed, public enterprise, market economies.
5. Pat Devine's ideas about democratic planning as "negotiated coordination" where consumers and community representatives as well as workers have seats on the boards of publicly owned enterprises is spelled out in *Democracy and Economic Planning* (Westview Press, 1988).

Michael Albert, Al Campbell, Paul Cockshott, Alin Cottrell, Robin Hahnel, David Kotz, David Laibman, John O'Neill and I all share a commitment to democratic, participatory planning as the eventual replacement for market forces. But while there are many other points of agreement among all or some of us, there are also disagreements over fundamental principles and values as well as details.

Left greens such as Howard Hawkins,[6] and social ecologists like Murray Bookchin[7] propose replacing environmentally destructive market relations with planning by semi-autonomous municipal assemblies who they argue would have reason to preserve the ecological systems necessary to their own survival and well being. There has also been renewed interest in classic writings from the anarchist and utopian socialist traditions[8] among young people disgusted with both capitalism and communism. All these economic visionaries believe equitable cooperation and environmental preservation require replacing markets with some kind of democratic planning. One of the more fully developed models of democratic planning is called *a participatory economy*.[9] I think of participatory economics as a "full program" to secure the economics of equitable cooperation. To provide readers with a concrete idea of what the economics of equitable cooperation might look like, I briefly describe

6. See Howard Hawkins, "Community Control, Workers' Controls, and the Cooperative Commonwealth" in *Society and Nature*, Vol. 1 No. 3, 1993, and articles about green visions in *Synthesis Regeneration*, a journal of the Green Party in the US available on their web site: www.greens.org/s–r/
7. See Murray Bookchin, *Post Scarcity Anarchism* (Black Rose Books, 1986) and *The Politics of Social Ecology* with Janet Biehl (Black Rose Books, 1998).
8. Some anarchists whose writings have been rediscovered are Michael Bakunin, Peter Kropotkin, Emma Goldman, Alexander Berkman, Errico Malatesta, Anton Pannekoek, Isaac Puente, Diego Abad de Santillan, and Rudolf Rocker. Utopian socialists whose writings seem even more compelling in the aftermath of the death of communism include William Morris, G.D.H. Cole, and Sidney and Beatrice Webb.
9. This model was first presented in *The Political Economy of Participatory Economics* (Princeton University Press, 1991), and *Looking Forward: Participatory Economics for the Twenty First Century* (South End Press, 1991), both by Michael Albert and Robin Hahnel. Other essays about participatory economics and a forum where participants discuss and debate participatory economics can be found on the ZNet web site: www.zmag.org/parecon/

how a participatory economy could work, and consider the major concerns critics have expressed.

Participatory economics

The major institutions in a participatory economy are: (1) *democratic councils* of workers and consumers, (2) *jobs balanced* for empowerment and desirability, (3) *remuneration according to effort* as judged by work mates, and (4) a *participatory planning* procedure in which councils and federations of workers and consumers propose and revise their own activities under rules designed to yield outcomes that are efficient and equitable.

Production would be carried out in *workers' councils* where each member has one vote, individual work assignments are balanced for desirability and empowerment within reason, and workers' efforts are rated by a committee of their peers and serve as the basis for consumption rights. Every economy organizes work tasks into jobs. In hierarchical economies most jobs contain a number of similar, relatively undesirable and unempowering tasks, while a few jobs consist of relatively desirable and empowering tasks. But why should some people's work lives be less desirable than others'? Does not taking equity seriously require trying to balance jobs for desirability? And if we want everyone to have equal opportunity to participate in economic decision making, if we want to ensure that the formal right to participate translates into an effective right to participate, does this not require trying to balance jobs more for empowerment? If some people sweep floors year in and year out, while others review new technological options and attend meetings year in and year out, is it realistic to believe they have equal opportunity to participate in firm decisions simply because they each have one vote in the workers' council? Trying to balance jobs for desirability and empowerment does not mean everyone must do everything, nor an end to specialization. Each person would still do only a few tasks – but some of them will be more enjoyable and/or empowering and some less so.

In economies where remuneration is determined by competitive forces in labor markets, people are rewarded according to the market value of the contribution of their labor. But the market value of the services of a skilled brain surgeon will be many times greater than the market value of the services of a garbage collector no matter how hard and well the garbage collector works. Since people will always have different abilities to benefit others, those with lesser abilities will always be disadvantaged in economies where remuneration is determined in the market place, regardless of how hard they try and how much they sacrifice. Therefore, a participatory economy seeks to reward people according to the effort, or sacrifice they make in work, rather than the value of their contribution. If someone works longer, harder, or at more dangerous, stressful, or boring tasks than others, then and only then would she be rewarded with greater consumption rights in compensation for her greater sacrifice.

In a participatory economy every family would belong to a neighborhood *consumers' council*, which, in turn, belongs to a *federation* of neighborhood councils the size of a city ward or rural county, which belongs to a city, or regional consumption council, which belongs to a state council, which belongs to the national federation of consumption councils. The major purpose of "nesting" consumer councils into a system of federations is to allow different sized groups to make consumption decisions that affect different numbers of people. Failure to arrange for all those affected by consumption activities to participate in choosing them not only entails a loss of self-management, but, if the preferences of some are disregarded or misrepresented, a loss of efficiency as well. One of the serious liabilities of market systems is they do not permit desires for social consumption to be expressed on an equal footing with desires for private consumption. Having consumer federations participate on an equal footing with workers' councils and neighborhood consumption councils in the planning procedure avoids this bias in a participatory economy.

Members of neighborhood councils present consumption requests along with the effort ratings their work mates awarded them. Using estimates of the social costs of producing different goods and services generated by the participatory planning procedure described below, the burden a consumption proposal imposes on others can be calculated. While no consumption request justified by a person's effort rating can be denied by a neighborhood consumption council, neighbors can express their opinion that a request is unwise, and neighborhood councils can also approve requests on the basis of need in addition to merit.

The participants in *participatory planning* are workers' councils and federations, consumers' councils and federations, and the Iteration Facilitation Board. Conceptually participatory planning is quite simple: The Facilitation Board announces current estimates of the opportunity costs for all goods, resources, categories of labor, and capital stocks. Consumer councils and federations respond with their own consumption requests while workers' councils and federations respond with their production proposals – listing the outputs they would provide and the inputs they would need to make them. The Facilitation Board calculates the excess demand or supply for each good and adjusts the estimate of the opportunity cost of the good up, or down, in light of the excess demand or supply. Using these new estimates of social opportunity costs, consumer and worker councils and federations revise and resubmit their proposals until the proposal from each council and federation has been approved by all the other councils and federations.

Essentially this procedure "whittles" overly optimistic proposals that are not mutually compatible down to a "feasible" plan in two different ways: Consumers requesting more than their effort ratings warrant are forced to reduce their requests, or shift their requests to less socially costly items, to achieve the approval of other consumer councils who reasonably regard their requests as greedy. Just as the social burden implied by a consumption proposal can be calculated by multiplying items requested by their opportunity costs, the benefits of the outputs a workers' council proposes can be compared to the social costs of the inputs it requests using the same indicative prices from the planning procedure. Workers' councils whose proposals have lower than average social benefit to social cost ratios are forced to increase either their efforts or efficiency to win the approval of other workers. Advocates point out that because consumer federations propose and revise requests for public goods on the same basis that individuals and neighborhood consumer councils do, there is no bias against social consumption in participatory planning. Moreover, because federations of residents are stewards of their natural environment and empowered to set charges for any who emit pollutants in their area, participatory planning is designed to only permit emissions whose benefits outweigh the damages they cause. Proponents argue that as iterations proceed, consumption and production proposals will move closer to mutual feasibility, and estimates more closely approximate true social opportunity costs as the procedure generates equity and efficiency simultaneously.

Reasonable doubts

It is understandable why people are skeptical of those who propose alternatives to capitalism. At the beginning of the twentieth century socialist activists assured people that central planning would make rational use of productive resources and put workers in charge of their destinies. But revolutionary dreams turned into Stalinist nightmares, and talk of equitable cooperation among "associated producers" turned out to be just that – talk – that real world socialism resembled less and less. In light of twentieth-century history, people have every right to demand that advocates of a new kind of economy address their doubts.

Critics worry that since talent is scarce and education and training are costly, balanced job complexes would be inefficient. It is obviously true that not everyone has the talent to become a brain surgeon, and it is costly to train brain surgeons, so there is an efficiency loss whenever a skilled brain surgeon does something other than perform brain surgery. Roughly speaking, if brain surgeons spend X% of their time doing something other than brain surgery, there is an additional social cost of training X% more brain surgeons. But advocates of balanced job complexes argue there are important benefits to sharing unpleasant tasks more equitably and empowering people in their work environments. Moreover, advocates point out that virtually every study confirms that participation increases worker productivity, so if more balanced jobs enhances participation, any efficiency losses from failure to fully economize on scarce talent and training should be weighed against the productivity gain from increasing worker participation.

Critics worry that rewarding effort rather than outcome is not efficient. Advocates of participatory economics argue that the only factor influencing performance over which an individual has any discretion is effort, and therefore the only factor we should reward to enhance performance is effort. Critics worry about how effort could be measured. Proponents admit that measurement will never be perfect, but argue there is no better way to decide if some deserve to consume more than others than a jury of one's fellow workers who serve on an effort rating committee on a rotating basis.

Critics worry that it would prove difficult for people to know what they want and plan their annual consumption in advance. Advocates respond that people would have ample opportunities to make changes during the year, and even if a third of people's consumption requests were changed, a participatory economy could still plan production efficiently for two-thirds more than can be planned in advance in market economies where 100% of consumers' desires is guess work for producers. Advocates also point out that when consumer federations take responsibility for providing information about available products, and R&D in new products, consumer sovereignty is better served than when producers control advertising and product innovation.

Critics worry that some people might not want their neighbors to know what they are consuming, and want to know if people could borrow or save. Advocates point out that people can submit anonymous consumption requests, or submit to a council made up of people who are not their neighbors if they wish. People can save simply by not asking to consume as much as their current effort rating warrants. People can borrow – consume more than their effort rating currently warrants – by promising to consume less than their effort warrants in the future. As in any economy ultimately someone must judge the credibility of borrowers' promises to repay. Instead of loan officers at privately owned banks, neighborhood consumption councils and federations would be the arbiters on consumer loan requests in a participatory economy – much as fellow members are in credit unions today.

Some critics worry that the Iteration Facilitation Board could hijack the planning process, and best intentions notwithstanding, we would end up with Soviet-style central planning again. To those critics advocates of participatory planning point out that the Facilitation Board is only a convenience and not actually necessary. Excess demands and price adjustments could all be done by formula – the only drawback being that more rounds of proposing and revising would probably be necessary. Other critics worry that democratic planning would take too much time. To them advocates point out that (1) planning time is not zero in market economies – it's just done inside corporations by elites rather than by those who must carry out the plans – and (2) in participatory planning, councils and federations *do not meet or debate proposals with one another at all.* Instead, looking at estimates of social costs, each council or federation decides what to propose to do *itself,* and whether to vote thumbs up or down on others' proposals about what *they* want to do. But no doubt democratic deliberation *is* more time consuming than autocratic fiat. Advocates believe the gains in economic democracy and in the superior quality of the decisions are well worth it.[10] Other critics,

10. Pat Devine put it this way: "In modern societies a large and possibly increasing proportion of overall social time is already spent on administration, on negotiation, on organizing and running systems and people.

citing the work of Austrian economists Friedrich Hayek and Ludwig von Mises, argue that without markets and private ownership of productive resources there can be no accurate or objective determination of the human costs and benefits associated with producing and consuming different goods and services. Advocates point out that this criticism does not apply to participatory planning because the estimates of social costs and benefits that emerge from the planning process are precisely the result of a real social process in which individuals and groups express their desires about using productive assets knowing they will live with the consequences of their proposals.

Critics worry there would be insufficient innovation. This is an important question since even after people come to recognize that environmentally and socially destructive growth is no longer in our interest, raising living standards for the poor, reducing work time, improving the quality of the working environment, and restoring the natural environment will require a great deal of innovation. However, an economy based on the principle that only above average effort in work merits above average consumption privileges cannot reward those who succeed in discovering productive innovations with vastly greater consumption rights than others who make equivalent personal sacrifices. Moreover, successful innovation is often the outcome of cumulative human creativity for which a single individual is rarely responsible, and an individual's contribution is often the product of genius and luck as much as effort. Finally, it would be inefficient not to make innovations immediately

---

This is partly due to the growing complexity of economic and social life and the tendency for people to seek more conscious control over their lives as material, educational and cultural standards rise. However, in existing societies much of this activity is also concerned with commercial rivalry and the management of the social conflict and consequences of alienation that stem from exploitation, oppression, inequality and subalternity. One recent estimate has suggested that as much as half the GDP of advanced western countries may now be accounted for by transaction costs arising from increasing division of labor and the growth of alienation associated with it (D. North, "Transaction Costs, Institutions, and Economic History," in the *Journal of Institutional and Theoretical Economics*, 1984). Thus, there is no *a priori* reason to suppose that the aggregate time devoted to running a self-governing society would be greater than the time devoted to the administration of people and things in existing societies. However, aggregate time would be differently composed, differently focused and, of course, differently distributed among people" (*Democracy and Economic Planning*: 265–6).

available to all enterprises once they are discovered. Critics wonder if all this implies there would be too little innovation in an equitable economy that shared innovations immediately.

First, advocates argue that recognition of "social serviceability" should be a more powerful incentive to innovation in a participatory economy where acquisition of personal wealth is unnecessary and elicits no social esteem. Second, proponents argue that a participatory economy is better suited to allocating sufficient resources to research and development because R&D is largely a public good which is predictably under-supplied in market economies, but promoted by participatory planning procedures. Workers' federations would run research operations whose purpose is to develop more efficient and pleasant methods of work. Consumers' federations would manage equally extensive research facilities to develop new and better products. The performance of these R&D operations in promoting innovation would be judged by those whose interest they serve and who control their resources. Third, advocates observe that while the only effective mechanism for providing material incentives for innovating enterprises in capitalism is to slow their spread through patents at the expense of static efficiency, temporary extra consumption allowances could easily be granted to workers in innovative enterprises while their innovation is made available to all in the participatory economy who could make good use of it. In other words, while social incentives for innovation are more equitable and should be emphasized, advocates point out that material reward for innovation would be easy to provide with no loss of static efficiency if people in a participatory economy decided their economy was not sufficiently dynamic.

Finally, some critics worry that democratic planning would violate people's freedom, i.e. not be sufficiently libertarian. But what is a libertarian economy? If people are not free, for example, to buy another human being is the economy not libertarian? There are circumstances that would lead people knowingly and willingly to sell themselves into slavery, yet few would refuse to call an economy libertarian because slavery was outlawed. If people are not free to hire the services of another human being in return for a wage, is the economy not libertarian? There are familiar circumstances that lead people knowingly and willingly to accept "wage slavery." Does this mean public enterprise market economies are not libertarian because the employer/employee relation is outlawed? Critics of capitalism argue that to equate libertarianism with the freedom of individuals to do whatever they please is a misinterpretation that robs libertarianism of the merit it richly deserves.

It is, of course, a good thing for people to be free to do what they please – as long as what they choose to do does not infringe on more important freedoms or rights of others. I should not be free to kill you because that would be robbing you of a more fundamental freedom to live. I should not be free to own you because that robs you of a more fundamental freedom to live your own life. I should not be free to employ you because my freedom of enterprise robs you of a more fundamental freedom to manage your own laboring capacities. I should not be free to bequeath substantial inheritance to my children because that robs the children of less wealthy parents of their more fundamental right to an equal opportunity in life. Although advocates of capitalism would not agree, there is little disagreement about any of this among those who believe we must go beyond capitalism if we are to achieve the economics of equitable cooperation. But are there additional freedoms and rights that others should not be free to violate in choosing to do what they please?

Advocates of participatory economics think everyone should have an equal opportunity to participate in making economic decisions in proportion to the degree they are affected. We think self-management is the only way to interpret what "economic freedom" means without having one person's freedom conflict with freedoms of others. We think self-management, in this sense, is a fundamental right, so when people are free to do what they want this should not mean they are free to infringe on others' right to self-management. In other words, we do not think some should be "free" to appropriate disproportionate power, or "free" to *oppress* others with their greater economic power. But we do not think ourselves any less libertarian for wanting to outlaw oppression, any more than abolitionists thought themselves less libertarian for fighting to outlaw slavery.

Advocates of participatory economics also think when people enter into economic cooperation with one another they have a right to a fair distribution of the burdens and benefits of their joint activities, i.e., people should enjoy economic benefits in proportion to the effort or personal sacrifice they incur when fulfilling their economic responsibilities. So we believe economic justice requires that nobody be "free" to appropriate more goods and services than warranted by their personal sacrifice, i.e. nobody should be "free" to *exploit* others. But we do not think ourselves any less libertarian for wanting to outlaw exploitation, any more than reformers thought themselves less libertarian for fighting for progressive income taxation in the early twentieth century.

Does this take all the fun out of freedom? If freedom does not include the freedom to oppress and exploit others does it lose its appeal? Is a "politically correct" economy a drab and regimented world – as some critics would have us believe? Proponents of participatory economics see little reason to think so. Consumers in a participatory economy are free to develop and pursue desires for any goods and services they wish. They are free to consume whatever they want – paying prices that are more accurate reflections of true social costs than market prices are. People are free to choose more consumption and less leisure, or vice versa. They are free to distribute their effort and consumption over their lives as they please. They are free to apply to work wherever they want, free to bid on any job complex at their work place they want, and free to organize a new enterprise to produce whatever they want, by any means they want, with whomever they want. People are free to educate themselves in any career they want, and train for any tasks they want. *People are just not free to do any of these things in ways that oppress or exploit others.*

But there is another way to look at participatory economics – from the bottom up. The first priority is to guarantee economic justice and self-management for those who have never enjoyed it by making sure people's consumption is commensurate with their sacrifices, and by making sure people's work experience equips them to be able to participate in economic decision making should they want to. And there is another way to look at talent and education. A participatory economy encourages people to use their talents. Outstanding abilities used to benefit others will be highly regarded in a participatory economy. People will be encouraged to pursue education and put it to good use in a participatory economy by the esteem and recognition this earns them. Nobody is told what kind of education or work they must do. But there is no material reward for anything other than effort and sacrifice – since this would be inequitable. And while those with greater talent and education will be asked to play the role of expert, and may have their opinion more highly regarded because historically their opinions have proven more insightful, they are not given greater decision making authority in a participatory economy because this would infringe on others' right of self-management.

CONCLUSION

The question boils down to this: Do we want to try and measure the value of each person's contribution to social production and allow individuals to withdraw from social production accordingly? Or do we want to base differences in consumption rights on differences in sacrifices made in producing goods and services as judged by one's work mates? In other words, do we want an economy that obeys the maxim "to each according to the value of his or her contribution," or the maxim "to each according to his or her effort and sacrifice?"

Do we want a few to conceive and coordinate the work of the many? Or do we want everyone to have the opportunity to participate in economic decision making to the degree they are affected by the outcome? In other words, do we want to continue to organize work hierarchically, or do we want job complexes balanced for empowerment?

Do we want a structure for expressing preferences that is biased in favor of individual consumption over social consumption? Or do we want to it to be as easy to register preferences for social as individual consumption? In other words, do we want markets or nested federations of consumer councils?

Do we want economic decisions to be determined by competition between groups pitted against one another for their well being and survival? Or do we want to plan our joint endeavors democratically, equitably, and efficiently? In other words, do we want to abdicate economic decision making to the marketplace or do we want to embrace the possibility of some kind of participatory, democratic planning?

Those willing to work for the economics of equitable cooperation need not agree now on how far we will have to go to secure it. There is an overwhelming consensus among opponents of the economics of competition and greed on reforms needed to make capitalism more efficient and equitable. That does not mean all agree on what reforms should be accorded greater priority in light of limited financial and organizational resources. But few who favor the economics of equitable cooperation would disagree that most of the reforms and programs described briefly above move us in the right direction, and most of us would agree on other reforms that could be added to the list as well. Since the road leading beyond capitalism must travel through capitalism for the foreseeable future in any case, there will be time, and a great deal of new experience to evaluate, while we continue to discuss and debate (1) whether it is necessary to move beyond capitalism, (2) how far beyond capitalism we must go, and (3) what a sustainable economics of equitable cooperation will eventually look like.

Index

Compiled by Sue Carlton